THE HIGH PRICE OF HEAVEN

THE HIGH PRICE OF HEAVEN

DAVID MARR

ALLEN & UNWIN

All works illustrated are details from John Pule, *Angelu*, lithograph, 755 × 565 mm, courtesy of the artist and Gow Langsford Gallery, Auckland, NZ.

First published in 1999 by
Allen & Unwin
9 Atchison Street, St Leonards NSW 1590 Australia
Phone: (61 2) 8425 0100
Fax: (61 2) 9906 2218
E-mail: frontdesk@allen-unwin.com.au
Web: http://www.allen-unwin.com.au

National Library of Australia
Cataloguing-in-Publication entry:

Marr, David.
  The high price of heaven.

  ISBN 1 86508 201 5.

  1. Christianity—Social aspects—Australia. 2. Christianity—Australia—Influence. 3. Christianity and politics—Australia. I. Title.

261.70994

Set in 11/14 pt Bembo by DOCUPRO, Sydney
Printed and bound by McPhersons Printing Group, Maryborough

10 9 8 7 6 5 4 3 2 1

TO
S.T.
WHO BELIEVES
IN PLANTS

CONFESSION

'I've been to the other side and let me tell you, son, there's fucking nothing there.'

Kerry Packer

I was a Christian. It's best I confess this right from the start. I took Christ into my life on a dark night on the shores of Port Hacking in the summer of 1960 and spent the next few years caught up in the dramatic business of my Faith. I was a loud-mouth, lumpy boy desperate to be Good. I read the Bible. I prayed. I shopped myself round Anglican parishes looking for somewhere exciting and convincing to worship. I found they all served the same sweet and sour port. For a time I toyed with the idea of going into the Church but the ambition faded even before it was fully formed. In the meantime, with Christ's help, I fought masturbation and temptations too terrible to name.

I ditched my faith five years later. It was on a midwinter morning at Sydney University as I was doing an exam under the mural of Great Thinkers in the Philosophy Room. No one had prepared us for the second question: 'Reconcile the propositions that God is both all powerful and all good.' I couldn't. I found myself arguing the opposite with terrible fluency. Words poured onto the page. Without knowing it until this moment, I'd already decided my life as a Christian was over.

I was eighteen. I'd discovered politics and the world was full of disasters God couldn't fix. I laid this on thick for the examiners but didn't hint at what was really gnawing at me. I'd fallen in love. It was fraught, unfulfilled and extremely heady. All the Christian teaching I'd clung to about the who, the when and the how of sex now seemed arbitrary and cruel. If this was sin, I wanted to sin. The sooner the better. My pen was driven by a sense that the old Christian bargain I'd been living by — renunciation now in return for rewards in the life to come — felt like a dud.

Perhaps I'd never had a strong grasp of heaven. Anglicans think it's a bit vulgar to go into detail about the ultimate reward and the ultimate punishment, about heaven and hell. At school I'd spent forever in chapel staring at stained-glass pictures of heaven with lambs grazing in green fields, but they looked too like the Goulburn paddocks I knew from winter holidays to trust — pretty for now but the weather would turn nasty soon enough. Dante's *Paradiso* in the Penguin translation didn't set me alight. I'd fallen asleep trying to read the college library's chalky copy of Augustine's *City of God*. By the time I found myself sweating over that exam paper in the Philosophy Room, I'd already decided the only way to find out about heaven was to look for something like it on earth. It wasn't a great wrench to give up my seat on the all-stations train to the afterlife.

Or that's what I thought I'd done . . .

Twenty-five years later I was writing about censorship, wondering why people still *bothered*, when it came to me that what's at stake here is heaven. The enemies of films and books and magazines, of sex and music and drugs and television, of drink and dancing are Christians. And what they're campaigning about is not this life but the next. They're careful not to talk about heaven and hell, but what they want goes way beyond the nation's good: their ambition is salvation for us all. Because so much is at stake, no issue is too small, no gesture entirely wasted that can save even a single soul from damnation. Popular support is irrelevant. Dissent doesn't count. The voices of those who want to ban, censor and jail for our salvation are never silenced. All that changes is that from time to time governments choose to listen. We're living in one of those times.

This is a book about the role salvation plays in the politics of Australia. Ours is a very secular country but the churches remain the most resilient, most respected and the best-connected lobby in the nation. Sin is their business. Heaven is their aim. Government is their partner. There's a certain instinctive generosity in wanting to keep all us sinners on the train, but there's also a bullying indifference here to those who count on living only one life — this one. For those who have no faith in the afterlife, the price we're expected to pay for getting us all to heaven is too high. Too much waste, too much cruelty, too much pain.

We've inherited a tough strain of Christianity in this country. From the moment the first priest and missionaries were rowed ashore watched by assembled felons — with Godless savages hovering at the edge of the timber — these men of God felt called on to perform particularly urgent work for the Lord. They still think that way. One quality we've never lost from those early times is larrikin distrust for authority. Another is Christianity still geared to the task of ministering to human beings at their worst. The churches brought a simplified faith to build a simple society; they worked hand in hand with the governor's men to achieve the little civilisation of Sydney Cove; and they developed a particular fear that the work of the Lord in this new land could so easily be sabotaged by pleasure — by sun, surf, sensuality and prosperity. Without the mercy and humanity of some of these early Christians, Australia would not be the place it is today. But the inheritance of that time is still felt in the mood of today's churches. Catholic and Protestant, old and new, they love authority and suspect pleasure.

Nothing much changes with the churches. That's their boast. Each claims to be the authentic expression of values going back a couple of millennia. So as we start into the next one, it's perhaps no surprise Christians are engaged in an old crusade against sex, last-ditch battles with women inside and outside their congregations, guerilla campaigns against homosexuals, harassment of AIDS- and HIV-prevention programs, outbreaks of civil war in church schools, persecution of books and grim collaboration with governments to pursue the War on Drugs. To understand what's going on here, the theology has to be disentangled from the politics. That's my purpose.

ONE

LEAVING THEM TO DROWN

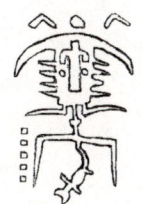

'We're frightened to put forward the hard teaching of Christ.'

Archbishop George Pell

Pastor Wayne Magee and I are sitting in a cold church waiting for the urn to boil. The Rock Christian Faith Centre in Sydney's Camperdown is unimaginably forlorn on this autumn morning. Life has fled the place, leaving behind a baby grand and a drum kit, rows of mauve chairs and a peculiar text from Revelation nailed high on a crossbeam: 'Behold I come quickly'.

The Rock is Magee's city parish and he uses a corner of this dismal hall as an office for the PR work he does for the New South Wales Council of Churches. He assures me this place doesn't give a true picture of the Foursquare Gospel Church. Out in the new suburbs of the city where he lives there are a dozen congregations preaching, healing and working miracles. 'The God I worship is the God of miracles.' Miracles count in the drugs war. He volunteers that only a miracle will make Australia drug-free. This doesn't leave him downhearted. 'I've seen ships turn amidst the storm of life where one would have said, "No, there is no hope, they are destined for the rocks". That is not foolhardy or pride in me. That's reality.'

Since 'Flower Power' arrived on these shores, the New South Wales Council of Churches has been rallying governments to take tough measures against drugs. But with Magee's appointment as PR for the council four years ago, it's been pushing an even more combative line.

Magee is a wheeler-dealer at the Protestant end of church politics. 'I am regularly at Parliament House. I speak with members, ministers, shadow ministers. I have actually got phone calls from a minister's office: "How do you think the church would react to this?" That was about euthanasia, not drugs, but we are having an impact.' The council PR is particularly proud of the impact they're having on John Howard. 'I have put a release out on a Monday, and the Prime Minister has come out very strongly on the Tuesday or the Wednesday with something that is very close to what we have said.'

A few days before the Prime Minister's drug summit in 1999 Magee issued a bombshell press release in the name of the huge Sydney diocese of the Anglican church, the Salvation Army in New South Wales plus half a dozen little Protestant churches: THE CURSE OF DRUGS — IT'S NOW TIME FOR AN ALL OUT WAR. The Twelve Point Initiative called for more police, more sniffer dogs, more surveillance planes, more customs officers, tougher censorship of films, television, radio and songs plus forced rehabilitation for addicts and mandatory jail terms for dealers. The immediate target of the release was the Prime Minister. Magee summarised the message he wanted to get across thus: 'You've got a summit coming up, John, on Friday. Take this and grab hold of some of this stuff that we believe will rectify the problem.' Pastor Magee hadn't consulted the member churches but cobbled his dramatic Twelve Point Initiative together from old council motions, old press releases and old quotes from the Baptist minister who was, at the time, the council's acting president. The release was something of a sham, but the politicians weren't to know.

The drugs debate looks on the surface like a contest between two views: drugs as crime and drugs as disease.

But the political complexity of this issue — and the reason we're stuck in such a quagmire here — is a third view almost always forgotten in public discussion: drugs as sin. In the eyes of warrior Christians against drugs, cocaine and marijuana and heroin users are quite literally taking a hell of a risk. Those warriors have enlisted the world in a crusade against sin.

Slabs of Magee's Twelve Point Initiative were run in newspapers and on television the weekend before the Prime Minister's drugs summit. Christians rarely speak in terms as uncompromising and scornful as this: 'The New South Wales Council of Churches said today the majority of the general public has had enough of the politicking, the cries for legal supply of heroin to addicts by some members of the legal profession and the ludicrous endorsements for heroin shooting galleries from some people who should know better.' The central message from the churches was that heroin must never, under any circumstances, be given to anybody. A heroin trial is out. 'It just won't work. For anyone to even consider giving heroin-addicted people a daily supply to help them through life is utter nonsense. It is just as stupid as to suggest that one give alcohol to an alcoholic. It just will not help them get off the stuff.'

The churches now fighting drugs hardest are the churches that mobilised a century ago against booze. The terms of victory are the same: total abstinence. Heaven is for the sober. The image of 'war' comes out of the Salvation Army's struggle with gin in the slums of the Protestant world. Now the Sallies — or at least those that come under the sway of Sydney — are bringing the same high hopes, moral fervour and dramatic language to bear on the devil of drugs. Intoxication is wicked. Addiction is a disgrace. Drug taking is a sin. For such hard headed Christians, the core evil here is pleasure itself. Christians talk disease, abasement, prostitution and crime, but their horror stories of extreme addiction mask deeper worries that go back to the earliest days of the Faith: the fear of pleasure.

But the Churches are divided against each other. Congregations are split. The Uniting Church opened a safe injecting room in Sydney and a Uniting Church preacher called the cops to shut it down. While the Catholic Archbishop of Melbourne, George Pell, calls for stiffer measures to combat drugs, the Sisters of Charity prepare to open the first legal safe injecting room in Australia. So different are attitudes in Melbourne and Sydney that it's hard to credit sometimes the same God is guiding the churches north and south of the Murray. Baptists in Sydney preach war and Baptists in Melbourne talk peace. On the whole, Melbourne churches are having doubts about the war, while the heartland of the warriors is Sydney. That's Sydney's great contribution to the spiritual life of the nation: the sensual, chaotic, superficial city that's attracted the toughest churchmen right from the start. Men like Magee and the Salvation Army's Major Brian Watters.

John Howard is listening to the Sydney churches. His 1999 summit didn't go as far as the New South Wales Council of Churches was urging, but the decisions taken sat comfortably with the council's advice: no safe injecting rooms, no drug trials, no talk of legalisation. There were to be more millions spent on treatment and education, but lots more money to pour into the war — money for jails and courts and police and sniffer dogs. These are harsh policies and Howard can impose them with a Christian gloss. The churches are divided but the political bottom line is this: no major church has yet called for the war on drugs to be abandoned. Governments are now fending off police chiefs, QCs, doctors, prosecutors and scientists who are fed up with the war. They are having to deal with the angry parents of dead heroin users who want the war to end. But governments don't have to grapple with protesting archbishops. No matter what doubts there are in their own ranks, the churches are officially holding the line.

The Rev. Howard Moody is from the Deep South, born and raised in the land of the great hellfire preachers. That Southern Baptist childhood is still strong in his voice but its dramatic certainties are long behind him. 'There are fourteen different kinds of Baptist in the United States,' he explains. 'I'm American Baptist now.' Moody has seen a lot of life in his 35 years as a pastor in New York's Greenwich Village. Since he retired a couple of years ago he has been mobilising religious leaders in North America to oppose what he calls the war against drug users, 'Because that's what it is, a war against drug *users*'.

Religious Leaders for a More Just and Compassionate Drug Policy is bankrolled by the international speculator George Soros who uses a little of the cash he earns busting currencies to underwrite drug reform in America where the war against drugs takes a particular toll on blacks. Most of the users are white, but most of those who go to jail for long, mandatory terms are black. And the health toll on intravenous drug users is terrible because supplying clean needles to addicts — a policy that's made Australia a world leader in HIV prevention — is still considered a radical option in America. Clergy join with politicians to preach against the evils of needle exchange.

As Moody sees it, change has to come from within the churches. He blames them for 'consciously or unconsciously' fuelling the moral crusade against drugs, a crusade that's not only failed to make America free of illicit drugs but has 'constructed laws that are highly unjust, racist in application, a threat to individual freedom and a danger to our public health'. Moody says unless the churches change, America can't change. And unless America — 'which has so corrupted the other nations' — changes, the world is stuck with the drugs war.

'Remember Nancy Reagan's "Just Say No"? Church people love that. Church people of all stripes love that line. The church has a prohibitive gene in its DNA. That whole negative thing is there through its history. These are the people who say no to drugs, no to sex, no to pleasure.' Moody sees pleasure, not addiction, as the key. 'There's a primitive policy of opposition in churches to anything that gives you pleasure. If you take opiates for pain, it's okay. If you take them for pleasure, it's wrong.'

American churches haven't learnt from Prohibition. Moody laughed gruffly at my suggestion that they might look back and learn from that fiasco. No. The victory was theirs. Sure, things went wrong afterwards but it was their victory against great political odds. 'So when you talk about Prohibition not working, it's hard for the church to accept. It's their baby.' And banning booze from the community is a live political issue in the United States. 'There are still counties in this country where you can't buy liquor.' Whatever the rest of the world might think, American Christians see those few years of Prohibition in the United States of America sixty years ago as a model for the universal and permanent prohibition of drugs.

Fame was thrust on Major Brian Watters of the Salvation Army when John Howard announced at the Albert Street Uniting Church in Brisbane in March 1998 the formation of a new drugs council with Watters as its chair. 'Government cannot do it on its own,' said the Prime Minister. 'It must be a combined strategy involving governments, law enforcement agencies, churches, social and welfare groups and the community.' By 'it' Howard meant the search for a way through the drugs mess while remaining absolutely 'tough on drugs'. Those instructions were fine by Watters.

Scrubbed and plucky, the major sits among his eagles. There are eagle statuettes on his shelves and eagle photographs on the walls. Behind his desk hangs one of those novelty posters that seem only abstract squiggles until you shift focus and the squiggles resolve — or so he assures me — into the image of another fierce eagle. 'One of my favourite passages of scripture is Isaiah 40:31. "They that wait upon the Lord will renew their strength. They shall mount up with wings as eagles. They shall run and not be weary."'

This man who chairs the Prime Minister's Australian National Council on Drugs is a total abstinence Christian who grew up in the shadow of his father's addiction to booze and believes he too would be an alcoholic but for finding Christ through the Salvation Army. When he enlisted, he took the salvationists' vow of abstinence and has spent most of his career working with alcoholics. Booze and the fear of booze are the key to his thinking. He knows the bigger problem out there is drink. 'Heroin gets 90 per cent of the publicity and it's about 5 per cent of the problem.' Another man might conclude that if society can live with the problems of alcohol, there's not much point mounting a war to purge heroin from the community. But Brian Watters takes the opposite tack: the war against drugs is necessary to stop heroin becoming as bad a public scourge as booze. He believes it must unless we fight.

Watters' logic rests on two articles of faith unshaken by science. First, he believes pure heroin is as physically destructive as pure alcohol. Second, he believes heroin is irresistibly addictive. He speaks of the heroin rush with awe. And for him it's axiomatic that the greater the pleasure, the greater the power to seduce. He tells me he has never seen scientific studies that rate the addictiveness of heroin slightly *below* that of alcohol. He says, 'I have never met a successful recreational user of heroin.'

'Never? Perhaps without knowing?'

'The people I deal with, like every alcoholic I deal with, started off as a social user of the substance. Now I know it's got a highly addictive potential. It's physically addictive and also psychologically addictive.'

THE HIGH PRICE OF HEAVEN

'But so is alcohol.'

'And the reality is we can't do anything about alcohol. We're stuck with it.'

'But aren't we stuck with heroin too?'

'No we're not. Why on earth would we ever consider making more available and acceptable and normalising the use of substances which are going to compound the problem enormously. At the moment at least they're contained.'

This is a further article of Watters' faith. He is not blind to the shortcomings of the drugs war but he believes absolutely the campaign is keeping things in check. 'I don't believe we'll ever stamp out illicit drugs, but I believe what we're already doing in a remarkable way has contained things.'

Watters has been around for years, rising through the ranks to command the Salvation Army's Eastern Division Rehabilitation Services. But his appointment as chair of the Prime Minister's new council not only surprised the name players in the drugs debate but was controversial in the Salvation Army. The major is a Sydney man and the Sallies in Sydney are Sydney hardline. Where Watters sets policy for the Army — in New South Wales, the Australian Capital Territory and Queensland — the only goal and measure of success is total abstinence.

Elsewhere in Australia, the Army sees things differently: abstinence is not the only goal, harm is to be minimised, addictions can be managed, heroin trials are not ruled out. When Watters led a successful campaign to stop Ansett putting syringe disposal bins in aircraft toilets — for 'sending a message of tolerance of the use of illicit drugs' — his opposite number in Melbourne, Major David Brunt, countered on the ABC Radio's 'Religion Report' that these bins were really an occupational health and safety issue: 'I didn't see it as anything actually to do with the drug problem at all.'

Melbourne sets policy for the rest of the Army in Australia. Relations between the two headquarters have been difficult for some time. In March 1999, after a series of meetings with Watters, the Melbourne command publicly dissociated itself from the major's role as adviser to the Prime Minister, and from the hardline advice he was giving John Howard. 'There are major tensions and concerns over Major Watters' commitment to a policy of total abstinence and no heroin trials,' Brunt hold the press. 'We believe we have to get the debate focused back on saving lives.'

Safe injecting rooms save lives. And there are many to be saved. About six hundred men and women — mostly men — die every year in Australia from overdoses. Providing users with somewhere safe and supervised to take drugs, would seem to be in obedience to Christ's teaching that life — no matter how debased — is holy. From this springs Christian pacifism and absolute Christian opposition to abortion and euthanasia. But another tradition collides with this reverence for life, puritan contempt for lives enslaved to the 'pleasures' of addiction. Puritans will not feed a man's addiction, for is that not conniving in their sin?

'One of the great fallacies of all this is that if in some way we supply injecting rooms the death from heroin overdose will cease,' says Watters. 'I don't believe that's so. Now bear in mind and I hope this comes through very clearly. I've given my life to saving these people's lives and I never talk about them as "those addicts". These are individuals I know by name. They're somebody's son and daughter and without being pretentious in any way, God's given me a love for these people, I believe and I work very closely with them. But to some extent it's trying to stop the spread of a disease in our society. We have to contain it for the sake of the broader community. Sometimes I think about it as the navy's rule that you don't stop and pick up survivors if the U-boat is still lurking.'

That's a tough picture: bodies in the water, cries for help, the captain on the bridge signalling his ship to steam on . . .

'But isn't keeping people alive the fundamental obligation of Christians?'

'I believe that life is sacred and precious and we should do all we can to sustain it. We've also got an obligation at the same time to make sure that's a meaningful life, that it's worth living.'

'But life is life isn't it? How can you say as a fallible human that you will judge the meaningfulness of a life — to play God?'

'Let's get real. If you see a person covered with scabs sitting in a corner unable to feed themselves, who doesn't attend to their basic ablutions and cuts themselves off from their family and loved ones and makes absolutely no contribution to society — it's not some sort of moral judgement to say that's not a meaningful life is it?'

'But it's still a life isn't it?'

'Yes. That's obvious. Let's not get lost in the realm of some sort of philosophy about this.'

'But isn't philosophy crucial?'

'No, but let's keep it in the realm of practicality and reality.'

'But some Christians would say that that debased poor bugger sitting in that corner in that state is a *life* and isn't keeping that person alive a principal Christian obligation?'

'And I don't argue with that.'

'And if that requires a shooting gallery, then you give them a shooting gallery?'

'Well I don't know too many Christians who would say that. If you're talking about that debased poor bugger who's sitting in the corner there whose life is where it is because of the use of this substance, I don't know too many Christians who would say let's help that person continue using the substance. I don't know of any.'

'Any?'

'Well, I've never met anybody who would talk in those sort of terms. This might sound hard: I believe that at some point we have to say to people, you have to accept the consequences and the outcomes of the decisions you make and if you deliberately chose to start using highly addictive substances then you need to make an informed choice and understand that this is the likely outcome and it's not incumbent on the rest of society to facilitate you to do that and we're not going to provide you with the means. We will do all in our power to help you get away from it, but it is not part of our contract with you to supply you with the means to continue doing this.'

THE HIGH PRICE OF HEAVEN

'And if you've got the poor bugger in the corner and the one thing that will keep him alive is a shot of heroin, he doesn't get it?'

'A shot of heroin won't keep him alive. Heroin doesn't keep anybody alive.'

Brian Watters' wife bustled in with some papers. Like her husband she's shining clean and dressed in Army rig. There is someone to see the major. We mustn't be long. She exits. I ask Watters if he's happy with the cut of the drug budget spent on treatment compared to policing. 'It's getting better.'

'Well, it's 84 per cent policing.'

'No it's not. That's Wodak's figures isn't it?'

Dr Alex Wodak, Director of the St Vincent's Hospital Alcohol and Drug Service in Sydney and president of the Australian Drug Law Reform Foundation, is in every way Watters' secular opponent. He is for injecting rooms, heroin trials, and an end to the war. He calls for 'Zero tolerance on unnecessary deaths'. I assured the major these were not Wodak's figures but came from the most recent United Nations World Drug Report: in 1997 Australia spent 84 per cent of its drugs budget on policing, 6 per cent on treatment, 10 per cent on research and prevention.

'I haven't seen those. All I know is that the Prime Minister's Tough On Drugs strategy has given out about $500m recently and probably the best part of $400m of that has gone to treatment, education and prevention.' As Watters sees it, the proper balance is 50:50 between policing and care. 'There are two ways we can deal with the drug problem: we can reduce demand and we can reduce supply. They are equally important I believe.'

Demand is to be reduced by reminding people that all this is sinful. God wants our bodies to be His temple. He has given us a natural desire for euphoria, 'But I believe there are natural ways of achieving this and rightly so: everything from sex to mountain climbing. I get some spiritual highs and they're wonderful too. These are God-given things. But with these substances, it's an effortless move towards these rewards. It's a short cut. A quick fix. It's a quick high.' And then comes addiction. 'I believe essentially addiction is a spiritual struggle. I think it's the souls as well as the bodies of people that are involved in this. It drags them down to hell literally, now.'

Very politely Major Watters walked me past his next visitor and down the stairs of the Rehabilitation Services Command in Surry Hills. A few paces short of the street he paused and asked me gently not to portray him as a hard man. 'The way of the Salvation Army is to be hard on the sin not the sinner.' He was sick of being written up in the press as a hard man. Did I think he was hard? I said I did. He looked blank. We shook hands.

Life in various shabby guises flows towards the Ashfield Uniting Church on the fringes of Sydney's old respectable suburbs. Kids are having lessons, the poor are waiting for lunch and upstairs the Rev. Bill Crews is simultaneously being interviewed by me and filmed for 'Australian Story'. He has been helping addicts for the last 25 years and has kept his battered face in the limelight all that time to protect himself and his projects from hostile forces in his own church. Those Methodists, Presbyterians, Congregationalists and the rest who came together as a new church in Australia were right to call themselves Uniting. They aren't united. Even though the more extreme puritans stayed out, there is within the Uniting Church continuous underlying tension between the innovators and the puritans. It's a church always on the brink of radical transformation, but the butterfly never quite comes out of the cocoon.

'Drugs are morally neutral,' says Bill Crews. But the heroin plague? 'It's not going to get much worse.' And the addicts? 'Just keep them alive.' Crews wonders if church backing for the war on drugs is religion addressing politics or politics dressed up as religion. 'Religion is a summons to love, not to be a moral policeman. The trouble is the two things have got muddled up. Why? I don't know. It may be religion ultimately divides people between those who love life and those who fear God. So one group of people are in awe of God's creation and the other fear God's wrath.' He's for creation. 'If you're in awe of creation you're more tolerant of life.'

I'd come to see Crews because word was out — this was April 1999 — that clergy in the Uniting Church were planning to set up safe injecting rooms. Crews had no plans for Ashfield. He suggested I ring a couple of numbers. Over the next few days I often heard clergy using the word Crews had used with me: sanctuary. In a hostile political climate, the Church might be a sanctuary where this could happen. The model of these Uniting Church men is a Rotterdam parish of the Dutch Reform Church which in the late eighties opened an injecting room, trusting the prestige of the pastors and old traditions of church sanctuary in the Netherlands would protect them. The Dutch government found it impossible to arrest the clergy and that room in Rotterdam precipitated all the radical policy developments that followed in the Netherlands — safe injecting rooms, heroin trials and now heroin maintenance programs.

I discovered there were two projects on foot, one in Sydney and one in Melbourne but coordination between them had broken down. Melbourne wanted a permanent facility with guarantees of immunity from prosecution. Sydney's Wayside Chapel wanted a 'strategic' four-week operation before the drug summit Bob Carr had promised in the election campaign just past. The Wayside Chapel 'T-room' opened, alone, on 3 May in a blaze of publicity. The point was press attention. Addicts had to negotiate a gauntlet of cameras and reporters to reach a room where they were given a fit and watched by a nurse as they injected. The rules were strict: no one under eighteen, long-time users only, no sharing drugs, injection only in arms or legs, no help from the nurse. Everyone involved — the chapel's Rev. Ray Richmond, the nurse and perhaps even the security guards at the door — faced fines and jail for 'aiding and abetting self-administration of a prohibited drug'.

The brief life of the Wayside Chapel safe injecting room caused a national sensation. The Prime Minister condemned the 'bad signals' being sent to youth. The newly defeated leader of the New South Wales Opposition, Kerry Chikarovski, called for the arrest of everyone involved. When Carr refused to direct the police to act, Fred Nile — an unattached Uniting Church preacher and member of the State Upper House — laid a formal complaint and police then entered and filmed the injecting room. No arrests were made. Changes were laid later. Nile turned up for the television cameras as the police were leaving the building to denounce, 'Illegal activity going on in the Wayside Chapel. I'm glad the police have acted, otherwise the law becomes a joke in this State. They should have closed it down.' Both the Sydney Anglicans and the Catholics distanced themselves from this act of civil disobedience.

But at St Vincent's, a few blocks from the chapel, plans were already far advanced for the hospital to open the first *legal* safe injecting room. Alex Wodak, who had been a figure hovering in the background at the Wayside Chapel, was the instigator of the St Vincent's plan. The Sisters of Charity who run the hospital settled the details while the summit was still sitting at Parliament House in Macquarie Street. When that was all over Carr made two announcements: he would 'trial' a safe injecting room and it would be run by the Sisters of Charity. Both announcements signalled brave decisions. Carr was abandoning his absolute opposition to any policy that suggested tolerance of drugs. The sisters were putting themselves in the path of Archbishop George Pell.

Through 150 years of antagonism between Catholics and Protestants in this country, the two divisions of Christianity had more in common than they ever cared to admit. That missionary belief that Australia was a place where the Gospel must be preached to humanity at its worst was matched by an Irish conviction that good has to be pummelled into human beings. We're so familiar with the impact on Australia of the hostility between Catholics and Protestants that we overlook how deeply affected we are by their hard, shared view of humanity. Their common message in Australia was this: distrust your senses, sacrifice pleasure, submit your will.

The leadership of the Catholic Church was all for fighting the drugs war. The enemy was pleasure, a *new* pleasure. But among Catholics working with addicts, the attitude was very different: addicts were not indulging in pleasure but caught in pain. What's more they were dying. So Catholics divided between those in the field and those making the rules back in town. More profoundly, this was a split between the men and women of the church. Just as it's hard sometimes to imagine the same God works north and south of the Murray, so it's difficult to believe the priests and religious women of Catholicism are members of the same institution. Division over the drugs war is only one example of a rift that runs through the church between men and women — between power and care. But as the death toll from heroin overdoses rose in the nineties, the bishops began to have second thoughts about their commitment to the war. Canberra was hit by wave after wave of overdose deaths, and in their aftermath Bishop Patrick Power came out in support of injecting rooms and even a heroin trial, 'simply because everything else has failed'.

For a time the church was moving away from the war. It isn't now. The reason is George Pell, a very Sydney figure appointed Archbishop of Melbourne in 1996. Pell is a big presence, a man of hard views who is not afraid to contradict his brother bishops. He's done that with drugs. Where Power spoke of tolerance and saving lives, Pell praised a 'stiff model with stiff penalties' to compel abstinence. In the aftermath of the 1998 Prime Minister's drug conference which the New South Wales Council of Churches had so zealously sought to influence, the Catholic bishops met and issued an opaque communiqué that endorsed nothing much except the vigorous prosecution of criminals. I rang Power and asked what had happened to the radical plans of a few years ago. 'We had to stop short. It's one of the difficulties you have putting out a statement 40 bishops can put their name to. But to say the solution to the drug problem is simply to get tougher and tougher with harsher penalties is not getting to the heart of the problem.'

The true test of a bishop's authority is to see him naked in a business suit. Pell's body is slumped but strong. His face is cut in slabs with a surprisingly small, busy mouth. Of the priests who'd joined the lawyers and businessmen to hear him speak about 'religion and freedom' at the Centre for Independent Studies, he seemed by far the most alive. Pell doesn't have the face of a man who has given up much. He may not be the cardinal — not yet — but this is what he wants to be: head of the biggest Catholic diocese in Australia with the personal backing of the man he calls 'our philosopher-Pope'. When Pell began to speak, he pitched his nasal baritone automatically to the resonance of the room. It's the habit of someone who talks in cathedrals. And he speaks at that particular pace priests, doctors and headmasters use for giving complex instructions — a slow, clear pace that says, if you fail to obey you don't have the excuse of mis-understanding me. The threat is in the rhythm.

Pell accused the Catholic Church of losing its nerve. 'We're frightened to put forward the hard teaching of Christ.' And he provoked a warm chuckle from his audience by quoting his hardline colleague at the Vatican, Cardinal Joseph Ratzinger: 'Christians are called to be the salt of the earth not the sugar of the earth.' George Pell is the messenger of hard teaching — not just on drugs. He is hard on those of us who want to read and watch what we like; hard on the old who want to choose their own time to die; hard on women who want contracep-tion, abortion or divorce; hard on religious women who want to be priests; hard on homosexuals who want sex, especially if they want to go to Mass too; and hard on dissidents who challenge the authority of the Pope and his bishops. In short, Pell is hard on freedom.

His analysis of freedom for the Centre for Independent Studies was not distinguished, just the usual sloppy equation of secular liberty with indecision and then — having made the obvious point that society requires authority — the easy assertion that this might as well come from the Catholic Church. Without God, freedom cannot flourish, hence a long riff on the evils of communism with quotes on torture from Solzhenitsyn: '. . . a ramrod heated over a primus stove would be thrust up their anal canal . . .'

Pell's idea of freedom must not be confused with the exercise of individual conscience. 'Catholic teachers should stop talking about the primacy of conscience. This has never been Catholic teaching.' Individuals who follow their own path are not free but followers of the Donald

Duck heresy, 'which rests squarely on the fallacy of overwhelming natural virtue. All you have to do to fulfil yourself is follow your natural impulses. Donald Duck always does this and always gets into trouble. It is a heresy which sanctifies mistakes, provided one is genuine, being oneself. Donald Duck is amusing, even loveable up to a point . . . '

Pell's own natural impulses are what count here, a familiar impulse deep in him to see the world on the brink of ruin. Parental values have been rejected. Restraint has been abandoned. The violence of the United States is heading our way. The great challenge to freedom is social disintegration caused by family breakdown, unemployment, alcohol, gambling, sexual irresponsibility — and drugs. A teacher rose at the end of Pell's speech to challenge his claim that adolescents these days are morally aimless: 'In thirty years I have never taught kids so concerned with spiritual issues.' Pell dismissed him with a few remarks about young people today not going to Mass.

And what did he think of the Sisters of Charity opening a safe injecting room? The archbishop's voice took on a warm burr. 'I can well understand the move is motivated by the very best intentions.' He paused. 'Everything we try in the drugs war isn't working. This particular initiative is not going to make a great deal of difference in the war against drugs.' Again he paused. 'We believe drug taking is wrong and sinful. The question is — is such a place weaning people off drugs? I'm not terribly optimistic.'

That Pell lines up with the abstainers — those who

measure success by habits kicked rather than lives saved — has important consequences for Australia's response to the drugs mess. He can't order the nuns to shut down and he can't drag the whole church with him, but Pell is a powerful Christian voice calling for war. Governments have been hunting for bishops to bless warfare as far back as the earliest days of the church. In this campaign, Pell is their man. He has a record of intervening in politics, either as an individual when he proposed the republic at the Constitutional Convention, or as the voice of Catholicism in campaigns against euthanasia and abortion. And now he's speaking as if with the voice of the church on drugs. He makes no apologies for these political interventions. 'The public benefits and consequences of Christian living,' he told the Centre for Independent Studies, 'need to be spelled out and defended at the ballot box.'

George Pell, Wayne Magee, Major Brian Watters and all who fall into step behind these Christian warriors have a hard question to answer every time they oppose a program that will save, here and now, even a single life. It's a question of faith, their real expertise. What would a Christian rather see, a death by overdose which sends a sinner straight to Hell, or a life saved that offers even an addict a chance for repentance and thus salvation? But that's a question never asked and never answered. Sitting among his eagles, Major Watters said, 'God has got some mandatory sentences. You know that, don't you? The wages of sin is death.'

TWO

NO MORE THAN THEY DESERVE

'The purpose of this motion is to generically express in relation to a number of issues the regret that the people of Australia feel . . . '

John Howard

John Howard has been walking towards this impasse all his life.

He can't say sorry. The word won't pass his lips. He can't accept the slightest trace of guilt, the least feeling of shame. When he speaks of what whites have done to blacks in this country, he uses the language of a careful solicitor admitting mistakes, errors, injustices or mistreatment that are not his own and happened way back in the past. He sees no present injustices standing in the way of reconciliation between black and white Australians, only lingering hurt and qualified pride in Australia's great achievements. As near as he could come to an apology in August 1999 when he proposed a carefully-drafted, seven part reconciliation statement in the House of Representatives, was the deep, sincere and 'generic' regret of the Australian people.

Crucial to John Howard's story is the man's unshakeable sense of himself as civilised and tolerant in his dealings with black Australia. Yet he has shown all his career that he's uncomfortable with contrary ideas on race. When he is challenged here, he responds as if his integrity is at stake. This matter is deep and personal. It all goes back to his Methodist youth.

Imagine a skinny kid with a quick tongue and a hearing aid. His father is dead. His mother shelters him from undesirable playmates. The family is teetotal, standoffish and proud. They don't mix. At sixteen, the boy is already in the Earlwood Young Liberals with ambitions to be a politician but his deeper commitment is to his faith. He's a devout adolescent Methodist. The church lies over the road. He spends summer weeks in the hothouse of Methodist youth camps down the coast. Salvation in Christ is his ambition. For Methodists the road to salvation calls for sobriety, respectability and hard work.

Those who search Howard's Sydney childhood for clues to this mysterious man cite a redoubtable mother, bad hearing, a working-class white suburb — 'It was what Australia was then' — the constant talk of politics around the table, pride in prosperity hard-earned in the family service station at Marrickville. All this mattered. So did the homely snobbery of the Howards that reassured a Protestant family nowhere near the top of the heap that they were, at any rate, in the right heap.

But the boy was profoundly marked by Methodism. We discussed this one day in an easy long talk on the phone. He's not a Methodist now but he's proud of what he learnt from the church and sees its plain, non-conformist beliefs as the core of his values. He has preached work and respectability all his life. Charity must be earned. He'll have a drink these days but he still loathes gambling. This is Methodism. And through the Methodist church he had his first contact with Aboriginal Australia. Methodists ran missions. 'It was very much a Christian mission to assist, so it was thought, people towards a better life. The Methodist Church did put a heavy emphasis on that.' The Methodist missions were strong in Fiji and Samoa and Tonga. The same Methodist Overseas Mission Board that ran the work of the church in the Pacific, managed the Methodist missions in Arnhem Land. 'Overseas' meant blacks.

What Earlwood kids knew about black Australia they learnt from holidaying missionaries who thrilled the Sunday School with first hand accounts of Christ's work among the Polynesians, the Micronesians and the Aborigines of Yirrkala, of Croker and Elcho islands, and of Ernabella and Milingimbi. Every quarter copies of *The Missionary Review* arrived at the church with pictures of neatly dressed women with very clean babies and working men dressed all in white. These were the hardworking, respectable, polite, sober, educated success stories of Methodist endeavour among the blacks. Christ brought more than goodness to these people. He brought character. The Rev. H. V. Shepherdson writing of the natives of Elcho Island, told the readers of *The Missionary Review*, 'We are convinced that to hold his own his character must be strengthened. To build his character, Christ must come into his life giving him moral power and a new outlook'.

Methodists didn't take it entirely for granted that they were doing good. By the time John Howard was in his mid-teens in the 1950s, Methodists were talking about a fresh direction that would test old practices and old prejudices. Politicians and missionaries were working together on this. They called it 'assimilation', helping natives come in from the wild and survive with dignity in the white community.

Methodists didn't deny the horrors of dispossession. It's a theme of *The Missionary Review* that Christians had a special obligation to deal charitably with people who had been so badly done by in the past. But it was taken for granted by the church at this time that the era of injustice was past. Dispossession was a subject of some moral anguish, but it was over and done with. The debates in Methodism were all about charity and education, not justice and restitution.

'And that's roughly your view now?'

'My view is very much that the best thing we can do is to give them opportunities. I don't hold the view that our society should be forced upon them. I don't know that I ever did hold that view. But it's not something that was so intensely debated then. You have to be fair to that generation, in that the debate about recompense for past misdeeds and the whole question of formal national apology and so on, they were not issues that were on the agenda. All came later, much later. And it was a different society.'

'But you haven't come to those either.'

'A lot of Australians haven't. You shouldn't speak as though mine is a starkly minority view on this.'

And it was an article of faith for Methodists that they were not racist. Their idea of racism was bad manners. It was racist to be impolite, to be rude. 'To be fair to those people and to the church,' Howard continued, 'it was not something people were especially conscious of. Because there wasn't a lot of mixing with people of different races it was hard to say that people reacted badly. But as an ethic, racial equality was something I was taught both by my parents and also by the church.'

But the Methodist Church didn't see it as racist that

whites made all the decisions in those black Methodist communities. Black and white weren't equal in the bush. In those years only the most radical Methodists in the field were expressing the hope that black and white might one day sit down together when deciding policies for Aboriginal Australia.

These were the missionary values that seeped into John Howard as an adolescent believer and lay dormant in him for over thirty years. In that very white suburb of Earlwood they were the only ideas on race in the air. They were by no means entirely contemptible. Education, training, responsibility, sobriety were part of the deal. The key for Howard was — and remains — giving blacks opportunities: 'It was very much founded in improving their opportunities and including them in the benefits of a society that was then regarded as a pretty good society.' But it was all so limited. Black Australia was expected to put behind it all the wrongs that had been and were being suffered. Life was to start anew, a good life on earth leading to Salvation in the life to come. Whites owed Aborigines the Christian obligation of decent treatment and charity. Blacks owed whites gratitude.

In the late fifties, young John Howard wasn't going to learn any different at Sydney University, especially as the only campus he knew was the Law School in Phillip Street. He didn't plunge into university politics — an early profile by Craig McGregor in *The National Times* blames the deaf aid — and his political world remained the Earlwood Young Libs. But he was exposed to racial issues which friends from those days believe subtly confirmed what his church had taught him. As a student,

Howard worked for a Jewish solicitor and had many Jewish friends at the Law School. These days there's a growing identification in the Jewish community with the situation of Aborigines. Holocaust lessons are being applied. But in the late fifties that shift lay far in the future. The Jewish community John Howard got to know was conservative, hard-working and mainstream — a model of successful assimilation.

Marriage finally carried the young man out of the reach of the Methodists, just as the church was changing. The Parkers were a social cut above the Howards and when Janette married this gawky young solicitor in 1971 she carried him into the Church of England. Her influence was profound. John and Janette were born to support each other: a pair of Young Libs, ambitious, old-fashioned, confidently decent. She didn't change him so much as make him almost invulnerable to change. The attitudes of the man Australia elected Prime Minister in 1996 were the attitudes of the man Janette married 25 years before. Had he stayed in the Methodist Church he might have been changed by the new spirit that blew strongly through Methodism in these years. Rather appalled by their own record in the mission field, Methodists were leaders of the push for redress, justice and respect for Aboriginal rights that developed in the seventies and eighties — with cautious but bipartisan support in Canberra. But this new spirit hardly touched the Anglican parishes of Sydney's lower North Shore where the Howards worshipped. In the judgement of that veteran Methodist leader Sir Alan Walker, John Howard was left, 'stalled in his old attitudes'.

Among the core lies of Pauline Hanson's One Nation Party is the claim that race has never been candidly debated in Australia: that politicians and élite commentators have been silenced by a moralising herd-mentality that's now called 'political correctness'. It's a picture John Howard has often endorsed, of a country reduced to a sort of coy silence on race. The truth is the subject of race — immigrant and Aboriginal — has hardly ever been off the political agenda. The history of Australia is punctuated by great public and parliamentary discussions which saw Canberra ditch white Australia, abandon assimilationist policies, bring Aborigines and Torres Strait Islanders under the federation's constitutional umbrella, give land rights to traditional owners in the Northern Territory and then, under Malcolm Fraser, extend those rights to include the power to veto mining on Aboriginal land.

This continuous process of enquiry and debate produced a bipartisan understanding in Canberra that Aboriginal Australia was owed both help with education, jobs, health and housing plus some restitution and amends for past injustices. This understanding produced some very patchy laws and each step of the way was contested — ferociously by Queensland and Western Australia — but from before the time of Whitlam, both sides of politics in Canberra had more or less agreed on what should be done. Then in the mid-eighties, Bob Hawke tried to extend land rights to the states. The uproar this caused was the end of bipartisanship. Faced with a hostile Opposition and under great pressure from Brian Burke, the West Australian Labor Premier and party bagman,

Hawke abandoned land rights and turned his attention instead to negotiating a treaty or compact between black and white Australia.

This was the point at which John Howard became Leader of the Opposition. One of the most curious things about his political career is that he rose to power with only one purpose: to transform the Australian economy. To that he gave intense, shrewd consideration for decades. More than once he put his future on the line to pursue the policies that made politics worthwhile for him. His public life has been a long, dry economic argument. Since reaching Canberra in 1974 he had hardly given race a thought.

'Howard showed no interest in land rights or Aboriginal matters,' recalled Ian Viner, Minister for Aboriginal Affairs in Malcolm Fraser's Cabinet. As Treasurer, Howard didn't contest the direction being taken by the Fraser government. Without complaint, he signed off on land rights, the Aboriginal Development Corporation and the first capital fund to compensate for the dispossession of traditional lands. He very rarely saw the outback. Aborigines very rarely, if ever, came into his office. South Africa was one of his enthusiasms. He hankered to travel there in the eighties but friends and advisers warned him this would be unwise. He wasn't pro–South Africa, he told the *Sydney Morning Herald*, 'It is a question of not treating South Africa any worse than other countries which have regimes which to me are even more unacceptable.' He cited the Soviet Union and Argentina.

Fraser fell, two years later Andrew Peacock walked out in a huff and in September 1985 Howard became

Leader of the Opposition, a man with no interest in race and no ideas on race. Rather than pursue the policies of his party, he fell back on the certainties of his adolescent faith. White Australia's duty was to give Aborigines 'opportunities' and address their 'current disadvantage'. Redressing wrongs was not on Howard's mind. The nuances of this shift are complex and still being worked out in practice but old hands like Viner saw the outline of what was happening in clear-cut terms: 'Under Fraser we recognised we had to address both needs and questions of justice. Howard acknowledges the needs but doesn't recognise there are issues of justice involved.'

The new atmosphere of partisan hostility over race suited him. Howard is an instinctively adversarial politician. Few if any issues have ever been considered by him to be too sensitive or too important for the ordinary brawling of Canberra politics. If there was party advantage to be had squabbling over race, Howard was happy to squabble. At first it just looked like brawling. The fact that he had come to power in the aftermath of the breakdown of the old bipartisan approach to black Australia disguised how radically Howard was going to shift policy on race.

He denounced Hawke's plans for a treaty as a 'cruel trick' on Aborigines. He attacked the treaty as if it would put a fence across the continent. 'There is no way the Australian people will ever accept that in some way we are two nations within one — nor should they.' Where others hoped a compact would heal division, Howard saw it creating, 'tensions and antagonisms that could well reduce public sympathy for, and understanding of, the real disadvantage and deprivation which is the lot of so many of our Aboriginal citizens. Whatever may be the history of the past 200 years, the reality of 1987 is that Australia is one nation with one destiny.'

Keeping Australia 'one nation' has been Howard's great theme in the years since. Time and again, he has argued with flat passion that Australia is at risk of 'legal fragmentation' if Aborigines are given more than 'an equal dispensation of justice'. Ask Howard precisely how this break-up is going to happen and he talks about a fragmenting sense of that egalitarianism which is 'such a valuable bond'. Press him further on his idea of Australian egalitarianism and it comes to seem peculiarly racist. Our egalitarian identity can survive ceaseless jockeying by everyone from Queenslanders to brain surgeons for a better-than-equal dispensation of justice, but apparently it can't survive a deal where Aborigines are the winners.

A few months after attacking the 'compact', Howard turned his guns on plans for an Aboriginal and Torres Strait Islander Commission to be elected by black Australians. 'If there is one thing, above everything else, that we in this parliament should regard as our sacred and absolute duty, it is the preservation of the unity of the Australian people. The ATSIC legislation strikes at the heart of the unity of the Australian people.' He warned: 'The government will not lift up Aborigines, embrace them, and right their wrongs by signing treaties or creating black parliaments. It will bring upon them more distrust, more hostility and more misunderstanding.'

Today Howard makes no apologies for that high-flown rhetoric of 'sacred and absolute duty' to protect

Australia's unity. Ask why the nation is so vulnerable on the question of black advantage and Howard starts talking about white resentment in the bush. 'There is a very different view about a body like ATSIC in rural Australia, than there is in urban. Deeply different.'

I said, 'When I look at your career you've fought extraordinary battles to change Australians' minds about industrial reform, about taxation systems. But yet I don't see in you this kind of fight against ordinary white resentment.'

'I suppose I have a more optimistic view about the ordinary white than you do. I think that is the answer. I do not believe the average white Australian is racist. I do not believe the average white Australian does not want Aborigines to be properly treated. I do not have a pessimistic view about Australians. I think they are a generous people. What I thought you were saying was that I lacked the determination to fight to change their attitudes.'

'That is what I was saying.'

'Well I think their basic attitude is decent where you apparently have a different view.'

The great talent Howard has for parliamentary debate was never really engaged to explain his views on race. All he did, year after year, was talk up the dangers of a white backlash that would imperil national unity. He began to be called a racist. He didn't like it but he couldn't answer the charge with any eloquence. Instead he rather haughtily objected to it being levelled. 'Whenever one disagrees with the minister or the Prime Minister one is bashing Aborigines or one is a racist,' he complained. 'One is not allowed to have a different view. If one does, one lacks compassion for Australia's black citizens. If one disagrees with the minister, one does not understand the Aboriginal people. If one disagrees with the Prime Minister's constant professions of moral concern, moral outpourings and moral outrage about the Aboriginal people, in some way one is forgetting the history of this country.'

Howard's own grasp of history was feeble. He personally reversed his party's pioneering support for land rights, claiming it was an unfair deal to rectify wrongs that all lay far in the past. This was to become one of his signature arguments in Opposition and Government. 'Land rights is fundamentally wrong, because what land rights inevitably leads to is large-scale alienation of enormous sections of Australia to a very few people. I do not accept the doctrine of hereditary guilt. I acknowledge that, in the past, wrongs were done to Aboriginals, but they weren't done by me. They weren't done by my parents. They weren't done by my generation. We are a separate, distinct, Australian nation of which the Aboriginals are a part, an honoured part, a special part, and I am all in favour of giving them special help. They need it. But I am strongly against dividing the country between black and white. I think that is a recipe for disaster.'

Yet Howard's generation and his faith were deeply implicated in the scandal of the stolen children. While he was still an active member of the church, the Methodists ran two notorious homes for children. One was the 'half-caste training institution' on Croker Island off the Arnhem Land coast. The other was Mogumber on the Moore River, north of Perth, a home for 'God's neglected children' which the Methodists had only taken over in the early 1950s. Congregations across Australia, including Howard's Earlwood parish, contributed cash to this work which continued until the late sixties on Croker Island. Mogumber was still going until about the time Howard entered Parliament. By this time word was already out about the stolen children. The men and women who ran the homes in their last years were leaders in awakening first the Methodist Church and later Australia to the evil of what had happened in these institutions — contemporary evil.

No one ridiculed Howard's history. His combative attitude to Aborigines paid him, instead, modest political dividends. After prolonged attacks on the administration of both the Department of Aboriginal Affairs and the Aboriginal Development Commission, Howard forced the Prime Minister to sack his Minister for Aboriginal Affairs, Clyde Holding, and the first senior black Commonwealth public servant, Charles Perkins, was forced out of the department. Not everyone on the Liberal side agreed that this campaign had been very useful. 'We found numerous examples of petty maladministration,' said the frontbencher Michael Wooldridge years later, 'But after the 100th time of saying we are attacking the administration of Aboriginal Affairs, all people heard was we are attacking Aborigines.'

In retrospect the most remarkable gesture of hostility to Aborigines in Howard's first stint as Leader of the Opposition came the day parliament first sat in its new palace on Capital Hill. Bob Hawke had proposed that the first resolution in the new House should be a bipartisan parliamentary declaration recognising prior Aboriginal occupation of Australia. Under John Howard, the Coalition refused.

Race was his undoing a few month's later. But it says a great deal about the politics of this country that the crisis came not over his long-held, clearly expressed attitude to Aborigines but because of a few unguarded remarks about migrants from Asia. At issue was his old familiar concern for the survival of Australia as one nation. Discussing Asian immigration on television one night, he said: 'It would be in our immediate-term interests, and supportive of social cohesion, if it were slowed down a little.' There was uproar. He would neither retract nor explain. He insisted he didn't have 'a prejudiced bone' in his body. For months the pressure continued from the churches, the press, Labor, migrant groups and the 'wet' faction of his own party. Lee Kuan Yew attacked him from Singapore and Malcolm Fraser from Nareen.

Trailing Hawke by more than 20 points in the polls, with the 'wets' in open revolt and an election coming within months, Howard was dispatched in a party-room putsch on the evening of 9 May, 1989. Andrew Peacock was leading the Opposition once again and promised a 'fairer' and 'more compassionate' country with a return to bipartisan policies on immigration and Aborigines.

Politicians in exile, reflecting on their downfall, can use these fallow years to remake themselves as great leaders. That was so for Howard's heroes, Churchill and Menzies. But the six years that passed before Howard was again

Leader of the Opposition had little impact on his attitudes to race that so largely precipitated his own downfall. He made a number of apologies in later years to the Asian community: 'I stuffed up on that.' But Howard was very bitter about those who turned against him in the immigration debate. His old staffer Gerard Henderson sees this as the time Howard began complaining about élites and the press, especially the ABC. Howard calls them all, 'Left-liberal by instinct and personal disposition'. This antipathy to 'élites' was tied up from the start with race, and closed him off to a range of contrary views on race. He sees the ABC as a particular source of manipulated history, false contrition, bogus sympathy and partisan Labor influence. The ABC doesn't help Aborigines. 'I think the apparent obsession with certain indigenous issues does go down very badly in the bush because the feeling is that the interests of the bush are being ignored.'

Howard remained just as stubborn about Aborigines and no more interested. It's not that he dislikes them. Those who have dealt with Howard on Aboriginal issues don't sense antipathy, just a lack of engaged interest. Rick Farley, both with the National Farmers' Federation and the Reconciliation Council, often watched Howard with Aboriginal delegations. 'You can see him just sitting there. He honestly doesn't understand where they are coming from. There's no dislike, just a very narrow personal frame of reference.'

What always interested John Howard was power and regaining power. That brings us to Mabo. The Opposition might have been able to make a more generous response to the High Court's landmark decision except that the Liberal Party was embroiled in another leadership brawl. Peacock had long gone and Hewson was hanging on to the leadership after losing the 'unlosable' 1993 election. Howard was still a contender and mobilised support in the party for a tough anti-Mabo line against Hewson's initially more accommodating approach. Hewson had tried to convince the party room that Mabo was one of those issues where they should rise above party politics. Howard attacked him in reply for denigrating politicians.

All the leadership contenders — Howard, Peter Reith and Peter Costello — were economic rationalists and they bid the party down on Mabo. And as most of the land at stake lay in Western Australia, Hewson had at his heels the same men of the west who'd killed off Hawke's land rights legislation a decade before. The leader needed their votes to fend off challenges. Insecure after the election loss, circled by Howard, Hewson was rolled on Mabo and the Coalition decided to oppose, absolutely, the native title legislation. Many Liberal MPs were appalled by this but Howard rallied the troops in the party room to maintain absolute opposition to legislation 'rotten to the core'.

Howard's instincts on race were untouched by Mabo though the court's rejection of terra nullius — the doctrine that Australia wasn't owned by its inhabitants in 1788 — presents a direct challenge to those like him who see no obligations of justice owed to Aborigines for lands lost. Under terra nullius Australia was there for anyone to take and the whites took it. End of story. But the High Court put a lie to that, both as law and as history. What whites took, blacks had once owned, and owned absolutely by rights older than the common law.

After Mabo, strange skirmishes over history offered a way out to those who wanted to go on denying obligations from the past. Warriors in these history wars don't deny the dark side of our national story, but deny that current obligations arise from killings, rape and dispossession. Howard is a keen skirmisher in these little battles. He explained to me that history is a balance sheet. What really matters is the bottom line. 'I fully acknowledge that there are plenty of blemishes and plenty of mistakes' but on balance the history of Australia is not 'negative and shameful'. So we have a right to take a sunny attitude to the situation today. It's a view Howard shares with Geoffrey Blainey whom he regards as the quintessential Australian historian. The two men see eye to eye on the fundamental political obligation of preserving national 'cohesion'. Howard found in Blainey support for his disastrous public remarks about the need to slow down Asian immigration.

Around the time of Mabo, Blainey began to speak of 'black armband' historians who are false to the real Australia by always mourning for the country's past. The black armbander, he wrote, 'laments . . . above all the treatment of Aborigines'. Howard adopted this expression and along with it the notion that what's really going on here is a contest between optimists and pessimists. The Blainey forces see themselves as optimistic, realistic and patriotic. Ranged against them are troops once commanded by gloomy Manning Clark and now by Henry Reynolds, cataloguing the horrors and illegalities of dispossession. Howard calls the optimists patriots. 'By contrast, the apologists take a basically negative view of Australian history and light upon every great national occasion not to celebrate Australian achievements but to attempt the coercion of us all into a collective act of contrition for the past.'

Contrition is what young John Howard wasn't taught by the Methodists. They were only learning it themselves as Howard was leaving the church. Howard neither shares contrition nor does he respect in others that contrition towards Aborigines that is shifting the moral map of this country. His view remains that sympathy to Aborigines is due but contrition is bogus. He ravels false history up with false guilt and false contrition in the catch-all term of abuse that he has made his own: 'political correctness'.

Howard accuses the press, the 'wets' of his own party and the churches of aping 'politically correct' sentiments. This is not feigned. It's a source of both great frustration and tactical weakness in the man that he is so sure his position is morally and politically unassailable. It leaves him sincerely puzzled by the part black issues play in Australian politics. Locked into the missionary idea that Aborigines deserve decent charity, he's baffled by the continuous demands of what he calls — without embar-rassment — 'the Aboriginal industry'. He directs something like hatred towards those whom he blames for using Aborigines, egging them on, manipulating them for political advantage.

John Howard was once again leading the Opposition as Australia headed to the polls in 1996. While the campaign lasted he was very cautious about race. When the Nationals' Bob Katter complained about 'politically correct enviro-nazis and femo-nazis and all the rest of these little slanty-eyed ideologues who persecute ordinary average Australians', Howard forced him to apologise. When an unknown Pauline Hanson threatened to embarrass the campaign, Howard moved swiftly to have the Queensland Liberals disendorse her. As Howard's biographer, David Barnett, remarked: 'Whatever the merits of her opinions, there was no room for her in the campaign.'

But even before the elections were over and won it was clear Hanson was in many ways a woman after Howard's own heart. She complained about Aboriginal privilege. She talked of white resentment in the bush being fanned by their favourable treatment. She used the same rhetoric of 'equality' that Howard used on the election trail to argue against initiatives of redress and amends. She complained of money wasted by and on Aborigines. Above all she argued the need to preserve Australia as 'one nation'. On only a couple of crucial points are Hanson and Howard at odds. She evidently dislikes Aborigines. He doesn't. She denies Aboriginal need. Howard never does. 'I don't agree with her when she implies that Aborigines as a group are not disadvantaged,' he said after her maiden speech. 'I think they are.' Despite the frantic urging of his colleagues, that was the only answer Howard would make to that speech, the naked racism of which made headlines everywhere. Pauline Hanson was soon the most famous Australian on the globe.

As Prime Minister, Howard was determined to be true to himself on race. The first meeting of the Howard

Cabinet decided to put special auditors through ATSIC. The government's first budget cut ATSIC's funds by more than $400m. When the furore over Hanson reached such a height that it was decided to make a bipartisan parliamentary declaration on racial tolerance, Howard's side banned the language of shame, past injustice and spiritual needs. When an enquiry into the stolen children begun by the Keating government reported to Howard's parliament in May 1997 and formal apologies were being made for these outrages by churches and governments, the new Prime Minister refused absolutely to apologise on behalf of Australia.

Even his old church, now subsumed into the Uniting Church, was urging him to say sorry for the nation. The head of Keating's enquiry, Sir Ronald Wilson, was a former president of the Uniting Church. For Howard this was all very close to home. The church had already made its own apologies for Croker Island and Mogumber, acknowledging to the Aboriginal community that it thought it was acting, 'in a loving way by providing them with homes but was blind to the racist assumptions that underlay the policy and practice'. Howard would not follow suit.

When a test case on the stolen children began in Darwin in early 1999, his government instructed lawyers to fight the case tooth and nail. No mistreatment would be conceded. Assimilation would be defended. The forced removal of half-caste children from their mothers was described by the government's lawyers as noble in both intention and outcome. It might have been Howard addressing the court. 'The motivation was not one of doing evil or doing harm,' he said of the Methodist missions of the 1950s. 'The motivation was noble. It may, with the benefit of hindsight be seen as misguided and inappropriate and all those other things, but people at that time who were involved acted out of the best of motives.' He will not concede the racist assumptions that underlay it all.

When Australia was trying to define its sense of itself in a new preamble to the Constitution, Howard refused — despite Mabo and Wik — to allow mention of prior ownership of the land by the indigenous people of the continent. That, too, is an old cause. Ten years earlier Howard had condemned as 'an exercise in national lunacy' the words of the preamble to the ATSIC legislation that spoke of 'prior occupiers and original owners of the land'. For the first time, terra nullius was to be declared a sham. Again Howard argued national survival. 'We're not in the business of undermining the basis of our Constitution in establishing a plethora of claims for compensation for dispossession.' He has always been absolutely true to himself here.

His government has the uncertain distinction of being the first in the history of the Commonwealth to deprive Aborigines of rights and property already granted. The Hindmarsh Island Bill was designed to silence Aboriginal women who claimed their spiritual life would be compromised by the building of a bridge to a little resort island in the Murray. The politics of Hindmarsh were ferocious. A minister fell. Labor eventually supported the legislation. When it was challenged before the High Court, the Howard government instructed counsel to argue Canberra had the very widest power to legislate *against* Aborigines, powers as broad as Nazi Germany and South Africa if necessary. Canberra won and so established a legal and political precedent for denying Aborigines protection when white Australia wants something of theirs badly enough. It's the old familiar principle of pre-Mabo Australia: what whites want, whites get.

That is the lesson of Howard's response to Wik. The High Court in Mabo had said blacks might still own the wasteland whites had not taken. That was a psychic, legal and political shock for Australia. Paul Keating's response was to regulate those rights by legislation. In Wik in December 1996 the court told white Australia it might have to share some of the good country that was already in its hands. Howard's response to this second shock was a Ten-Point Plan to cut back black rights. Now the man who had so often preached the 'sacred duty' of preserving national unity divided Australia more deeply than it had been on any issue since the upheaval of 1975. The Opposition parties and Brian Harradine saw he didn't get everything he wanted but he clawed back from black Australia as much as he possibly could of what whites wanted for themselves.

What would history make of this, I asked him? 'Racial dispossession all over again?'

'I don't think history will do that,' Howard replied. 'I think history will judge that we went through a difficult period of adjustment to a new concept and in the end got the balance right.'

'By taking most of it away?'

'I don't agree with that. We haven't taken away the original Mabo decision in any way. David we haven't.'

'If you step a long way back from this it's going to look like just another transfer of rights and property from black to white.'

'I don't agree with that. That won't influence your writings but that is not my view.'

He believes it will all calm down now. 'The issue will go off, will disappear, not totally but it will largely disappear as a bone of contention.' Again, he doesn't trust the history that lies at the heart of the story of Australia: injustice keeps trouble alive. But John Howard is one of those politicians for whom issues are finished with once they are won. Winning is everything. He once said, 'I am the bloke who ultimately wins the last battle, and in political terms that is Churchill'.

Black Australia's verdict is a little different. They see John Howard as a familiar figure from their own recent past. 'There has never been a sense that the Prime Minister had any interest in what we said or represented,' concluded the distinguished Aboriginal leader of ATSIC, Dr Lowitja (Lois) O'Donoghue. 'He was just the missionary type.'

John Howard made much of having changed his mind when he rose in the House of Representatives in August 1999 to move his 'historic resolution' of regret. 'People are entitled to reflect on what I have said in the past . . . Some will criticise me. Some will say that I have changed my position on some aspects of this. I do not mind if they do.' He told the nation he had changed in response to magnanimous compromise by indigenous leaders. Their compromise is clear. His change of heart is all but invisible. The official resolution he hammered out with the Democrats and their new black senator Aiden Ridgeway is roughly what Howard has believed all his political life — and longer. The regret he expressed was not new, nor was his refusal to apologise. What poetry he had in him that day he spent on 'the scale and the immensity of the Australian achievement' and the 'celebration of unity' that awaits us when we reach the centenary of Federation in 2001. Injustice is a thing of the past. What matters now are 'practical measures leading to practical results' for black Australia

The resolution called for no change of heart, no change of mind, no change of attitude from white Australians. Howard spoke only of changing indigenous minds, to allow them to be reconciled to us, to remove what hesitation or constraints might make them reluctant to join us in the big party in 2001. 'In order to do that, our indigenous Australians must feel a proper sense of reconciliation and a proper sense of being, in every way and totally, part of the Australian community.'

Too much can be read into a single word, but that 'our' chimes with the spirit of Howard's speech and the spirit of his career on race, to suggest that the unified Australia of his imagination is as white now as it was when he was a kid in Earlwood and the church over the road talked of 'our' missions to the north bringing the benefits of Christ Jesus to 'our' natives, to help them one day join 'our' community. What made that seem virtuous back then was the sense deep down that 'our' obligations to black Australia was decent Christian charity. Their obligation to us was gratitude. This makes sense of Howard's thinking still.

THREE

ORDINARY MEN

'Immediately after his arrival at the police station, the appellant admitted killing the deceased. He never resiled from that admission. He told the police: "Yeah, I killed him, but he did worse to me." When asked why he had done it, the appellant said: "Because he tried to root me."'

Justice Michael Kirby
Malcolm Thomas Green v. The Queen.

Investigations of bigotry take us to strange times, strange places and strange corners of the human heart. Tracking the hatred of homosexuality — a commonplace sexual variation as old as the human race — takes us back to the Judea of Abraham's day, to Alexandria in the very early years of the Church and to Rome in 1179 — from whence it's been a long, straight, bumpy ride to Botany Bay and its outlying suburb Canberra, where lately a brutal young killer engaged the sympathy of the High Court by pleading that he was provoked to kill when a naked man climbed into his bed, hugged him, and gently touched his groin.

Most of us go through life with the moral values of faiths we've long ago abandoned. But the Chief Justice Sir Gerard Brennan who led the court to this grim conclusion is a man deeply influenced by a living belief in Catholicism and an intimate understanding of its values and history. Brennan's brand of Catholicism brings with it not only an instinct for racial justice that gave Australia Mabo but a freight of bigotry about homosexuality which he has now helped fix in Australian law.

Eight appeal court judges have now examined the case of Malcolm Green who in May 1993 killed a gay real estate agent in the prosperous town of Mudgee, west of the Blue Mountains. Two out of three judges of the New South Wales Court of Criminal Appeal called it murder. But three out of five judges of the High Court opted for the possibility of manslaughter. Ferociously complex questions of law were involved but these didn't really divide the judges. Green's case was decided by the gut feelings of those eight men about the values of ordinary Australians.

As it happened, the Catholics carried the day. Sir Gerard Brennan, Michael McHugh and John Toohey held that to kill as Malcolm Green said he killed may not be murder. The judges saw where he was coming from, they didn't forgive him but they offered a little consideration. Green's case establishes in Australian law the proposition that violence will be looked on a little kindly by the courts if it's provoked by one man making a pass at another.

Malcolm Green turned up in blood-splattered clothes at the Mudgee police station before dawn and said, 'I've killed Don Gillies'. Was he sure the man was dead? He was sure. In a house a few blocks from the station police found a very dead man. Gillies lay face down in a pool of blood beside a blood-soaked bed. Sprays of blood reached the walls and even the high old ceiling of the room. These experienced officers had never seen such a battered corpse. The skull was smashed and there were nearly a dozen stab wounds. They found one weapon — a pair of gourmet chicken shears — but searched in vain for some heavy object that Green might have used to batter the man's skull. The police couldn't believe he'd done such damage with his fists alone. They photographed Green's hands that night, hands unmarked after apparently landing three dozen heavy blows.

What the dead man's friends couldn't understand — and still can't — is how skinny young Malcolm Green could overpower Don Gillies who was a big fit man of 36, built like the truck driver he once was. He had a gym in the garage. He worked out. He ran. Gillies had been drinking heavily that night but that would make him an even tougher customer to deal with. The dead man is remembered for his generosity, his charm, his music, his endless laughter — but also for his one failing: when he drank he turned nasty. He wasn't violent — and Green never claimed he was — but there was a taunting, aggressive edge to Gillies when he got stuck into the whisky. What blood there was left in his body gave a reading of .225 next morning. His friends ask, how could this man have been overpowered and killed by Green unless he was caught unawares?

And why in that meticulously neat house were those chicken shears lying accidentally by the bed instead of hanging where they always hung on the wagon wheel in the kitchen? And why was there a bottle of amyl nitrate by their empty glasses in the sitting room? And why was Green so sober and Gillies so drunk? And if Green was asked for sex and didn't want to have sex, why didn't he just leave the house and go home? Why did he bash and stab to death a friend of six years?

Australian country towns can be comfortable places for gay men to live. The rules of acceptance are those that everyone lived by three or four decades ago: you can be as queer as you like so long as you're not the mayor, the priest or some other figure of authority round the place, and the locals aren't made to acknowledge you're actually having sex. This is, in its way, a secular version of the Christian distinction between the predilection and the act: being homosexual is unfortunate; having sex is a sin. And if they like you enough out in the bush they'll go to some lengths to hide the obvious truth from themselves.

They liked Don Gillies: he didn't act queer and if he was having it off with the locals, no one in Mudgee ever heard about it. Sure, he was unmarried, he lived at home with his Mum, he drove a little red coupé and played the organ at St John's but — as the old ladies who thought him so wonderful said — 'That was just Don'.

He was still driving trucks when he met Malcolm (Mootch) Green in about 1988. The kid was then sixteen, the product of a wretchedly unhappy childhood in Condobolin. He had no money, little work and lots of troubles with the police. Over the next few years Green was in prison for stealing, later for growing dope and then for a few days in 1992 for assault. Gillies helped him with advice, sometimes a bit of cash and introduced him to the church (not a success). Over the years they'd been drinking, swimming, and jogging together. By 1993 Gillies was managing rental properties for a Mudgee real estate agent and a couple of times had found places for Green and his girlfriend to live. Winter was coming on and Gillies had gone over there in May to give them a heater. Perhaps this generosity was coming to an end. Gillies was saying in Mudgee he'd had enough of Green hassling him for help.

Green's girlfriend shot through at this time. A day or so later the young man was hanging around the house of a Mr Dean Sirola in Mudgee. He asked Sirola if he knew of anyone who could 'knock someone off'. Who the victim might have been was never clear. Was it the girl? Was it Gillies? Was it — as lawyers later claimed — Green's father? What was clear to Sirola was that Green had killing on his mind. He reminded the young man that knocking people off was not right.

Next day Gillies invited Green round for a steak. At this time Gillies' mother was away in Sydney coping with the awful business of moving her own mother into a nursing home. The two men ate and watched television. Gillies drank a lot. Afterwards Green said he was persuaded to stay the night — he sleeping in Gillies' bed and Gillies in his mother's bed — and had just fallen asleep when Gillies climbed in naked and began caressing him. He says he protested, 'I'm not like this' and pushed Gillies away but that Gillies' hands were all over him. It was, he said, when he was touched 'gently' on the groin that he began to punch while Gillies hugged and tried to soothe him. 'I hit him again and again on top of the bed until he didn't look like Don to me. He still tried to grope and talk to me, that's when I hit him again and saw the scissors on the floor on the right-hand side of the bed. When I saw the scissors he touched me around the waist–shoulders area and said, 'Why?' I said to him, 'Why, I didn't ask for this'. I grabbed the scissors and hit him again. He rolled off the bed as I struck him with the scissors. By the time I stopped I realised what had happened. I just stood at the foot of the bed with Don on the floor laying face down in blood.'

He called his brother-in-law to come and collect him then made a few perfunctory attempts to clean up. Somewhere on the journey home he decided to turn himself in. He was dropped near the police station. Don Gillies had died, he said, because he tried to root him. During the long night of interrogation that followed, Green explained that he'd 'lost it' in bed because he suddenly recalled his father's sexual abuse of his sisters. 'Just that when I tried to push Don away and that and I started hitting him it's just — I saw the image of my father over two of my sisters, Cherie and Michelle, and they were crying and I just lost it.'

Talk to those who defend the terrible outcome of this case in the High Court and they will tell you it really turned on the abstruse technical question of whether Green was allowed to cite the flashback to explain why he was provoked to bash Gillies. That's technically so and all the appeal judges who looked at this case agreed the jury should have been allowed to take the flashback into account. But the flashback only gets Green halfway home. Even if everything he said about that night were true — the sexual pass, the flashback, the details of the brawl — he still had to convince the jury that an ordinary person provoked as he was provoked might be excused to some degree for so losing control that he decided to kill Gillies or cause him grievous bodily harm. If lawfully provoked it was manslaughter. If not it was murder.

A jury in the Blue Mountains' town of Katoomba had no doubt it was murder and Green was sentenced to fifteen years. But the condemned man appealed, claiming the judge had denied him the full benefit of the flashback.

The New South Wales Court of Criminal Appeal agreed the judge was wrong but by a majority of two to one decided no miscarriage of justice had occurred as a result. The court confirmed both the murder conviction and the fifteen-year sentence. Speaking for the majority, Justice Bill Priestley said: 'It is easy to see that many an ordinary person in the position in which the appellant was when Mr Gillies was making his amorous physical advances would have reacted indignantly, with a physical throwing off of the deceased, and perhaps with blows. I do not think however that the ordinary person could have been induced by the deceased's conduct so far to lose self-control as to have formed an intent to kill or inflict grievous bodily harm upon Mr Gillies.'

The failure of Green's appeal was greeted with relief by police and lawyers worried by the appearance in Australia of what's called the 'homosexual advance defence' — the argument that men can be excused even horrific violence if it's in response to a man trying to fondle or kiss them. This idea was born on psychiatrists' couches in America in the 1930s and reached the courts there in the sixties. It was a marvellous new device to give violence a respectable face in the courtroom. By the eighties the tactic had reached New South Wales and young — overwhelmingly young — men were being acquitted or convicted on lesser charges after bashing or killing gay men even where the evidence suggested they'd deliberately targeted them and even when these sprees ended in shabby robberies. What makes this worse are official figures that showed even in this tolerant country disturbing levels of violence against homosexuals. They are still four times more likely to be assaulted and about twice as likely to be murdered as Australians in general.

In a few New South Wales cases in the nineties the 'homosexual advance defence' was pleaded after violent killings.

- McKinnon said he was lured to the victim's house to buy marijuana and hit him with a wine bottle when he jumped on the bed and tried to seduce him. He also knifed and bashed the man, left him unconscious then stole his car and boasted he'd just 'rolled a fag'. Acquitted of murder.

- Turner said he was wandering down the road when a stranger invited him in for a drink then a little later grabbed his bum with both hands and 'said something'. Turner bashed the old man with a garden gnome, stabbed him a number of times, stole and later tried to sell the dead man's video. He was found not guilty of murder and sentenced for three years for manslaughter.

- Dunn was cycling along a bike path when a man in a frock appeared waving his penis, thrusting his hips and saying he was going to 'get' him. Dunn was seen punching and kicking the transvestite for forty minutes. The body was found next morning half-naked with a stocking tied round its penis. Dunn stole the man's keycard and cigarettes and boasted afterwards that he'd 'bashed a rock spider'. A jury found him not guilty of murder and he was sentenced to seven years for manslaughter.

- Richards, a man with a violent criminal record, collapsed in a stupor from drink and drugs in a friend's house. Weeks later he learnt something not quite amounting to 'sexual interference' had happened to him while unconscious. Returning to the house with two mates, he punched the man to death and they stole the television. He was found not guilty of murder and sentenced to four and a half years minimum for manslaughter.

The tactic worked best while violent kids could make an impassioned speech of horror and disgust from the dock without being cross-examined. Then the rules were changed so they had to defend their violence under close questioning. Green's case was an example of the new courtroom response to this — to argue both homosexual advance plus something extra. In this case the flashback: a sexual advance from a 'father figure' that brought the horrifying plight of his sisters (not himself) to mind with violent consequences. That the new double-barrel tactic had failed in Green's case was particularly gratifying to police and lawyers. It sounded like the death knell of the homosexual advance defence. Then Green appealed to the High Court — and won.

The five justices of the High Court were to spend a year mulling over their reasons. They devoted acres of complex argument to the provocation provisions of the NSW Crimes Act. But what they had to decide in the end was a question of values. Could Malcolm Green's response to that light touch on his groin be excused in any way as the response of an ordinary Australian? Three men on the court said yes. The reason why has to be found in their lives as much as their law books, in the values in which they were born and raised. That the court split along religious lines — Protestants for murder and Catholics for the possibility of manslaughter — wasn't entirely a fluke. Sex between men is a matter of particular moral difficulty for Catholics.

Among the handful of beliefs common to nearly every brand of Christianity from the most ancient Orthodox faiths of the Old World to the newest Pentecostal sects of suburban Melbourne are these two: that Jesus Christ rose from the dead, and that homosexuals are bound for hell. Of all the mainstream faiths it's Catholicism that remains most robustly convinced that for a man to make a pass at another man is a sin of the blackest kind. Such bigotry comes in the guise of plain teaching to Catholic children: to Michael McHugh at his mother's knee, to John Toohey at the Jesuits' St Louis School in Perth, and to the schoolboy Gerard Brennan swotting for his life under the direction of the Missionaries of the Sacred Heart at Downlands College, Toowoomba.

The Bible isn't neutral about homosexuality despite what clever gay scholars try to argue these days. The Good Book disapproves and it's as trivial to argue otherwise as it is to claim that a dozen or so verses scattered through the Bible settle the moral issues involved for all time. But those scholars are right to quarrel with the Genesis account of Sodom and Gomorrah for whatever brought fire and brimstone raining down on the cities of the plain it wasn't sodomy. Even the maths are against it. The Lord promised Abraham he would save Sodom if he could find ten righteous living within its walls. He couldn't. So whatever the unspecified vice — probably luxury — that provoked

THE HIGH PRICE OF HEAVEN

God to mass slaughter by molten lava, the women were in it up to their necks.

But there's no denying the book of Leviticus where homosexuality is listed among the prohibitions, sexual and dietary, that God dictated straight to Moses. These are the rules that set the Jewish nation apart from the tribes around them. They go on for chapters. They get down to things like forbidding dwarfs to make offerings to the Lord. It's in this part of the Bible we learn which of our relatives we can't marry. It's here the Jehovah's Witnesses find their fatal objection to blood transfusions. And at Leviticus 20:13 God told Moses: 'If a man also lie with mankind, as he lieth with a woman, both of them have committed an abomination: they shall surely be put to death; their blood shall be upon them.'

Centuries later, Christians took this Jewish distaste for homosexuality into the world of late Imperial Rome where it was, to say the least, unfamiliar. Pagan Rome was never Hollywood's wet dream of an erotic free-for-all. There were lots of rules of decorum, deportment and family life. Some of these touched on homosexuality, but homosexuality was neither forbidden by law nor stigmatised by society. The late John Boswell of Yale, a controversial historian of homophobia, wrote 'Neither the Roman religion nor Roman law recognised homosexual eroticism as distinct from — much less inferior to — heterosexual eroticism'. Of love poetry of that era Boswell wrote, 'It is extremely difficult to convey to modern audiences the absolute indifference of most Latin authors to the question of gender'.

Distaste for homosexuality was one facet of a new

Christian sense of the body that was to transform the moral universe in which we still live. The Romans saw the body as the sensual, sometimes unruly companion of the spirit. The body had to be taught and disciplined, but also needed sensual gratification. The spirit looked after the body in a mood of alert but friendly care.

But Christianity came out of Judea with the terrible idea that the body was the enemy of the soul. To conquer death, Christians had first to conquer the body so that body and soul together could make the journey to heaven. The Greeks and Romans taught that a measure of sexual abstinence made you strong but Christians believed it made you holy. The ideal of chastity, which was not unknown to ancient prophets and pagan cults, came in from the fringes to the heart of belief.

So keen were Christians for this new cult of abstinence that they had to be encouraged to marry. In offering the most famous sex advice of all time — 'It is better to marry than to burn' — St Paul was making the sensible point that celibacy is not for everyone. Paul praised celibacy very highly — 'It is good for a man not to touch a woman' — but also recommended a Christian brand of sex made holy by lots of rules and denials. One of these denials was homosexuality. And a century or so later, Clement of Alexandria came up with the formula that sex is *only* holy within marriage and for procreation. Christ said nothing of the kind. Not even Paul had taken such a stern view of the matter. But however foreign, however cruel, however artificial, however unconvincing, Clement's idea took hold at the end of the second century and Western civilisation lurched further down a very odd track.

It took time to work out all the implications of Clement's rule: no masturbation (very important), no contraception (simply unthinkable), no sex when conception is unlikely (lactation and menstruation), no sex in positions that inhibit or forbid conception (anal, oral), no sex for the barren (it would only be pleasure), and, naturally, no homosexuality.

Peter Brown in *The Body and Society* wrote, 'Strict codes of sexual discipline were made to bear much of the weight of providing the Christian Church with a distinctive code of behaviour. Sexual prohibitions had always distinguished Jews, in their own eyes at least, from the sinister indeterminacy of the gentiles. These were now asserted with exceptional vigor. Christian marital codes were rendered yet more idiosyncratic by a few novel features, such as the relinquishment of divorce and a growing prejudice against the remarriage of widows and widowers. Above the solid conglomerate of ancient, Jewish notions there now rose the peak of total chastity.'

That ideal haunts Western civilisation still — the moral heroism of saying no to sex. This is the ground from which the Christian fear of sensuality springs. Wherever churches want drugs policed, books banned, flesh censored, sex education curtailed and contraception forbidden they are acting from an instinct now deeply absorbed in old society, that of chastity itself as an ideal moral state. Priests were always the sex police of society. There are Catholic, Protestant and Orthodox priests who still find the role irresistible. So do civilian Christians. A judge can look at the killing of a man who tried to kiss and fondle another man and see not one but two moral problems here — not just violence but sexuality.

Not that Christians thought homosexuality was a major problem until quite late in the piece. Sex between men was a sensual failing which suddenly from about 1050 was transformed by dynamic zealots into a major sin — worse than sex with a beast or incest with your mother, as bad as cannibalism, a criminal wickedness, a blinding self-indulgence, a radical rejection of God, a violation of grace, reason and nature that calls down destruction in this life and banishment to hell for ever. It was at this time, a couple of thousand years after Genesis was composed, that the name of Sodom was first attached to this freshly demonised sin.

The reasons for this sudden panic are obscure but it happened as the Western church was coming to the momentous decision to enforce celibacy on its priests. This was a wretched development for straight priests who lost their wives when clerical marriages were forcibly dissolved. Meanwhile, gay monks and priests went on living as they always had. Scholars speculate that the reworking of the old distaste for homosexuality as an especially dark sin was institutional revenge by the straight clergy against the gay. What was done initially for internal purposes became a general rule for Christendom. At the Third Lateran Council in 1179 it was decreed for the first time that homosexual clerics were to be deposed from office and homosexual laymen should, 'suffer excommunication and be cast out from the company of the faithful'.

Whatever the catalyst within the church, the 12th century was an age of vengeful uniformity. Both church and state sought traitors in their midst. These usually came in threes: an evil trinity of sodomites, heretics, and Jews. The same council that condemned homosexuals, set limits to the economic and civil liberty of Jews in Europe. The propaganda of the Crusades claimed Moors were insatiable sodomites, having their way with Christian boys, priests and bishops. The Holy Land had to be rescued as much from anal sex as Islam. I like to think that modern fantasies about the extraordinary erotic refinement of the Arab world go back to the evil propaganda that launched those pointless Crusades.

From Leviticus to the Lateran, every step was bigotry. As with all bigotry, the moral at the heart of its history is that it didn't have to turn out this way. Other traditions that might easily have allowed homosexuality to survive with pagan dignity were stifled and crushed. Gay Christian historians try to present this as a series of unfortunate accidents. But it doesn't wash. What's remarkable about Christianity is its persistent focus on issues of sexual purity and its use of homosexuality — especially in this last millennium — as a dramatic example of impurity.

Wherever Christianity went on the globe, dogma was turned into criminal laws against gay men, laws that seemed to express a fundamental moral value of Western society. But the engine of homophobia was always the church. These days these laws are being repealed everywhere but always in the face of opposition from the churches. Australia took twenty five years from 1972 in South Australia to 1997 in Tasmania, to ditch laws that threatened homosexuals with life imprisonment for having sex. Catholic bishops fought the process nearly every step of the way. Then Green's case came along in 1996 to remind us that cleaning up old laws is not enough. Bigotry like faith is infinitely resourceful.

'When you say "amorous",' interjected the Chief Justice, 'you mean sexual.' His reproach hung in the air. Judges and lawyers alike were astonished. Couldn't Don Gillies be amorous? Can homosexuals only be sexual? In the way of such proceedings, Chief Justices are never challenged to make themselves clear. Brennan seemed to be reproaching the Crown's advocate for linking homosexuality and love.

Justice McHugh had the floor at the time. He was painstakingly assembling what details he could to show that Don Gillies had roughly handled young Green. 'He may have been gentle to start with but then there is the pulling towards him, he pulled him close to him so that there was no room between them, and that is when he got aggressive.'

'I do understand, with respect, what your Honour is putting to me,' replied Keith Mason, Q.C., 'but it remained in the context of an amorous, not a physically aggressive approach.'

That's when the Chief Justice intervened. Mason didn't want to brawl over the point. He reminded Brennan he was using the words of Justice Bill Priestley speaking for a majority of the judges of the New South Wales Court of Criminal Appeal. The moment passed. McHugh went on assembling his portrait of a young man gravely provoked by Gillies. 'It is a sexual assault.' Justice Michael Kirby corrected him: 'Not technically.' But

McHugh's mind was back in the old days before homo-sexuality was taken out of the Crimes Act. Back then, he argued, Don Gillies could have 'been convicted of indecent assault or indecent dealing'. The law had moved on but not McHugh.

Few in that courtroom would have been unaware that Justice Kirby was himself homosexual, though he was still a couple of years away from revealing the fact in the fine print of *Who's Who*. It was, like Pulcinella's secret, known to everyone. Kirby stood resolutely by the murder verdict. He asked, how would an ordinary Australian react to the situation in that Mudgee bedroom? 'He or she might, depending on the circumstances, be embarrassed; treat it at first as a bad joke; be hurt; insulted. He or she might react with the strong language of protest; might use as much physical force as was necessary to effect an escape; and where absolutely necessary assault the persist-ent perpetrator to secure escape. But the notion that the ordinary 22-year-old male (the age of the accused) in Australia today would so lose self-control as to form an intent to kill or grievously injure the deceased because of a non-violent sexual advance by a homosexual person is unconvincing. It should not be accepted by this Court as an objective standard applicable in contemporary Australia.'

Justice Gummow stood by the murder verdict also, citing 'contemporary conditions and attitudes' to find that even allowing for all the terrible events of his childhood that may have gone through his mind in that crisis, Green could not be excused in this day and age for so losing his self-control. To say otherwise, Gummow concluded, 'would undermine principles of equality before the law and individual responsibility'.

But ranged against them was a majority of the court willing to see the possibility of manslaughter in that horrific killing. McHugh and Toohey spoke mildly and pitched their argument in terms of refinements of the law of provocation. But the Chief Justice spoke with visceral disgust. He painted Gillies' behaviour in the darkest moral colours, not as unwanted 'amorous' fumbling but a potentially 'terrifying' and 'revolting' act of sexual abuse intended to coerce Green into providing 'sexual gratification'. A jury would be entitled, Brennan decided, to see Green's response as a loss of self-control provoked by moral outrage. 'The real sting of the provocation could have been found not in the force used by the deceased but in his attempt to violate the sexual integrity of a man who had trusted him as a friend and father figure.' He accused Gillies of abusing his hospitality and betraying the young man's trust, dependency and friendship — so much so that, 'Some ordinary men could become enraged and feel that a strong physical reaction was called for.' He deployed no equivalent language to condemn the horrific violence that followed.

So in late 1997, Green's case was sent to a new trial. Once again the Crown claimed Malcolm Green's whole story about the 'homosexual advance' was a cover for premeditated murder. Green again denied this. Now he was allowed to argue the flashback as that something extra to intensify his revulsion at finding Don Gillies' hands gently touching his groin. This time the jury convicted him only of manslaughter and his sentence was reduced by a third to a little over ten years.

Green's case was barely reported in the press but the High Court's verdict produced a flurry of hostile commentary in the law journals. It was called disappointing and dangerous. I call it bigoted in the drift of Brennan's rhetoric. The worst of it is that the court had an opportunity — just as it did in Mabo — to establish in law principles that few parliaments in the Commonwealth would be brave enough to legislate. Instead, it did the opposite and endorsed the 'homosexual advance defence'. So now wherever a gay man is bashed or killed in Australia, juries can expect to hear some version of Green's story — he tried to kiss me, he touched my balls, he came onto me, he said something, I had a flashback, he waved his dick at me — in the hope of winning a little sympathy for the violence that followed. It works often enough, and only because the High Court has said 'ordinary' Australian men might react that way . . .

Don Gillies was wondering what he should be doing with his life. He had no hang-ups about sex or being homosexual. Indeed, sex didn't mean a great deal to him. In that rather Roman way most of us really live by, he made sure his unruly companion body was disciplined, kept in shape and had its share of sensual satisfaction. That often included too much whisky. But his neatly compartmentalised country-town existence was all under control. He was loved. People mattered most to him in life, then music and through music, God. At 36, Don Gillies was thinking of going into the Anglican Church: from trucking to real estate to God. But death intervened.

FOUR

SOLDIERS OF THE CROSS

'The magic of light . . . is the creation of God, and it can only honour Him and glorify His own handiwork, to utilise this invention for the salvation and blessing of mankind.'

Herbert Booth

A serious question to start: why isn't the crowd that runs this country *funny* anymore? They were a joke in Opposition, but now we just moan about them. Where are the satirists? Where are the jokes? Where's the cabaret? Where's the laughter? I concede that it's hard these days getting laughs out of John Howard but the jokes just tumble out of Richard Alston — that bull of a Melbourne barrister, bursting out of his suits, dark-eyed and congenial, who sits at the Cabinet table as both minister for the arts and the most raucous advocate for censorship Federal government has seen for decades.

What a double: arts and censorship! Alston is so brazen he doesn't bother to be convincing. There was no 'extensive' internet industry support for the new censorship legislation. But Alston is happy to say so. And he's happy to smear critics of his bill — who range from computer geeks to civil libertarians — as a bunch of irresponsibles intent on making it 'easier for pedophiles, drug pushers, racists and criminals to pollute the internet'. This is so over-the-top it's a joke. But we're not laughing.

This tale of a government at war with the screen isn't going to make much sense until we clear away a fundamental misconception — that it was all about impressing Brian Harradine while that renegade Tasmanian moralist's vote counted for something, but once power shifted to the new Democrat senators Canberra liberty and good sense would reassert themselves. Don't be fooled. The shameless play for Harradine's vote in the dying days of his influence only made more dramatic and urgent developments that square perfectly with the politics of the Howard government.

And on the other side of politics? Where was the caustic ridicule from Labor at the developments of the last year? Nowhere. There's a second misconception lurking here: that Labor champions free expression and is in there fighting for the liberty of the screen. That's not so. Remember that Labor voted *for* internet censorship. There were umhs and ahs about a sunset clause. Doubts were raised about the technical effectiveness of the scheme. But when it came down to it, Labor voted for this ridiculous legislation. There were no Labor protests when *Salo* was banned, nor did Labor object to the new 'voluntary' code of television censorship imposed in April 1999 to take sex — or sex as romp, sex as fun — off free-to-air television.

Nearly every move along the censorship path in the last, gutless decade has been instigated or blessed by Labor. Ask around the Labor Party why this is so and you'll be told that publicly defending the liberty of the screen is bad politics these days — even though the polls suggest something like 70 per cent of us believe adults should be allowed to see and read and hear what we choose. In the autumn of 1999 the porn industry commissioned Roy Morgan Research to assess community feeling about porn videos. Porn is the very messy end of the liberty business but the response — from a thousand adults across all states — was a clear 72 per cent support for the sale of non-violent erotic videos.

There were no headlines here because it was just another poll that confirmed what politicians and porn merchants have known for ages: that the real Australia is a casual, live-and-let-live, secular, modern society. So why are the politics of film, television, video and the internet heading off in quite another direction? The answer is that during the nineties both sides of politics discovered it's not the 70 per cent — the confident, relaxed typical Australians — that decides who runs this country, but the anxious, at times vindictive, often militantly Christian 30 per cent.

A hotel kitchen. Close up on a plate of lamb. The camera pulls back to show 220 plates of roast stuffed loin. Through the walls comes the roar of a contented crowd. We follow the food into the James Cook ballroom of Sydney's Intercontinental Hotel. The camera notes blue dresses, blue balloons, happy red faces. This is election night, 13 March 1993, and John Hewson is about to wipe Paul Keating off the electoral map. Liberal grandees and party workers get stuck into their lamb. Cut to television monitors on the walls. John Elliott, craggy self-styled victim of the National Crime Authority remarks, 'something's up'. Intercut between tally room and ballroom. The camera lingers on cold lamb and disbelieving faces. Guests slip away. Keating claims victory for the true believers. In the ballroom women begin to weep and up the back a distraught Young Liberal shouts, 'Sieg Heil. Sieg Heil'. John Hewson has lost the unlosable election.

Five months later the Liberals set out to find new supporters. Out in the marginal seats the party's pollster

Mark Textor — who is for good reason the party's polling guru still — discovered an unhappy chunk of Labor voters who didn't like Keating, or Mabo, or the republic, or Asia or the sort of liberal social goals Australia was drifting towards in the eighties. They had been buffeted by change under Treasurer Keating and then Prime Minister Keating. Many of these disgruntled Labor voters were the survivors and heirs of the DLP, the right-wing, moralising wedge of the party that detached itself in the 1950s Split. Some had drifted early to the Liberals, the rest had never been entirely happy casting a vote for Labor. These disgruntled conservatives looked willing to change sides. There were enough of them in enough marginal seats to swing the elections.

As the Liberal teams under Textor were doing their research, Labor teams under Gary Gray were coming to roughly the same conclusions. Labor had an immense problem: the deserters in the marginals were not typical Australians but there were enough of them and they were unhappy enough to tip Labor out of office. Keating didn't listen. While you and I were enjoying the spectacle of a Prime Minister offering Australia a sense of what a fine place it might become — open to the world, free of the Crown, at peace with Aborigines — the leader's support was seeping away.

The Liberals, on the other hand, acted on their research. They chose John Howard. Since then, he has earnt a reputation for having some sixth sense for what the Australian electorate wants. He doesn't really. But he does understand the disgruntled wedge that was to take him to power. After all, as the son of a service-station owner in Marrickville, he was born into it. And his front bench knew what was going on. About a year out from the elections one of these men spoke to me guardedly about the shift in Australian politics they were trying to engineer on the basis of their polling. It was years before I understood the importance of what he was saying. The Coalition, he said, would offer disgruntled marginal voters what they wanted: reassuring policies about morals, sex, marriage, drugs and violence — in life and in art. One little promise they made along the way was to wage war on porn. It's a promise that's haunted them ever since.

Howard won by a landslide in '96. What worked for him in that election, worked for Carr in '99. Another landslide. The key to political power in Australia today is having the support of the most conservative, most anxious chunk of the electorate. But gathering these votes calls for great political skill because the big parties have no intention of ditching the economic policies that are actually producing the pain out there. Free-market economics are sacrosanct. So instead, the major parties are appealing to these unhappy electors' prejudices on blacks, Asians, drugs, violence and a general fear that the world is drifting out of control. Each party has its own rhetoric, its own emphasis. There are lines even the Nationals won't cross. But all of them are pitching for the same customers. And in this unhappy auction, promises to ban porn and clean up television are attractive, make politicians look morally sensitive — and they're cheap as chips.

The other day, seeking reassurance and insight, I rang the analyst Hugh Mackay. He calls what's going on here an appeal to insecurity being made by both sides of politics, but especially powerfully by the Coalition parties. 'The big growth of genuine swinging voters that's now about 30 per cent of the electorate are people with a deep sense of uncertainty: "I don't know what to do about my children's education, about my job, about my life — about my vote." This is the age of unknowing.' The strategy used to capture their vote is first to heighten their fears and then promise to allay them by offering laws and regulations — like censorship. Mackay says, 'The move against freedom of speech is a subset of Getting Things Back Under Control.'

Terrible things can happen in Australia but this is one of the safest, most peaceful countries on earth. Those politicians who prosper by talking up the horrors of crime and violence at every opportunity are the same politicians who demonise the screen. The violence and crime they reckon is eating away at society can be nipped in the bud, they say, by censoring television and video and film. The argument is circular, but logic is beside the point here. What matters is that the old rhetoric of censorship has been absorbed into the new language of law and order. Liberty is not the issue in the nineties, it's the problem.

Film and television plays into the hands of those who fear change. There's something I call trailer terror: every trailer for the next episode of the 'X Files' or the latest blockbuster set in the Valley of the Kings makes wild claims to be shattering taboos, boasts new horrors, promises experiences of unprecedented intensity. This is all advertising flim-flam of course — as old as the movies — but it aggravates the terrors of those who project their fear of change onto film and television.

Mackay said when we were talking the other day: 'The central irony of John Howard as Prime Minister is that he says he wants us to feel relaxed and comfortable but at the same time he is putting people through economic change — downsizing, deregulating, opening the markets — that makes them uncomfortable, uncertain and anxious. This is where the media (and especially television) is used as an ogre. Howard can deregulate and privatise and let the banks loose, but then he'll say, "We'll clean up television", and it looks like a fine moral crusade.' This isn't going to change, said Mackay, just because Brian Harradine has lost his crucial vote in the Senate. 'He could disappear and it would go on, just as Hanson could disappear but her movement would go on. Harradine isn't driving it but being driven by it.'

Nevertheless Brian Harradine is a mighty figure in the politics of censorship and deserves to be honoured even as he fades to black. He is one of a cohort of militant Christians who have led the fight for censorship around the world since those dark days when all seemed lost for goodness and modesty in the swinging sixties.

The first of these Christians was that Boadicea of Birmingham, Mary Whitehouse who, in 1965, delivered a petition to the British government with half a million signatures asserting that, 'the men and women of Great Britain believe in a Christian way of life; deplore present day attempts to belittle and destroy it and in particular object to the propaganda of disbelief, doubt and dirt that the BBC pours into millions of homes.' From that 1965 petition grew the Festival of Light which spawned in turn, the Rev. Fred Nile's New South Wales Festival of Light. But then along came Harradine whose shrewd grasp of minority politics makes Nile look like an amateur.

It's another of the great misconceptions that these militant Christians despise the screen. Not so. Indeed they are fans — thwarted fans, but fans nevertheless. It isn't hypocrisy of Harradine to list film among his recreations in *Who's Who*. These men and women are actually the last people left who really believe that when we go to the movies our souls are up for grabs. Yet that is the core belief on which all censorship relies, a belief that's pushed with particular urgency by Harradine, by his Christian colleagues in parliament, by Christian pressure groups and by the parishes running letter campaigns against the new *Lolita* or the sight of the Mardi Gras on television. The crucial 30 per cent of the community is somewhere behind them, but the only groups actually campaigning for censorship in Australia are Christians. We're not going to find a way out of the mess of censorship into which we're sliding unless we look beyond the politics of the situation and into its religious depths.

The first great screen creation in Australia, *Soldiers of the Cross*, was filmed by the Salvation Army on the tennis court of their Girls' Home at Murrumbeena with a martydom in the Tiber staged at the Richmond Baths. The history of *Soldiers of the Cross*, which was made, and almost certainly later destroyed, by the Salvation Army, is a window into the theology that still powers the push for censorship in this country.

Joe Perry shot the film. From the early 1890s he and his wife ran the Army's Limelight Department with

Mrs Perry doing the Bible readings and Joe operating the lantern. Christians have always been among the first to admire new technology and put it to use. They have an urgent evangelical duty to do so. The printing press printed Bibles; radio and television preached the Gospel; rickety aeroplanes took missionaries deep into the godless wastes; Christians had some of the first sites on the internet. So there was nothing incongruous about the Perrys and their magic lantern show. Joe was good and he had the best projectors. The triple lantern — with double racking lens and dissolve — could turn Westminster Abbey by Day into Westminster Abbey by Night and then bring colour pouring through the stained-glass windows.

In 1896, moving pictures and a new commander for the Salvation Army arrived in Melbourne in the same month. Perry was at the Opera House in Bourke Street to see a conjurer called Carl Hertz show a few reels in a vaudeville show. Probably the very first reel seen in Australia was a London street scene: a couple of minutes of buses and carriages. Perry reported to the new commander, Herbert Booth, who at once ordered one of the new 'kinematographe' from Lumière in Paris.

This Booth was the showman son of General William Booth, founder of the Salvation Army. Herbert was a musician and poet. Despite all the bitterness that would soon surround his name, Herbert Booth's songs are still sung by the Army in Australia. What he grasped was that film — which at this point was essentially a newsreel of races and boxing matches and the Boer War — could also be used to tell stories. He was not the first person in the world to think this, but in this country at that time it was an important intuitive leap. 'I saw at a glance that the living pictures, worked in conjunction with life model slides would provide a combination unfailing in its power of connecting narrative. In fact, I see no end to the possibilities of Limelight instruments in the service of the Kingdom of Jesus Christ.'

Perry's first efforts with the Lumière unit were little reels showing the work of the Army: a man chopping wood to earn a bed for the night in the Metropole shelter or the Sallies helping a poor sinner on his release from jail. These were shown in a kind of religious vaudeville: you came for the flicks and had a few prayers and songs and then you were asked to commit your life to the Lord. The Army paper, *The War Cry*, would boast about the size of the crowd, the cash taken at the gate and the conversions: four souls saved, five souls saved. And it was to boost the salvation rate — he had a new training college to fill — that Booth and Perry conceived *Soldiers of the Cross* which was acted entirely by amateurs drawn from the ranks of the Salvation Army and filmed in the Melbourne winter of 1900.

God knows how to describe what was created. This was not the first feature film in the world but it was a unique film entertainment that used thirteen short films plus 200 slides, a band and a full score as well as hymns and preaching to tell the story of the early church from the Crucifixion to the martyrdoms in the Coliseum. Booth, who was a terrific spruiker for his own work, called this two-and-a-quarter hour epic 'the greatest thing ever produced in the limelight world'. There was early on — and I think even now — an umbilical connection between preaching and film hype. It's something Bob Ellis demonstrates still . . .

All this happened in the first three minutes — 'As the film opens, the patient faces of the martyrs are seen through the rising smoke to be encouraging each other to look with joy to the glory of the crown which waited on their martyrdom. In the rear are seen the waving plumes of the Roman soldiery. A pagan priest comes with his attendant to the front. The incense is offered, an opportunity is given to recant, but neither man, woman nor child can be found unfaithful enough to touch the unholy incense. Then, without waiting [for] the onrush of the soldiers to compel them into the burning kiln, you see them joyfully commend themselves to heaven and deliberately plunge over the brink, disappearing amid the thickening vapours of the pit beneath, and the soldiers coming cautiously forward, peer through the smoke with blanched, awestruck faces into the boiling cauldron.'

The show opened at the Melbourne Town Hall in September 1900 and it was a huge sensation. *Soldiers of the Cross* made its stately way around Australia pulling in cash and saving souls. For the Melbourne revival in 1901, *The War Cry* put a banner slash across the full-page announcement: 'Sixteen souls won.'

But at about this time, Booth fell out with the Army and 'deserted' with a copy of *Soldiers of the Cross* to start his own church in San Francisco. His name was chipped off foundation stones. For a time, Perry's Limelight Department still prospered. He was engaged to film the Federation procession to Centennial Park the day Australia was declared a nation. It's iconic news footage courtesy of the Salvation Army. But a faction was growing in the army that believed picture shows had been lost to God. When a Scot with a flair for real estate arrived to take charge of the Army in 1909, he immediately shut down Perry's Limelight. In his memoirs, *Aggressive Salvation*, the new commander wrote curtly: 'Cinema as conducted by the Army had led to weakness and a lightness incompatible with true Salvationism, and was completely ended by me.'

He probably ordered the destruction of *Soldiers of the Cross*. None of the reels have ever come to light. What we have was picked up by the National Film Archive on the American market in the 1950s, presumably all that was left of the copy Booth had taken to America. By the time he returned for a preaching tour in the 1920s — now styling himself Ambassador of the Christian Confederacy — Booth, too, had turned against film. And the Salvation Army for the next forty years regarded it as a sacking offence for officers to be found at the pictures.

That absolute ban testified to their continuing Christian belief in the power of film. Film can save souls — they'd seen that — but the pictures had become too secular and disreputable, so film threatened to damn souls. In the fleapits of Australia, Christians could see ankles exposed — there had, in fact, been complaints about men in tights in *Soldiers of the Cross* — they could see people necking; they saw men finding wives not through prayer but in dance halls; they saw lives lived for pleasure; they were invited to worship success and money. This only worried Christians because they never doubted the power of film to set people off on the track to hell.

THE HIGH PRICE OF HEAVEN

The rhetoric of hell is used these days very sparingly. Canny politicians refuse to discuss censorship in language that even faintly evokes theology. Christian lobby groups rely heavily on the rhetoric of 'family values'. But if we are to make sense of what's going on now in Australia, we have to learn to listen to the old puritan arguments that linger, no more than half-hidden, behind the new secular language. Christians may talk of protecting women and protecting children, but what's really at stake is the fate of adult souls. If you believe in heaven and hell, there are no higher stakes.

Three specifically Christian traditions converge on censorship. I don't for a moment mean all Christians share these beliefs, or even voice them in the same way, but they have been around from the earliest times and continue to power specifically Christian calls for censorship.

The first is rare but potent: it's the Christian charge of triviality brought against all fiction. It's what that Salvation Army commander was getting at when he shut down the Limelight Department as a distraction from God's work. And while it's rare these days to come across someone arguing bluntly that we should be concentrating on God and the real world rather than wasting our time with film and novels and theatre and television and video — nevertheless, this puritan haughtiness about fiction is always there to contest our commitment to art.

Second, there's Christian affection for authority. This fuels calls for censorship of political satire, or more subtle appeals 'in these difficult times' — times are usually difficult — for art to show respect to the state, indeed to authority all the way down the line. A few months ago I was doing a few rounds on radio with a leader of that influential Christian lobby group, the Australian Family Association. Talking together during an ad break he confessed that what really disturbed him about television — apart from tits and bums and bad language — was the message in American sitcoms that fathers are weak and foolish.

Third, there's the far-reaching Christian suspicion of the body. Brian Harradine can maintain his poise through the most heated, most difficult Senate debates. If it's Wik or the GST, he's a gentleman through and through, but when it's tits and bums on Channel 10's 'Sex/Life', he turns into a passionately bad-tempered old man. This is where puritan Christians can least tolerate the attitudes of the secular world. Yet of all the traditions feeding censorship this one — wanting to keep sexuality private and within the bounds of heterosexual marriage — is the most obviously theological. And it's at the heart of nearly all censorship, ancient and modern.

Theology matters especially when we are arguing whether censorship is necessary for the protection of women. For 25 years, Harradine has been condemning porn or even sexy television because it depicts, 'women in general as being highly promiscuous and available'. That's the mantra of Christian censorship. But what's he talking here? The welfare of women or theology? He's suggesting the danger of violence and rape, but to my mind he's asserting the essentially theological proposition that women are only properly 'available' within Christian marriage. That's not a real foundation for censorship. That's for the true believers.

When the issue is violence, the Christian belief in the power of the screen heightens fears that the sight of violence on the screen can do permanent moral harm. We can't deny there may be men and women capable of being inspired to violence by violent films. The world is a place where very strange things happen. Almost anything is possible. But so uncertain is the science that tries to link violence on the screen and violence in life, that in the end the conviction that the two are inevitably linked has to be seen — and contested — for what it is: essentially a matter of faith.

But the challenge of disentangling secular good sense from church teaching is nowhere more difficult than in the fourth tradition that feeds calls for censorship: Christianity's respect and care for children. The rhetoric of child protection used by Christian groups in Australia grows more florid every year. It was the principle justification for censorship of the internet. But if you use the net you know it's all but impossible to see big dicks or big tits out there unless you've got a credit card. Porn costs money. Banks won't give you a credit card until you're eighteen. Capitalism in its greedy way was already working to protect children. The real task of Senator Alston's Broadcasting Services Amendment (Online Services) Bill was always to nobble adults.

Not that it's going to be very effective. But the last great misconception of the censorship debate is that censorship has to be — or is even meant to be — truly effective. I used to think it was a knockout argument to show that such and such a censorship law wasn't going to work. Back in the seventies I'd be raging that book censorship was useless because no matter how many customs officers were employed at airports rifling through the lingerie, copies of *Lady Chatterley's Lover* would still be smuggled in. But I was missing the point. Censorship is essentially gesture. Alston's internet laws are a gesture. They'll be intrusive and a nuisance; they'll limit what adults can see and read on the net; but they won't keep porn out of the country and everyone concerned knows that or will learn it soon enough.

Alston has devised a law that will work in only one limited respect: as a gesture of reassurance to a wedge of the electorate that wants government to protect them and their children. That so much about censorship in Australia is gesture only, explains what's otherwise inexplicable. *Salo* had exhausted its small audience here by the mid-nineties, so why should a small group of politicians led by the militantly Christian Senator Julian McGauran bother fighting for five years to have it banned again? The answer is that putting *Salo* back in its can was a gesture of power. Just as it would have been to ban the new *Lolita*. Many of us had a good laugh at the push to ban tedious, inoffensive *Lolita* while that black master-piece *Happiness* was being screened around the country at the same time. But the point of the campaign against *Lolita* was the hope of bagging another trophy. They didn't care about *Happiness* because no one knew about *Happiness*. They wanted infamous *Lolita*.

Gesture unites politicians and Christians. Neither is deterred when people tell them they're ineffective. Their duty, as they see it, is to try. As Richard Alston kept saying in one way or another during the internet debate, are we supposed to do nothing? For the faithful who believe that what's at stake here is the fate of our souls, the high Christian obligation is to do the best that can be done to bring us to our moral senses, even if the best is a futile gesture of censorship. After all Christians live in a tradition that has honoured the futile gesture from early on — as witnessed by the tennis court martyrs of the Murrumbeena Girls' Home running before the cardboard swords of those amateur gladiators to plunge to their deaths in a pit of Melbourne fire. I just don't want to go in with them.

We're not going to emerge from this censorship mess until we get God out of the picture, leaving faith to the faithful and the screen to us. And somehow we have to start laughing at the government again. Howard and the boys deride this sort of talk as élite. Perhaps the best proof that we're speaking for 70 per cent of Australia here is to get them laughing again at the silly prudery of government in Australia. I'm old enough to remember that last time — back in the sixties — what did the trick was laughter.

FIVE

HARRADINE

'The greatest foul-ups in my own public life have occurred when I've said, "How am I going to get out of this? And what am I going to do about this problem?" Instead I should have said, "Jesus, how are we going to turn this into an opportunity for good? How are we to meet this challenge?" '

Brian Harradine, 1998

Five television cameras, dozens of journalists and most of the leaders of the National Indigenous Working Group were waiting for him, yet Brian Harradine managed somehow to materialise out of thin air a few feet from his chair and look about Committee Room 1R1 with pained — and feigned — surprise. What a turmoil of feelings this old stager provokes: ridicule as he throws himself in the path of condoms, IVF, 'dirty' movies and every method of birth control except counting the days — and fierce relief as he interposes his single vote between the Howard government and Aboriginal Australia.

It was December 1997. Harradine had never disguised his support for the High Court's Wik decision. 'I can't see why certain rights which are associated with native title can't co-exist with farming and mining leases,' he'd told me matter-of-factly soon after the verdict. But how far this quirky Catholic union official from Tasmania would go to thwart Howard's legislation was the focus of the most urgent speculation across Australia. The bill had already been four days in the senate. Most of that morning Harradine had voted with the government. His decisive 'no' is hardly audible, a dry sound muttered towards the floor yet heard right round the chamber. Was

Harradine buckling? Had he ever held out against the Howard government when it really mattered? The senator had yet to signal where he stood on the fundamental issues buried in a fat bill with 600 often-overlapping amendments still to be considered. Being hard to read is one of Harradine's strengths. Another is infinite patience. He warned all sides in the senate, 'I'm happy to stay here till Christmas to discuss in detail, in this chamber, what it is all about'.

To a crowd of journalists a Prime Minister would be glad to pull, Harradine now set out his position with exaggerated patience. He signals with his hands: 'bottom line' is hands out flat, palms a few inches above his papers. He has big, pale hands. 'Let no one run away with the idea that I'm doing a trade union job. This is not an ambit claim . . . this is the bottom line.'

After lunch on the eighth day of debate, he sat for a moment on his Senate bench, steadying himself perhaps, before walking over to Nick Minchin to whisper a few words. Minchin, the government senator in charge of the bill, is a man almost devoid of gesture. He strikes no poses. As Harradine left him, Minchin looked very, very still. Before lunch Harradine had delighted the government by denouncing as 'a lawyer's picnic' Opposition plans to give native title owners the protection of the Racial Discrimination Act and angrily told Labor senators to 'face up to the real world'. But as he left the chamber to grab a sandwich with his staff, he was ambushed by Ron Castan, a Melbourne QC advising the National Indigenous Working Group. 'Senator, you've made a terrible mistake. This will send the wrong message to all of Australia.' Over lunch the lawyers changed Harradine's mind. One of the things that makes this stubborn man so fascinating is that except on issues that touch fundamental religious belief he *can* change his mind. People say, you always know where he's coming from. The same people say, he's a mystery to the last.

After delivering the news to Minchin, Harradine sat with an old-timer on the Labor benches for a few minutes. A weak patch of sunlight fell on the two men as they spoke. Senator Harradine's big hands were working. They nodded. Harradine returned to his seat to await the moment. Everyone all week had taken their time. The result of every important vote was unknown until it was taken. This was parliament working as textbooks say it should work. There was a sense of the whole building being in play, feeding the chamber. Senators talked on the white phones that hang under their desks. Notes went in and out. Up in the galleries it was all but impossible for the public to follow the amendments and counter-amendments. But they sat waiting for bursts of rhetoric, or vital votes. Early on there was a bit of a showing by graziers. They didn't last long. The Aborigines, of course, were the stayers. There were Harradines among them.

'I have been giving this further thought,' he began. Ron Castan, hitherto invisible in the debate was sitting at the back of the senate, slumped forward in an attitude of prayer. 'Much of the power under this Act is going to devolve to the states and that's a matter I've been concerned about.' He now laid it out: the states had to be made to deal with Aborigines as fairly as they dealt with all other Australians, so the Wik bill had to be 'constrained subject to the Racial Discrimination Act'. Then came the moment of pure Harradine. With a gesture of atonement he said: 'I do apologise to the senate and I indicate now that I am supporting the amendment proposed by the Opposition.'

This was a very big loss for the Howard government and the white men of the bush. 'I don't know what Senator Harradine had for lunch,' said Minchin, cool as ever. 'I retain my respect for Brian Harradine but he was right before lunch and is wrong after lunch.' The vote was taken. The gallery applauded. Harradine looked pleased. After that, the vote that sent the bill back to the House of Representatives was an anticlimax — except for the sight of the Nationals' Senator Ron Boswell, weeping.

Those who forget the history of Labor attack Brian Harradine for his contradictions. But he grew up in a Catholic trade union tradition where all that now seems at odds once fitted neatly into a single parcel of beliefs. There's an old-fashioned sense of fairness he's shown when he rejected the GST with that famous, 'I cannot'. There's a Catholic commitment to Natural Law which he saw at work in Mabo and Wik. But political savvy is an important part of the Harradine bundle, too. He let the — still disgraceful — Wik legislation through the senate out of fear for what a race election might do to Australia. And there is the bedrock prudery of the man that's driven his long war on porn, and the religious orthodoxy that sustains his absolute opposition to euthanasia, abortion and birth control wherever they are practised in the world. At the centre of the parcel, deep inside all this political wrapping and string, is Harradine's Catholic God.

Harradine is on his way to the Kingdom of Heaven via the Australian senate and means to take us with him whether we're keen to go or not. Christian legislators have a particular duty to the 'immature — I use the word deliberately — and the naïve', the senator told the St Thomas More Society in 1998. They are the ones who seem most to need direction from politicians: 'working in harmony with Our Maker's revealed guidelines on the meaning of life to reach the goal of perfect happiness, peace and union. By those guidelines we can discern right from wrong, good from evil, light from dark, truth from deceit, justice from injustice, life from death.'

This speech was a remarkable exception to Harradine's policy of not publicly discussing the doctrinal basis of his politics. Indeed, he insists his beliefs on birth control, in-vitro fertilisation, euthanasia and censorship are 'non-sectarian' views formed after independent reflection 'on the basis of what is considered just by persons of goodwill — of all of the religions and none'. He added, 'If you're trying to paint me in a situation of being a confessional politician, then you're barking up the wrong tree'. I asked the senator if it was just coincidence, then, that his views on birth control match exactly the official teaching of his church? He parried softly and swiftly. 'I'm talking about questions of justice in Third World countries in which I've been involved for many years.'

On this summer afternoon, he sat hunched in a chair in a corner of his Hobart office, all limbs like a grasshopper in grey daks. His face is a wedge separating slate-blue eyes. When he's puzzled, his brow furrows and his upper lip comes down like a tiny prehensile beak. He lets his doubts and confusions show, even parades them a little. They're an attractive mask for a man of fundamental certainty. He was restless. He seems locked in a struggle with his hands. He grasped them tightly, fingers in paw, but they broke free and slid up and down his arms until he brought them under control again. 'If you want to know what I believe,' he said, 'just go back through Hansard.' Twenty years of these scarlet volumes filled the shelves in this impersonal, government-issue office on the waterfront. Almost the only individual touch in the room was a faded colour photograph of horses hitting a finishing line. Racing is listed among his recreations in *Who's Who* along with 'family', bushwalking, reading and films. The track is part of Harradine's subterranean political territory.

'I do think there is too much emphasis on the individual in all of this. There are 76 senators. If one is important, they all are. If one is powerful, then they're all powerful.' Harradine delivered this line without a trace of irony. His position is, in fact, extraordinary. The deal at Federation was that every state would send an equal number of senators to parliament, so Tasmania — with the population of a couple of Melbourne municipalities — has twelve senators in Canberra. Harradine has become the longest-serving Independent parliamentarian since Federation, the father of the senate and a walking veto on government legislation for a few years in the early eighties and then for most of the nineties — courtesy of the Federation Fathers and about 32 000 Tasmanian supporters.

Reproduction is his central parliamentary interest: issues of life and death, mothers and babies, pills and coils, embryos and vasectomies. Outsiders see doctrine. Insiders see logic. Non-believers argue that religious doctrine should not be imposed beyond the parish. True believers like Brian Harradine see doctrine as a way to the common good. He has managed, remarkably in this secular society, to keep the Vatican's position on the table, a position that does not even enjoy the unequivocal support of Australian Catholics. In pursuit of his campaign to end aid for population programs abroad, Harradine takes public servants every year through Ausaid programs line by line with sometimes passionate ferocity: can they guarantee this, and this, and this contains no 'coercive element'? It's a nightmare for the bureaucrats and ties their departments up in endless research and paperwork.

Since John Howard took office, the Tasmanian senator has seen Medicare benefits for IVF reduced and benefits cut altogether for the reversal of vasectomies. The 'morning-after pill' RU486 which is available in many countries is effectively banned here. All Australian contributions to the Population Council and the International Union for the Scientific Study of Population have been cut and we have reduced our contributions to the United National Population Fund (UNFPA), the International Planned Parenthood Federation and the World Health Organisation's Human Reproduction Program. Harradine wants Australia to go even further: to abolish all Medicare payments for abortions and IVF, cut all government support for IVF research and all government funding for family planning organisations advocating artificial contraception. He wants refugee status for any Chinese family wanting to have more than one child and an end to all overseas aid for population programs. In 1993 he told the senate the $34 million Australia then spent on such programs could be better spent on milk biscuits for the Third World, biscuits that would discourage conceptions by allowing mothers to breastfeed longer. 'It could buy a lot of biscuits.'

'You remember how Hitler came to power?' Hitler was Harradine's answer to a poll in the Hobart *Mercury* that showed 54.3 per cent support for euthanasia. 'Hitler came to power by popular vote.' For a few minutes we argued history back and forth. What made the exchange so absurd was not Harradine's shaky grasp of Germany in 1933 but that Hitler is clearly a trump card he plays all the time. If it was news to the senator that Hitler never won a free election, it didn't faze him. He argues that fundamental issues aren't settled by opinion polls. True. But can he ignore what they say and declare, as he had, that euthanasia is 'anathema' to the people of Tasmania? And what about those UN surveys that show women in the Third World *want* access to artificial birth control?

'Oh, where do you get that?' he snorted. 'The United Nations Population Fund? Of course they do. The UNFPA would because there is a whole heap of them who would be out of a job if they didn't. Let's face it, it's not a question of whether people have available information relating to contraception, it's a question of the rights of individuals, like, for example, China. The PRC has got a one-child family policy which is a gross violation and a gross violation of women's rights. And I've got heaps of information about that, and the United

THE HIGH PRICE OF HEAVEN

Nations Population Fund gave them a gold medal. The PRC! I wouldn't worry about what the United Nations might say.'

This is not argument of a high order but it reaches to the heart of Harradine's situation: he is a numbers man who, ultimately, despises numbers. For all his skill in mustering and exploiting votes — in Hobart Trades Hall, in the little electorate of Tasmania and in the senate — his efforts are directed to issues where popular mandates are meaningless. He has devoted his remarkable career to advancing the minority positions of his faith.

Downriver from Harradine's waterfront office, at Mount St Canice overlooking Sandy Bay, the vicar- general of the Tasmanian archdiocese, Father Adrian Doyle, reflected with some pride on the senator's achievement. 'He is doing God's work, doing what he was encouraged by the church to do as a committed lay person out there in the wider world, out in the marketplace, on the front line . . . He heard very young the call of the church to be an apostle on behalf of Christ out in the wider world. He has done that extremely well.'

Lately, Harradine has been going through his papers. The story of his family has been much on his mind. They were railway people in South Australia and union from way back. He grew up with a grandfather, two uncles and three of his brothers all in the union movement — where he sees himself still. 'Never left it. Definitely don't feel that I've ever left it. There was that incident of my expulsion from the Labor Party but I don't feel I ever left it.'

He was born in the railway town of Quorn in the Flinders Ranges in 1935. The Harradines were English and Irish and Aboriginal. There were a lot of black Harradines around Quorn. During the Wik debate when the senators were laying out their bush qualifications, Harradine recalled, 'My father, who was a great hunter out bush where I was born and raised, used to tell me and show me how the Aboriginals tracked their prey'. The boy opted for the priesthood and was still a kid when he began his training with the Passionist Fathers, finishing school with them in Sydney, serving a year's novitiate in Goulburn before entering their Adelaide semminary.

Harradine didn't last the distance, but the decision to pursue his vocation among the Passionists is revealing. In the early 1950s they were rigid, authoritarian, punitive and still enthusiasts for flagellation. They would whip themselves to chastise desire and unite their suffering with the suffering of Christ. Suffering was essential to life, to virtue and to Salvation. Their fetishistic concentration on punishment came with a decent if narrow attention to the fate of ordinary men and women. A key ambition of the Passionists was humility.

He left to work on trains, in farms and factories. For a few months in 1958 he was at the very least 'associated with' the DLP. Labor had split in South Australia and the sympathies of the Harradine boys were with the Catholic, conservative, anti-Communist rump of the party and its union wing, the National Civic Council. In 1959 Harradine was sent by the Federated Clerks' Union to organise in Tasmania. The party hadn't split in the Apple Isle and he joined the ALP there in 1961. Yet there was always the suspicion — always denied by Harradine — that he'd been sent to Tasmania to organise for the NCC.

From his earliest days in the movement, Harradine showed three exceptional qualities: persuasion, persistence and a grasp of the rules. He does not have an original or speculative mind but he can master union rule books, *Humanae Vitae* and Odgers' *Australian Senate Practice*. He has a genius for turning campaigns for radical objectives into dry fights over the rules. He knows the value of a well-crafted constitution. When he became Secretary General of the Tasmanian Trades and Labor Council in 1964 — a position he held until 1976 — he added 'spiritual development' to the council's objectives. There was, he admitted in those years, some doubt about these new words. 'But I was able to convince the boys it was not going to be a hymn-singing session. This is where the workers get their freedoms — not from a material basis but from something immaterial, beyond the grasp of the materialists.'

This was essentially code for anti-communism. Harradine had swiftly wrenched the Tasmanian union movement out of Left control and ran Trades Hall for fifteen years with the single purpose of keeping it that way. He was a hard man to reach. The outer office was protected by the formidable Miss Maloney with shocking pink lipstick and fingerless gloves. 'She shielded Harradine from behind a sliding window of frosted glass,' wrote Bruce Montgomery in the *Australian*. 'Whenever one asked for him, he was never in, according to Maloney, and he certainly had nothing to say as she slammed the window shut.' Harradine is one of those loners who always find just the people he needs to work for him. It's a rare knack.

As head of Hobart Trades Hall, Harradine was elected in 1967 to the ALP federal executive and made his fatal claim that 'friends of the Communists' would prevent him taking his seat. There was uproar. By the narrowest margin, the executive *did* vote to deny him his seat and persisted in keeping him out of federal forums for the next seven years. Whitlam put his career on the line for Harradine. For the Left, it was a brawl to consolidate their numbers. For Harradine, it was a crusade pursued with sometimes comic fervour: he accused the Left at one point of the psychological murder of a couple of senior Right officials felled by heart attacks. For the Labor Party, the Harradine Affair was immensely damaging — all its dreary, complex length. When one of Harradine's fiercest enemies, Lionel Murphy, was translated from the Senate to the High Court in 1975, it seemed the party would finally bring the Tasmanian in from the cold. The Left then produced information collected by Websters Investigation Agency that Harradine had been seen one day in the Sydney office of the NCC. That has always been wildly disputed, but Labor had finally had enough.

The Russian Parliament is said to have been haggling over the liturgy of the Orthodox Church when the Revolution struck. As Labor plunged towards the Sacking, it was furiously debating Brian Harradine. He was expelled in time to be elected as an independent senator in the landslide of December 1975 that all but annihilated Labor in Tasmania. He's been returned at every poll he's contested since. Once or twice he's tried to bring a running mate to Canberra, but Tasmanians don't want a Harradine party — they just want him. His supporters are white-collar working class. That's the demographic of Catholicism in Tasmania, but in the least Catholic state in Australia, Harradine has to rely on support outside the faith. He hardly ever issues a press release. He hardly campaigns. Harradine public meetings are all but unknown. Instead he speaks privately to parish groups or sporting clubs or local branches of St Vincent de Paul. There is no Harradine machine except at election time. His connections in the church and the unions provide men and women to man the booths. He polls best in isolated rural settlements and worst in the really poor suburbs.

These days in Tasmania, applause for Harradine can be heard on all sides. This is new. Tasmanians are used to their senators disappearing to Canberra and delivering the state very little. Harradine was in that mould. Indeed it's been a deliberate strategy to keep clear of most local controversies — he was *not* a player in the long campaign to keep sodomy a crime in Tasmania — and concentrate instead on big issues like communism, porn, workers' rights and support for 'the family' with its attendant doctrinal concern about contraception and the proper place of women in society. So over the years Harradine has campaigned against feminists on government boards, radicals in university radio stations, the World Bank, women's counselling services, safe sex advertising on Fathers' Day, ultrasound machines, the employment of communists by Amnesty International, lesbian access to IVF, retrospective tax legislation, protection for lesbians and homosexuals from discrimination in the workplace, plus any experiment on any embryo: 'It is a being.' And he's pursued phone sex, sex videos, sex at the movies, sex on television and sex on the internet.

Harradine was an almost invisible and eccentric legend for most Tasmanians until the sale of Telstra. He had the power to stop the sale in its tracks. When he allowed the first sale of shares back in December 1996, a shot of him on his red bench, his unfamiliar face raised in exuberant laughter was carried in newspapers across Australia. Back home the press lauded him. 'Harradine Joins Ranks of Greats,' said Launceston's *Sunday Examiner*. The hundreds of millions of dollars he has delivered Tasmania first in 1996 and then on the second sale of shares in 1999 make his votes perhaps the most dearly bought in the history of Federation. But this was a strange triumph. For years Harradine has scorned the economic rationalists of both parties and fruitlessly voted against bi-partisan legislation to flog off the farm. But now, when his vote would have defeated privatisation, Harradine went with the government. The image of Harradine changed. This man who claimed to be above horse-trading had pulled off a spectacular deal but in doing so showed his legendary moral courage doesn't always hold in matters of secular belief. Harradine was just a politician.

Faced with a long list of services available in many languages, the Attorney-General Gareth Evans dialled for information on cholesterol. This was August 1988 and Evans was inaugurating Telecom's new 0055 information lines. He might have chosen tips on gardening, investments, dog care, or the track. He could have rung for the insult of the day or predictions from Athena Starwoman. But Evans opted for a couple of minutes about clogged arteries. What began that day was instantly popular, instantly profitable and instantly controversial. Soon customers could dial for information on penis size and masturbation or listen to 'Dr Rosie's Sex Talk'. Telecom allowed subscribers very simply to opt out of the service — about 10 000 soon did — but the moral vigilantes of the churches so successfully demonised this innovation that in mid-1991 Brian Harradine negotiated the establishment of a senate committee to investigate 0055. He would never chair the Select Committee on Community Standards Relevant to the Supply of Services Utilising Telecommunications Technologies but it would always, rightly, be regarded as his own.

Pooled in the committee were a number of moral hardliners from both sides of politics, mostly Christian senators from Tasmania and the bush who brought the ethos of their tight, respectable communities to Canberra. Labor welcomed the committee as a way of keeping these whingers busy and the party made sure there were always a few liberal spirits sitting alongside the hardliners. But the sad history of the committee shows the freer spirits never committed themselves body and soul to the often ridiculous work of grappling with Harradine, John Tierney, Shirley Walters and Julian McGauran. They didn't put in the time. They didn't even issue minority reports. Harradine was always able to claim the committee's alarming demands for bans, cuts, and restrictions were unanimous. So with the authority of the senate, the tacit approval of governments and the appearance of speaking with a clear, single voice, the Senate Select Committee on Community Standards became a key player in the moral politics of the nation.

Phone sex was only ever a stalking horse. Catholic bishops and other churchmen were campaigning against the wickedness of 0055 but more was at stake than the danger of children hearing voices talk dirty on the phone. What worried the moralists were the phone lines themselves for these would soon be transmitting pay television and the internet right into homes. Shouldn't they be censored? The first term of reference when the committee was set up in June 1991 was 0055, but at the foot of the same list was a direction to inquire 'whether the content of pay TV, were such a service to be introduced, should include material classified . . . in the R or X categories'.

Brian Harradine is the formidable scrapper he is over censorship because he won't accept anyone's definition of porn but his own. The law distinguishes mainstream R from pornographic X. Anyone over seventeen can see R at Hoyts and Greater Union. In R, sex is only ever simulated: it's actors acting. There's violence, but not violence that's gratuitous or exploitative. X is something else. X is 'sexually explicit' porn with real erections and real penetration. X can't involve violence. And X can't be seen at the cinema. But Harradine sweeps aside these distinctions. If they're fucking, it's porn. If they're pretending to fuck, it's still porn. If we can work out what's supposed to be happening even under the sheets, then that's explicit. The only difference between X and R as far as the senator is concerned is the camera angle. 'The theme is the same, the content is the same and the intent is the same.' Nor does he acknowledge that X has a distinct status because it contains no violence. For Harradine, R is porn, so there's violence in porn. Indeed, there's violence in all porn — and anyone who argues otherwise is 'ignorant' or attempting to 'hoodwink the public'.

Harradine sees only exploiters and victims, the pornographers and their prey. The freedom of ordinary people to watch X and R is dismissed as irrelevant. 'That is not the issue. Adults are also free to take poison if it's produced.' By allowing X and R, governments are protecting the 'pornographers' right to freedom of expression' while shirking their duty to save men and women from degradation, and children from irreparable harm. Harradine notes some sort of censorship is supported by almost everyone, even if only at the extremes. So the real question to ask is not *whether* to censor, but the proper basis of censorship. He defines censorship as 'The application of a carefully balanced and judiciously evaluated assessment of that which is conducive to the essential good of an equal, free and life affirming society'. It's a formulation laden with religious significance: the 'essential good' of Natural Law and the particularly Catholic freedom that comes with obedience to that law. It's not freedom of choice but freedom from sin.

Why Harradine is so passionate about censorship is a question buried deep in his life. There's something oddly un-Catholic about the ferocity of his commitment to this cause. It's the sort of rage common in Protestant preachers like Fred Nile or in those Pentecostal sects where the hubbub of worship goes hand in hand with the most rigid codes of morality. Harradine's failed vocation as a priest may be the vital clue here. Back in the seminary, the struggle against desire was fundamental to everyone's vocation. Trainee accountants sinned if they succumbed to lust; trainee priests put their vocations on the line. Porn must seem particularly evil to anyone who's been through a regime of weekly scourging. Harradine has a particular eye for sadomasochism which he condemns as 'absolutely beyond the pale', the sort of thing 'any reasonable person' would ban. Harradine puts sadomasochism right down in the depths with child porn and bestiality.

Those who have followed Harradine's censorship battles from very early believe he's spent the last decade avenging the defeat of the senate's enquiry into porn videos in the eighties. Porn *made* the video industry. Video was just a clumsy storage method until pornographers saw the possibility of taking blue movies out of football clubs and into bedrooms. The rest of the film industry soon caught on, but porn was there from the start. Not long after Bob Hawke came to power, the government established category X. Labor didn't introduce X to Australia, it acknowledged its presence. The counterattack was swift and within a year the fate of the porn video was being investigated by the Joint Select Committee on Video Material on which Harradine was the guiding force. Three busy, ugly and inconclusive years later the Labor Caucus refused to ban X. Instead, X was to be shorn of violence. So began a process that continues today: caught between the huge popularity of porn and the ceaseless politics of its opponents, Canberra prevaricates with talk of cleaning it up — taking fetishes and violence out of X. Brian Harradine has always treated these as 'lame, sham excuses'. The thing itself is evil.

The Committee for Community Standards was his next chance and saw his most important victories. The committee turned fears of violence after Port Arthur to its advantage and made hay from the pedophile scare that swept Australia in the nineties, but the win that mattered most happened right at the start when the committee established the principle that what comes down the phone lines — 0055, pay television and later the internet — would be censored in the same way as movies and television. Other countries took other courses. They saw these new, more flexible, more private technologies as an opportunity to allow adults more freedom of choice. Australia decided instead to censor the new technologies in the same old way.

R films are the staple diet of cable television around the world. Here Harradine's genius for confusion paid big dividends. He managed to spread the idea that by allowing R, the Hawke government was going to put 'porn' into people's homes. In June 1992, the Community Standards Committee recommended no R on pay TV until the Australian Broadcasting Authority conducted an investigation into the levels of 'taste and decency' expected by the public on this new television service. The government accepted the recommendation. Almost alone in the world, Australia banned R from cable television. Special subscription channels with access by PIN number very late at night were later allowed — over furious opposition from the committee — but the general ban has never been lifted despite that ABA investigation concluding in 1994 that 82 per cent of the public supported the right of adults to watch R on pay TV. The attitude of the public hasn't budged since.

The end of the decade found Harradine attacking the same old 'commercial exploiters' sending the same 'hardcore pornography and violence' down the phone lines — this time from the world wide web. The Committee for Community Standards had been worried about the internet early on and after a public enquiry recommended in 1995 and again in 1997 that it should be an offence 'to use a computer service to transmit, obtain possession of, demonstrate, advertise or request the transmission of material equivalent to RC[1], R and X categories'. Harradine had been repeating this mantra for a couple of years, but in 1999 the government was taking notice at last because Harradine's vote was needed to sell another tranche of Telstra shares. It didn't matter that the best advice the government had was that local censorship would make the net slower, more expensive and inevitably send Australian services offshore — and still not stop porn. Censorship was going to happen.

Harradine hardly spoke on the Broadcasting Services Amendment (Online Services) Bill 1999, only emerging from time to time to protest his innocence when needled by that other gaunt independent from Tasmania, Bob Brown. 'He is either following or leading some of the narrow-minded, unintelligent members of the media by constantly suggesting that certain interests are to get

---

[1] RC or Refused Classification means banned.

my vote on this, that or the other. I challenge him and any of those small-minded members of the media to point to one case where I have not dealt with a matter completely on its merits. I am getting sick and tired of that sort of approach . . .'

These were the last days in which Harradine's vote was crucial to the fate of government legislation. He was about to lose that magic power to the Democrats. He parlayed it well just one last time. He got internet censorship, a few hundred million more dollars for Tasmania — and a little law to have another go at Telstra's information lines.

As it happens the story of Harradine's attempts to ban phone sex perfectly prefigures the fate of internet censorship. At first the services fled abroad but then they crept back during the nineties. The public loved them and wasn't really worried by them and no one put much effort into policing them. By the time Harradine had phone sex guillotined again in 1999, about one and a half million calls were being made each month to sex lines, mostly by drunks on Friday nights. Within a few days of the new law, these services had been relocated abroad — just as internet porn providers relocated their wares overseas beyond the reach of Canberra's moral warriors. Everything is still available if you punch in a few more numbers. Perhaps it's not been a complete waste of effort on Brian Harradine's part. One or two drunken souls might yet be saved as they stumble over the difficulties of dialling that extra 0011 . . .

Harradine urged me to get out into the bush. His eyes, which have a faraway look at the best of times, became bluer and vaguer still as he spoke of walking with his wife Marian in the mountains in the northwest of Tasmania. Whenever he comes home he likes to be out in the hills round Hobart within hours. I should do that, too. I should stop quizzing him about his insignificant career and go up Mount Wellington and get some perspective on things. But even the bush presents problems of theology. He has been ridiculed for how little he's done over the years to save the state's forests and rivers. He denounces his accusers in turn as heretics. Back in the days of the battle for the Franklin, he warned the senate, 'There are people so dogmatic about revering what they call the wilderness that they are prepared to deify it and seek to preserve each species of flora and fauna intact. Does not this reveal a pantheistic view of nature?'

Did he stand by this taunt of heresy even today? Of course. These things don't change. The wilderness is there to be used for our common good. Nature is not to be worshipped. Out in the mountains a distinction must be made between the error of regarding bush-walking as a spiritual experience in itself and the proper spiritual refreshment that comes from finding in the bush reminders of the existence of God. 'When you look at the stars you've got to say, well, they didn't come there from nothing.'

SIX

ALEXANDRA'S SCREAM

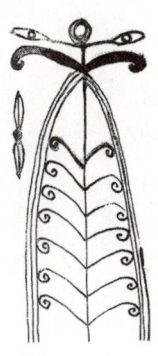

'When parents complain about sex and violence on the screen, always ask yourself what age are their children? When they're five they want to protect them absolutely. At thirteen they know they can't. At fifteen they give up.'

John Dickie, former Chief Censor

One night in the spring of 1992, the Keating daughters were watching television at the Lodge. They were watching alone. The days when families gather round a single set — father, mother and the kids in pyjamas ready for bed — are a long way in the past. In any case, television is not Paul Keating's idea of relaxation.

The girls had little to choose from in Canberra that night. They could hardly be expected to settle down to a documentary about bankrupt cattleman Bill Tapp on ABC 'Four Corners'. Perhaps they gave 10's *Teenage Mutant Ninja Turtles II, the Secret of the Ooze* a try but it's legendarily boring. At some point they found themselves watching *It*, the first part of a mini-series based on Stephen King's horror novel. *It* was rated Adults Only. The program in the papers that morning said the plot involved 'children who are being lured to their deaths by a deadly force that takes on the form of a circus clown'. Later that night Alexandra, who was only eight, had a nightmare about the killer clown and woke in distress. Keating arrived furious in his office next morning wanting an immediate 'Dorothy' to attack the television networks in the House. He was hosed down by his staff.

The repercussions of this domestic drama are still playing themselves out in Australia. There was nothing extraordinary in kids seeing stuff on television they shouldn't have seen. What happened that night at the Lodge reflected the occasional experience of families across Australia. What was extraordinary in this case is that Alexandra's very angry father was in a position to do something about it.

Keating called in the heads of the networks and castigated them for showing adult material so early in the evening. He tried to persuade them to push Adults Only material back an hour — to start at 9.30 p.m., not 8.30 p.m. The networks baulked. This was bad for business. Australians will stay up late for the tennis. We'll sit up all night for the cricket. But we won't stay up for films that end past our bedtime. One of the key elements of this story is that we like to get to bed early during the week. As a nation we're tucked up by 10.30 p.m. Two hours are needed to screen a film with its usual cargo of ads, so Keating's late start looked like a ratings disaster.

Having failed to achieve anything behind the scenes, the Prime Minister chose the launch of a national strategy to counter violence against women, to publicly reproach the networks. 'There has been far too much violence on television in the last few years,' he said. 'Way too much violence in my view, and this is encouraging violence to be seen as normal and acceptable.' He spoke most passion-ately about violence sending the wrong signals to children, 'and to those individuals who are wont to resort too readily to violence. We have to reaffirm the integrity of women and their equality as fundamental values which violence undermines. We have to instil in our children, especially in our boys, the notion that disputes should be resolved in non-violent ways.'

Keating was applauded. The political leaders of the day — John Hewson of the Coalition and Cheryl Kernot of the Democrats — backed the Prime Minister. The moral hawks of the senate were impressed. Christian lobby groups were happy. It was twenty years since a Prime Minister had spoken in these terms and longer, perhaps, since a political leader in Canberra had taken on the networks. Letters poured into his office by the hundreds. Many were hostile to the man and to Labor, but promised Keating if he did something about television he would have their vote.

The networks grumbled behind the scenes that Keating was projecting his problems onto the nation. If his kids in his house saw a show he thought was unsuitable, then he had to bear a measure of responsibility too. No one it seems had the courage to make this argument to the prime minister's face.

The nuts-and-bolts changes Keating forced through in the months after Alexandra's nightmare, changed film and television censorship. New codes were devised to warn that sex, violence or bad language was about to appear on the screen. The language of television censorship was brought into line with the language of film and video censorship. A new classification was invented. Christian and parent groups had been skirmishing for years over the border between 'M' (Mature — for those fifteen and over) and 'R' (Restricted — for those eighteen and over). There had been persistent minority complaints that too much that was too sexy and too violent was being allowed in M. So M was now split and the slightly tougher end was called 'MA' — Mature Accompanied. MA at the cinema meant kids fifteen to seventeen were allowed in the door only if accompanied by a 'parent or adult guardian'. On television, MA meant the film could not start until 9 p.m. at night.

What mattered far more than these mechanical changes were two assumptions being bolted in place at this point, undebated and uncontested. One was the notion that television is dangerous. The second was the understanding that the nation would be the ultimate parent to its children. In the United Kingdom there is a time of night when adults can watch what adults want to watch. It's assumed the nation's children are in bed — and if they're not, then that's for the parents to deal with, not the government. *Pulp Fiction* went to air uncut on British television. That is unthinkable in Australia. The Keating reforms of 1992–93 consolidated the Australian rule of television: that no matter how old we are or how late we stay up at night, we never see anything on commercial television a fifteen-year-old kid can't see at the pictures. Australian television is stuck, by law, somewhere in late adolescence.

One of the great achievements of censorship advocates in Australia has been to establish in the public imagination the image of the extraordinarily vulnerable and extraordinarily ingenious child who wanders about the house, barely parented, sleepless at 3 a.m., looking for mischief and finding it on television, on 0055, and on the internet. This is the child we know from talk-back radio, the child of Fred Nile's deepest fears and Dame Leonie Kramer's cool concern, this is the child of pedophilia witch-hunts in the New South Wales parliament. This is the only child Alan Jones will ever have.

Harrangues in defence of these scarecrow children are not directed at their neglectful parents but at the neglectful government. 'Those children will not be protected,' Brian Harradine thundered in the 0055 debate. 'It will be the fault of those senators who vote against this amendment that they will not be protected. That will be noted by the electors of this country . . . ' Debates for twenty years are littered with wildly exaggerated scenarios of horror and fear. Here's Senator Shirley Walters arguing why 'sexually violent' films should never be allowed on pay television, even with some sort of PIN card for adult subscribers: 'One can imagine a father coming home, having had a few drinks at the pub, putting his card through and watching the most violent pornographic video in front of the family, and perhaps leaving his card in the black box and enabling the children to use it.'

One can, as the senator says, imagine this. Just.

What's difficult to imagine is a government designing its television policy to meet the needs of badly parented children around the clock. The true object here is to restrict the freedom of adults. But out of real concern for kids and shrewd political assessment that danger to them is easier to sell than danger to their parents, advocates of censorship concentrate on perils to children. Like that child of Shirley Walters' imagination, forced by a drunken father to watch violent porn then left alone with a PIN card to explore deeper the horrors of cable television. Professor Kevin Durkin, a psychologist who has spent his career investigating these issues, remarked wryly to me that in such dysfunctional families videos and television 'are likely to be the least of a child's problems'.

Sometimes it seems there are more scientists investigating the mysteries of film and television than anything else on earth suspected of presenting a danger to children. Armies of scientists contend on this disputed battleground where facts are few and the principal ammunition is rhetoric. Both the science and the rhetoric take on peculiar meanings here because we're talking about children. Levels of risk that would otherwise be treated as meaningless are given tremendous significance — at least by one side of the argument — because what's at stake is the welfare of children and the terrible prospect of aggressive kids growing up to become violent adults.

Kevin Durkin has surveyed the work of the scientists in order to advise the Australian Broadcasting Authority (ABA) and the Office of Film and Literature Classification on the impact of violent television and video games on children. No one, he says, has ever demonstrated a true cause and effect relationship between violence on the screen and violence in life. All that researchers have turned up is a 'slight association' between viewing and aggressive behaviour. That's not really contested by anyone. Advocates for censorship build grim conclusions on the basis of 'studies that prove' such a link, but all that science has established after decades of trying is a very weak, very uncertain association. 'Neglected and abused children are undoubtedly at greater risk,' Durkin wrote in a paper a few years ago for the ABA. 'But it is not possible to maintain a serious argument that all television content should be regulated in accord with the viewing needs of neglected children. Television . . . could certainly be improved, but improvement will not be accelerated by gearing all content to what experts judge suitable for child victims. For their part, child victims do merit urgent community assistance, but better to deliver it to them rather than imagine that censorship will somehow cure all, or any, of the stresses they face in unsatisfactory homes.'

That conclusion is four or five years old so I rang Durkin at the University of Western Australia to see if anything had come up in the meantime to establish a link that many of us instinctively feel *ought* to be there between horrors on the screen and horrors in life. No. 'Everyone would leap at evidence that showed a link.' Researchers have still come up with nothing but a vague association. Statistically it's hardly there. The evidence is emotional, intuitive and anecdotal: very distressing accounts of death and rape put down to watching film and video. 'But you have to ask, was this some perfectly ordinary, decent guy who saw this movie and decided to murder his wife?' A disturbed individual can seek inspiration from any source. That *could* be a horror film. 'But two or three years ago there was that case in Britain where a man killed his mother and chopped her up and, I believe, cooked some of her. He was found gibbering over a book — and it was the Bible.'

On a Sunday in April 1996, Martin Bryant drove to the Seascape Guest House and shot two people dead. Then he drove deeper into Port Arthur killing as he went. At the Broad Arrow Café he took twenty lives. All this was done in cold blood, with a couple of powerful guns and hardly a word uttered. By the time he was captured — this was Australia, so he was captured — Bryant had killed thirty-five men, women and children in a few hours.

Peeking through the windows of Bryant's house in Hobart's New Town a few days later, journalists from the Melbourne *Herald-Sun* saw among the teddy bears and ammunition three videos lying on a coffee table: *A Nightmare On Elm Street*, *Missing in Action* and *Crime Story: The Final Chapter*. Bryant's former girlfriend, Jenetta Hoani, told them a couple of days later of two rooms full of videos. The country and western tapes she thought he inherited with the house, but there were also Scandinavian porn videos featuring sex with animals and a whole room of tapes she — or the paper — described as violent. 'Jenetta, a student at Hobart TAFE, said Bryant's favourite video — *Child's Play 2* — featured an "evil" doll. "He loved Chucky (the doll's name), he used to go on about it all the time," she said. "It comes to life and it has to kill this boy so that it can be real and then it just goes around killing all these people. There was a phrase out of that movie that he used to say: 'Don't f--- with the Chuck'. He used to get excited when he'd say that. He would think he was really cool."'

The horror of those videos in New Town seemed to grow in the imagination of a pulic appalled and baffled by what had happened at Port Arthur. Two days after Hoani's words appeared in the *Hearld-Sun*, Richard Alston was threatening a crackdown on violent films, videos and video games. He authorised the Senate's Community

Standards Committee to look into the Portrayal of Violence in the Electronic Media. By the time the militantly Catholic Australian Family Association came to make its submission to the enquiry, they were listing Martin Bryant among serial murderers and serial rapists whom 'case studies demonstrate time and again are heavy users of violent material and are pornography addicts'. The association added, 'Press reports indicate that he had some 2000 violent and pornographic videos in his house at the time of his arrest. It took two trucks to remove it all.'

Bryant's Hobart lawyer John Avery has confirmed there were 'a couple of hundred' videos of kids films, musicals and thrillers in the house. 'The videos were nothing out of the ordinary for a young man who had a lot of money and a lot of time on his hands,' he told me. No snuff films and only a handful of porn. Eventually all the videos went off with the rest of the contents of the house to be sold at public auction. Some of Bryant's favourites were 'of the violent action variety' but neither the police nor forensic psychiatrists who examined him thought they were an element in the shooting. Avery told the sentencing hearing in Hobart in November 1996, 'Mr Bryant described his pleasure in his life as watching the television, music and drinking. The music that he favoured was the sound track of *The Lion King* and records made by Cliff Richard. On direct questioning he acknowledged that he spent a considerable amount of time watching videos and going to the pictures. He listed as his favourite film *Babe*, his favourite videos as Steven Seagal's movie *Under Siege* and a film called *The Protector* which he claimed to have watched a dozen times.'

Under Siege involves Miss July 1989 jumping out of a birthday cake on the USS *Missouri* to team up with a meek hero working in the galley to save the ship from terrorists. Lots of gore. Lots of bad language. Rated M. *The Protector* (R) brought martial arts to the New York police force as Jackie Chan pursued kidnappers and narcotics smugglers all the way home to Hong Kong. Major flop. *Babe* is *Babe* (rated G).

Byrant's examination by psychiatrists and police revealed no evidence of an addiction to porn or violent videos. The picture emerged of an erratic, volatile, dumb, victimised and grandiose, often very drunk young man who came from a troubled family, had been in psychiatric difficulties himself since he was a child — and loved guns. He bought a lot of military magazines and a lot of guns. He never had a gun licence; that was never a problem. He spoke lovingly of his guns to the forensic psychiatrist, Paul Mullen. As Bryant began shooting at Port Arthur he thought, 'my power, so powerful and the guns and these magazines filled with bullets, I could just go bang, bang'.

The Community Standards Committee conceded that attempts to link violence on the screen and violence in life were 'largely inconclusive' but the recommendations they made took the link absolutely for granted. The suggestions they came up with for solving the problem were extreme: 'on the spot' fines of up to $100 000 for television stations breaching censorship guidelines, taking cartoons and other children's programs out of the hands of the stations' in-house censors, recutting films more stringently before releasing them on video, putting stickers on violent videos to warn of harm to 'the mental well-being of children and those adults suffering from depression and other mental disorders', removing 'disturbing footage' from early evening news bulletins and banning songs that mention 'suicide'. These recommendations lay fallow for two years.

Connoisseurs of kneejerk attempts to link film, video and television to terrible events like Port Arthur were struck by the appearance of *Child's Play 2* in the newspaper indictments of Martin Bryant. Two-and-a-half years earlier in Britain, Justice Morland remarked as he sentenced a couple of eleven-year-old boys to prison for the murder of two-year-old James Bulger, 'I suspect that exposure to violent video films may in part be an explanation'. Neither the police nor prosecution had made any such claim. The judge named no movie. The press pounced on *Child's Play 3*, the latest episode in the adventures of the demon doll Chucky. The father of one of the killer children had rented the video a month before the murder. When he said his son had not seen it, the press disbelieved him. When the Home Office insisted police had found no evidence linking the case with 'video nasties' this was ignored. Detective Superintendent Albert Kirby who led the Bulger murder investigation said he had seen no evidence to suggest the boys had access to videos any worse than might be found in many households — but yet the story did not die. Facts can't kill it. Among censorship advocates it's still an article of faith that James Bulger's death was a copycat killing based on *Child's Play 3*.

Not that Chucky is absolutely in the clear. As James Bulger's killers were being sent off to jail, a gruesome trial was underway in Manchester for the torture and murder of Suzanne Capper in the woods outside the city. One of the accused gave evidence of hearing her co-murderer Bernadette McNeilly say, 'Chucky's gonna play' as she injected amphetamines into her victim. Police denied reports the film was played in the torture chamber and denied Capper's death was a copycat crime, but the mantra 'Chucky's gonna play' was enough to condemn *Child's Play 3* all over again.

The *Child's Play* series was rated M in Australia: not suitable for the under 15s. This is not a sign that we're lax in classification. The truth is, these were never the savage films of their depiction in the press. Millions have seen them round the world. One person might have been unhinged. There is no evidence for this beyond a few muttered words. It was not the police but the press that came up with the video hypothesis but to blame Suzanne Capper's murder on *Child's Play 3* is to trivialise a terrible death. The fault was not in *Child's Play 3* but in Capper's four killers. Was Martin Bryant inspired by videos to shoot thirty-five people? There is no evidence to suggest this. The fault was somewhere deep — and undiscovered — in him. He may have gone about the house chanting, 'Don't fuck with the Chuck' but out in the open with his gun in his hand he was only heard to complain there weren't enough Japanese around to shoot.

Spot the movie has become a macabre American game in the face of violent deaths. The press was pointing to *The Basketball Diaries*, starring Leonardo DiCaprio even while bullets were still ricocheting round Colorado's Columbine High School. Why? Because the killings took place in classrooms and the killers wore long overcoats. The coats were the crucial detail. In the aftermath of the shootings, the National Rifle Association refused to cancel its Annual Meeting in Denver, but local video stores removed copies of *The Basketball Diaries* from their shelves. The killers were said — wrongly it turned out — to be fans of shock-rockers Marilyn Manson who then cancelled a Denver gig considering it 'inappropriate'. DiCaprio solemnly promised to turn down roles in violent films. The families of the victims are planning to sue the police, school officials, the parents of the killer children and the makers of *The Basketball Diaries* — but not the makers and the sellers of the guns.

Three days after the killings, an unexpected insight into the Columbine killers came from the *Courier-Mail* back home in Brisbane. Sports journalist Wayne Smith interviewed local psychiatrist Dr William Wilkie, president of the Beyond Bullying Association. 'It sounds to me like they got into a virtual reality area,' said Wilkie. 'They became more and more isolated and their sense of reality was influenced by whatever video game they were playing.' I rang Wilkie curious to discover what games these were. He didn't know. He didn't even know if the killers *were* playing video games. What really matters for Wilkie is his belief that shoot-outs are always the work of demons. 'I'm a Christian psychiatrist and I've seen some demonised people and I've had to deal with them.' The mark of men possessed by demons, he told me, are eyes like those of a cat playing with its kill and discomfort at the name of Jesus. 'The very strange thing is that they don't want you to mention Jesus. They get very uneasy with prayers. You try to get them to say the Lord's Prayer and you'd swear you were brandishing a red-hot poker. This is quite real. We seem to be seeing more of it.' Dr Wilkie describes himself as, 'Catholic by choice. I just believe in the ordinary things.' He's certain there should be tighter rules for the censorship of film and television. 'I think any society that doesn't look after its children deserves what it gets.' His last words to me were, 'We're just at the mercy of madness'.

When Paul Keating stormed into his office that morning after his daughter's nightmare and began to transform the censorship of television, his anger was only directed at violence, not sex. The general message of surveys through the nineties is that Australians generally are uneasy about violence on television but not worried about sex. Keating said sex on television isn't 'that offending to me'. But a few Australians are profoundly and inexhaustibly concerned about the nudity, bad language and lovemaking brought into their homes by television. So over the last decade, as politicians and the television industry tried to cobble together new codes to deal with public disquiet about violence, there was another campaign going on, hand in hand with the first, to chase sex off television. Oddly enough, when the new 'voluntary' code on violence and sex was finally forced on the industry in early 1999, it was the Christian campaign against sex that won the greater victory. But that's politics.

Channel 10's 'Sex/Life' was a catalyst. The sex code for television we're living with now is essentially the work of skilful politics by Christian lobby groups to make sure that nothing like this grab-bag of gynaecology, skits and marriage counselling is ever shown on Australian television again. Tottie Goldsmith anchored the show when it reached Ten in mid-1996. Television critics were sniffy about it from the beginning but over its first two years 'Sex/Life' built up an audience of a million viewers by working the same territory as *Cleo* and *Cosmo*: how to seduce, how to keep/drop your girl/bloke, how to have better sex. The aim was not marriage and kids but orgasm. The show's message — loud, clear and vulgar — was that sex should be fun. 'Sex/Life' became the most complained about show on television. The papers were full of the story. Ratings climbed. Channel 10 weathered the storm.

Commercial television stations censor their own programs under a 'voluntary' code drafted by the Federation of Australian Commercial Television Stations (FACTS) and approved by the Australian Broadcasting Authority. Quite by coincidence, FACTS was finishing a new draft code in the wake of Port Arthur just as 'Sex/Life' went to air. The new code proposed pushing the most violent permissible shows back to 9.30 p.m. — where Keating wanted them in the first place — but made no new restrictions on sex and nudity. The ABA declined to accept this draft so another, tougher draft was quickly produced and released for public discussion in December 1996. Violence was still the focus. The latitude once given to stylised violence disappeared and old restrictions on sexual violence were tightened further. Sex was now to be less detailed, more discreet. But the new code was left in limbo for nearly two years — partly because the senate Community Standards Committee was trying to impose its radical post–Port Arthur recommendations on the commercial networks but also because Harradine was running a peculiar campaign to convince the government that the latest FACTS draft code was actually *more* permissive than the old.

'Sex/Life' moved to a new 'adult' time slot of 9.30 p.m. in early 1997. The press had been sympathetic to complaints about the early starting time, and once the station dealt with these the papers lost sight of the story. But Channel 10 and the ABA were still fielding complaints about the show. Indeed, by the time this saga ended, the ABA was to conduct a dozen investigations into 'Sex/Life'. That they found only one breach of the code in all that time didn't stop the complaints. Instead, it generated an underground campaign for an even tougher code on sex than FACTS was proposing. Harradine was leading this campaign. By May of 1997, FACTS was alerting the commercial television stations that the government was very worried about antagonising the Tasmanian senator.

The government was nervous because they wanted to give the networks access to digital television and believed Harradine's vote was needed to make that happen. Digital will allow each station to broadcast several new, very high-quality services, both pictures and text, into the homes of the nation. Morals groups in the United States had used the digital revolution as an opportunity to impose a tougher censorship regime on television. Morals groups in Australia found themselves — courtesy of Harradine — in just as powerful a position. For those who knew what was at stake it was no surprise when, apparently out of the blue, Richard Alston began to talk about the concern of 'the entire community' over prurient programs on radio and television. In May 1998 he told the senate, 'I don't think anyone in this country wants to see an electronic version of Sodom and Gomorrah . . . and we will take efforts to make sure it doesn't occur.' Alston cited 'Sex/Life'.

There was no shift in community attitudes to sex on television. The ABA conducts regular surveys of community feeling on these issues and analyses complaints to television stations. The level of concern about sex was steady and low. But rage about sex on television continued to burn through Christian congregations across the country. It was particularly inflamed by a cheap effort screened by Channel 10 early one evening late in 1997 called 'Playboy's Really Naked Truth No. 1'. Again the ABA investigated these complaints and found no formal breach by Channel 10.

The commercial channels were in a difficult position here because the government was literally *giving* them digital. A fortnight after Alston's warning, the Community Standards Committee met and watched that week's episode of 'Sex/Life' which featured a topless woman having sex — simulated, of course — while wearing a Roman helmet. This segment carried a psychologist's warning, 'Make sure your partner understands what you have in mind, and don't become dependent on such role-plays for sexual gratification'. Afterwards, the committee grilled Tony Branigan the executive director of FACTS. Was this within the code? Was this discreet? Was this explicit? Their hostility was menacing. Channel 10 held its ground for another fortnight. After all, it had the support of somewhere near a million Australians who watched the show each week. But in late June 1998, Channel 10's chief, John McAlpine, capitulated. Citing pressure from Harradine, he announced they were canning the show. He added, 'I think Senator Harradine's pressure on this issue has gone much further than just "Sex/Life".'

He was right. Acting on complaints from Harradine, Alston told FACTS it would have to rework the sex and nudity provisions of the draft code which they'd been haggling over for nearly two years, 'to accommodate the concerns of the community'. The commercial networks now had not much choice but to do what they were told. The form of words was all but set. Nudity was to be raised as a serious issue of concern in order that nothing like 'Playboy's Really Naked Truth No. 1' should reappear on Australian television. And the sex provisions of the code would be altered not only to stop 'Sex/Life' rising from the dead but also to deal with several other shows like Seven's 'Full Frontal' and Nine's 'Pacific Drive'.

Soon after the 1998 elections were won, the ABA gave the nod to the latest draft of the 'voluntary' code with violence provisions born out of the massacre at Port Arthur and tough new bans on 'gratuitous, exploitative or demeaning' nudity and sex born out of 'Sex/Life'. 'These provisions are directed against romp,' said Branigan. 'It's ironic that something that's silly and mildly offensive should be knocked out of television when programs which many people would find more offensive and disturbing should survive. It's an odd approach to focus on one particular genre for reasons not very convincing to me.' He hopes the new rules will accommodate 'vocal groups' without disenfranchising too many viewers. 'But anyone who asserts this is logical and consistent with what you can see in an average home, on an average street, on an average beach is kidding themselves.'

The commercial channels will cut as little as they can. They know that now Brian Harradine has lost his crucial vote in the senate, the government won't be breathing down their necks as it has been for the last few years. But lots of television programs are taking nips and tucks. The lighter the show, the sharper the cuts. Trash is still appearing on the screen but the genitals are pixilated. Early evening news footage is less graphic, more cheerful. Shots that suggest drug-taking as an everyday part of our lives will now be rare on commercial television. Stylised violence will be cut as heavily as film of the real thing. Restrictions on violence will relax slightly after 9.30 p.m. but films aren't starting later as a result because Australians are still turning in at 10.30 p.m. Instead films are being cut more heavily.

More than ever the jealous eyes are being cast at the ABC and SBS which are not bound by these 'voluntary' codes. The next battle shaping in the senate is to protect children — and us of course — more systematically by bringing the public television stations under the censorship umbrella that hangs over the commercial stations. But the independence of the ABC and SBS is exaggerated. They still have to operate in the moral climate set by government. The ABC and SBS are stuck in adolescence too, showing television that's fit, maybe, for sixteen- and seventeen-year olds. By law it cannot show those R-rated films any eighteen-year old can see at any hour of the day in any cinema in the country. The hit English television series 'Queer as Folk' which was shown late at night back in the UK — where parents are responsible for seeing kids are safely in bed by 10.30 p.m. — was turned down by all the commercial stations here and turned down, too, by SBS and ABC. Australia can't take it.

Alexandra Keating is a teenager these days. She had a terrible dream a few years ago, a little nightmare we're all in some very distant way sharing now. My guess is she's doing just fine because she has good parents to guide her. Whatever side you take in the endless debate on the dangers of television and the vulnerability of children, all the studies conclude that Alexandra's parents will count for far more in her life than anything she ever sees on the box. From them she'll learn what matters most to her about morals and life. What she saw that night she shouldn't have seen, but I wonder if she remembers it now as anything but a bad fright. We're told these days that frights are bad for kids. They censor frights from Disney films in Australia. But I can't imagine childhood without them. I had one of the worst frights of my life one hot Saturday afternoon when I snuck into the Gordon pictures. I was seven. I shouldn't have been there. The film was *Twenty Thousand Leagues Under the Sea* and I was so terrified by the sight of Captain Nimmo's submarine charging towards me, its two great eyes blazing as it cut through the water, that I hid under the seat. I probably howled. My mother was furious. It haunted me for years but I reckon it did me no harm.

SEVEN

HEAVENLY WISDOM

'Form ever follows function.'

Louis Sullivan

D on't fall to your knees as you enter this place or the guards will throw you out. Secular Turkey decrees that no one must pray here, not even those godless pilgrims who come through these mighty doors and fall to their knees to give thanks to the god of architecture. They say it happens.

After nearly a thousand years as Hagia Sophia, the great church of Christendom dedicated to Divine Wisdom, and nearly five hundred years more as Aya Sofya, one of the most splendid mosques on earth, this mighty building was turned into a museum by the soldier who beat us at Gallipoli and created the modern state of Turkey. For Kemal Atatürk, the risky business of banning worship here in the 1930s was a symbol of his determination to disentangle all religion from government, an arrangement still honoured in modern Turkey even as it comes under renewed political threat.

So the furniture of the old mosque is still there on the floor pointing at an odd angle to Mecca, but high on the walls, plaster and paint have been stripped away to reveal patches of the finest Byzantine mosaic: of the Emperor Justinian who built the church only 500 years after Christ's death, of seraphim and archangels, saints and prophets, black-robed Virgins with and without child, and one surviving head of Christ — a little bad-tempered and infinitely wise.

Versions of this dome have appeared wherever Christianity and Islam have built for glory, but none of the great domed mosques and cathedrals, from Jakarta to New York, has the peculiar impact of the original. Justinian's two architects — teachers of geometry and mechanics — conceived Hagia Sophia and saw it built in six frantic years by teams of 5000 men working in competition, one team on each side of the building. The pile of domes was novel; the engineering to support them was (on that scale) unique; the span of the church was greater than anything seen before in the Roman Empire; and huge as it was, the building was filled with light.

Justinian had his propagandist, Procopius, on hand to celebrate the church: 'overwhelming to those who see it and altogether incredible to those who only hear of it, for it soars to a height to match the sky . . . and abounds exceedingly in sunlight and gleaming reflections.' When Justinian arrived in procession for the consecration on Christmas Day 536, he declared: 'Solomon, I have out-done you.'

In the degraded magnificence of Hagia Sophia today, it takes a little effort to imagine how it was on that day nearly 1500 years ago. But nothing can detract from the thrill of entering the place. You leave the touts behind, put down a wad of lire worth only $4, and pass a lazy security check. From the western door you cross a narrow lobby running the width of the building and then a second, much broader, sheathed in marble. The scale is already immense. Ahead you glimpse a dome in the distance and then a second perched above the first. This seems the big one, the dome that dominates the skyline of Istanbul, but it's an exhilarating trick. Only when you enter the nave through the imperial doorway is the real thing visible, floating high above the others: gold and ribbed, perched on a rim of windows that lift it into space.

Hagia Sophia isn't designed for gloom. It's not one of those Gothic monsters built to remind us how infinite God is and how puny we humans are. Hagia Sophia is made for glory and standing under that roof we are part of that glory. The roof is higher than any of the cathedrals of France, and that other great surviving Byzantine church, Saint Mark's, would fit into a corner of this building. As crowds pause below the dome, faces everywhere are lifted up smiling, sometimes even laughing with delight. This great space is designed to sweep us up to heaven, not cast us down as sinners. Procopius wrote: 'The mind is lifted up to God and exalted, feeling that He cannot be far away but must love to dwell in this place which He has chosen.'

Christianity has spent centuries denouncing pleasure but using pleasure too, pleasure that carries the faithful beyond the abstractions of their faith, to let them *feel* the existence of their God. This is pleasure the evangelist. No painter, musician or builder in the last couple of thousand years has faced a greater — or more familiar — challenge than proving the existence of God through art. Some of the mightiest music we know was written to make the Resurrection plausible. The more impossible the doctrines, the greater the efforts they inspire. Doubt and disbelief are at the core of Christian art — doubt especially about the power of the Word. In the last couple of millennia the most compelling arguments for the faith have not been made by books and preaching but by sound, light and sublime space. Hagia Sophia goes a long way further than mere words could hope to go to prove the existence of a magnificent God.

But then the reality of today hits. The walls and floor are so filthy it seems dust has been ground into the marble. The air smells damp, and everywhere there are signs of water damage: flaking paint and rotting, mottled plaster. The few Byzantine columns that have been cleaned make the rest seem even more pointlessly filthy. Black dust covers most of the upper walls. A quarter of the dome is filled by a tower of scaffolding rising 55 metres from the floor. The scaffolding — first wood, now steel — has stood there for fifteen years as a handful of technicians repair the mosaics.

Hagia Sophia has survived an earthquake roughly every century, though the whole dome fell early on and chunks have fallen two or three times since. And it has survived sacking by the Crusaders and conquest by the Infidel three or four centuries later. By chance the church was aligned south-east only a few degrees shy of Mecca. It was easy enough to convert into a mosque. Islam saved it from the fate of nearly every other great building of the former Roman Empire: it was not stripped of its marble, nor mined for building material.

Hagia Sophia weathered all this but it's not so certain it can survive its latest identity as a museum. Everyone is guessing what needs to be spent here: maybe as much as $100 million over the next decade. Turkey can't afford that and there is no prospect of such a sum from

UNESCO. Over the road stands the Blue Mosque, built in 1616 on the model of Hagia Sophia's dome. It's a mosque in perfect repair. The money comes from the state just as the state pays the budget of Hagia Sophia, but there's a lot more money in modern Turkey for the mosque than the museum. The state takes from Hagia Sophia where it should give. The museum earns nearly $9 million a year at the gate. That would meet almost all the foreseeable maintenance and restoration costs of the building, but half those millions goes into the coffers of the city council of Istanbul and the other half disappears into the Cultural Ministry in Ankara. Only a little makes its way back. In a poor country, Hagia Sophia is a minor goldmine.

In the heavy rains of autumn 1997, puddles appeared on the floor of the nave. There is no maintenance crew to find the leaks that spring in the acres of old lead on the roof. The museum's response to the puddle? A letter to Ankara. There are no cleaners. The staff of seven guards and ticket sellers work with brooms every morning for the hour before the doors open. The upstairs galleries are swept only once a week. Fragments of mosaic continue to fall from the ceilings. And these days, if one of the gaudy Byzantine sheets of marble falls from the walls, a replacement is bodgied up in paint.

Work inside the dome is proceeding at a snail's pace. Two UNESCO restorers work a few weeks at a time with syringes to re-glue the sixth-century mosaics chip by chip. They man the scaffold for only about eight weeks a year. It's said local restorers are hard to find and are only now being trained. The dome should have been finished already according to UNESCO, but not even the first quarter is done. At this rate, it will be another fifteen years before the dome is clear of scaffolding again.

Hagia Sophia is being examined minutely while it's spectacularly neglected. Academic teams from America, Austria and Japan are working with various Istanbul universities to investigate every peculiar problem of the building. The Japanese are monitoring the building's weather system. Istanbul is a damp city and the church was built close to a great underground cistern. Six thousand people a day enter and stand breathing under the dome. The humidity hovers around 80 per cent year-round and there's no ventilation high up in the dome where the air is always hot and wet. Condensation is rotting the plaster and loosening the mosaics.

The Austrians are at work on the mosaics themselves. The church was covered at first in patterned mosaic, mostly gold, and acres of this survive, rather blackened, on the ceilings. Not until three centuries later when the mad iconoclastic wars had calmed down were the figures of Christ and the Virgin, bishops and saints added to the walls. Those masterpieces that survive from that time — and alone make a journey to Hagia Sophia exciting — are only a fraction of what was once there. The hope has always been that more may have survived hidden under roughly painted 19th-century plaster that covers the upper walls. Old records show there was once a head of Christ in the centre of the dome, that spot in an Orthodox church from which He is traditionally shown staring down in judgement from heaven. That's gone. But with a new sonar device the Austrians have found, on the arch below the eastern edge of the dome, figures of Christ and John the Baptist. This wonderful discovery is still not fully revealed. From the nave you see the figures only in ghostly outline where the plaster has been crudely scraped away.

American universities are working on the structure of the building. It's a heap of damp mortar and brick, buttressed and reinforced at various times even as it was being built to make it carry the weight of the dome. By chance rather than design, this stack of domes and arches withstands earthquakes well. Hagia Sophia shakes but hasn't fallen. It didn't flinch in the big quake of 1999. The fact that this pile of brick is still standing earns the respect of everyone who tries to solve its mysteries. No plans survive and Justinian's architects carefully hid the bones of its construction behind sheets of marble and mosaic. The drama of most great buildings is expressed in showing how they hold themselves up. Hagia Sophia deliberately hides most of this. It was said for centuries that only God knew the secrets of this building, God and the architects to whom he revealed them in a vision. Now the university scholars are picking away . . .

It's hardly conceivable that the world would allow Hagia Sophia to fall into ruin but if this place were used again it would be cared for by the people of Istanbul as the Blue Mosque is next door. Atatürk's great achievement after beating us and a few other nations on the shores of the Dardanelles was to expel the clerics from Turkey's body politic. Keeping imams and priests at arm's length has been a duty of good government since before the days of Justinian, but it may be a death sentence to turn this ancient treasure into a symbol of wise politics.

Even gorgeously restored, it would be an empty shell unless there was worship here. It is the purpose of this place, one it served perfectly for nearly 1500 years. Hagia Sophia or Aya Sofya should be full of people praying and — if the Orthodox got the place back again — singing. This space is made for music, lifting to the dome, echoing through the galleries. But Christian or Moslem, it must be used again for its own sake. Turkey's main Islamic party has undertaken to turn this building back into a mosque if it ever wins power in Ankara. Let them do that. The mosaics would disappear behind a layer of fresh plaster but that's a small price to pay for the pleasure of those who should stand under this dome, worshipping God or great architecture — or both — for another thousand years.

THE HIGH PRICE OF HEAVEN

A NIGHT OUT AT THE CROSS

'Whosoever commits the abominable crime of buggery, or bestiality, with mankind, or with any animal, shall be liable to penal servitude for fourteen years.'

NSW Crimes Act, section 79

The steam had gone out of the 'mardi gras' by the time it reached the El Alamein fountain but as the demonstrators began to drift back towards William Street their way was blocked by paddy wagons. The side streets were also blocked trapping 200 people between the wagons and the strip joints. With sirens wailing, police began to make arrests.

'The noise of chanting and shouting was tremendous,' I wrote in the *National Times*. 'Police dragged people from the side of the road towards the wagons. Some of these resisted. The melee was joined by passers-by, bikies, and apparently by some residents of the Cross. "All the windows were full. Everyone on the Cross was watching," said a bystander. There was crying, screaming and panic.

'Politics had been played out on Sydney streets, violently, for over a decade. But the worst of the anti-Vietnam and anti-Apartheid rallies were rarely as nasty as this. Veterans of those demonstrations knew these police tactics — trap, bash and arrest — and knew there was always a chance of violence when you marched under a radical banner in Sydney. But this mid-winter night was supposed to be as much a celebration as demonstration — one of many celebrations round the world to mark the anniversary of a brawl outside New York's Stonewall Bar in 1969 that radicalised the gay rights movement across the United States. Stonewall was happening all over again in Darlinghurst Road.'

The paddy wagons were followed back to Darling-hurst Police Station by angry demonstrators. Arrests continued. One policeman dragged an unconscious woman by her hair through the station door. Four or five beat a young man's head against the station's iron gates. A woman was hit hard on the face as she sat in the dock. A man in the cells was beaten so badly he was taken, after some hours, to St Vincent's Hospital. Not till well after dawn were the last of the 53 charged, finger-printed and released. That night Neville Wran, Premier and Minister for Police, spoke on Channel 10: 'These sort of things happen,' he said. 'I don't suppose it's unexpected that the police have taken exception to a busy thoroughfare in Kings Cross being completely blocked off at midnight.'

Next morning outside the Court of Petty Sessions, Superintendent Reg Douglas deployed a cordon of police to keep sympathisers standing about in the rain. He announced: 'The court has been closed.' It stayed that way despite orders to police from the Chief Stipendiary Magistrate, Murray Farquhar, to let people through. A scrappy, ugly demonstration continued all morning. There was chanting. Eggs were thrown. I saw a woman tossed down the steps of the court and kicked in midair by a senior policeman.

Protests by homosexuals, lesbians, civil libertarians and lawyers continued through the winter of 1978. There were more mass arrests. Lawyers began to come out. Teams of civil liberties lawyers were joined by openly gay barristers and solicitors. All the charges against the demonstrators were eventually dropped. Police commanders were shown to have lied in court. Neville Wran was silent.

Homosexuals could live so well in Sydney that it seemed somehow impertinent to be campaigning for changes to the law. True, there were always a few zealots about like the old police commissioner, Colin Delaney, who reckoned homosexuals were the biggest threat to the nation. Worse than communists. But Sydney regarded this sort as cranks. No one fretted much about the city's homosexual Cabinet ministers, clerks, bishops, cleaners, judges, doctors, lawyers, truck drivers and teachers — as long as their sexuality didn't have to be publicly acknowledged. Sydney's civic emblem, since convict days, has been the blind eye.

Yet kissing was still a crime. Intercourse carried a jail sentence of fourteen years. At Prince Henry Hospital doctors offered to cure homosexuals with electric shocks. The churches promised damnation. Police entrapped, arrested, took bribes and ignored bashings. Nothing much in this line was reported in the press except the occasional celebrity arrest in a public toilet. Poor Claudio Arrau, one of the finest pianists in the world, was taken into custody after winking at a police provocateur in the infamous Lang Street lavatory. He left the country next day never to return.

Solicitors knew what was going on behind the façade of tolerance. They handled the cases. And they knew, whatever the political difficulties, that reform was technically simple. A neat cut of five sections from the Crimes Act would leave heterosexuals and homosexuals equal before the criminal law.

These laws — bequeathed by the church courts to civil authorities in Britain at the Reformation and inherited, in turn, by Australia — could never have survived so long on the statute books if so many men had not agreed with the terms of the 'civilised' deal that governed homosexual lives in this country: you'll be left alone if you keep quiet. These old hands reckoned Mardi Gras demonstrators sacked from their jobs when their names were reported in the *Sydney Morning Herald* were getting what was coming to them. 'They'll learn.'

But the world was absorbing the lessons of Alfred Kinsey, an Indiana zoologist who in 1948 announced that about one in ten white American men were 'more or less exclusively homosexual'. Kinsey's scientific reputation is shaky these days and his 10 per cent figure is certainly exaggerated but his fundamental conclusion has stood the test of time: homosexuality is commonplace. After the Kinsey Report, churches couldn't claim that homosexuality was in any ordinary sense 'unnatural'. As a saboteur of church teaching, Kinsey, for all his faults, has a place in the scientific pantheon not too remote from Darwin.

Reform took time. Nearly everywhere it was triggered by police. Britain eventually changed the law (badly) after a police campaign in the 1950s to round up homosexual aristocrats. Police intimidation and corruption led to the 1969 street brawl outside the Stonewall Bar in New York's Greenwich Village in which 'gay liberation' was born. Adelaide police were rumoured to bash homosexuals for sport along the banks of the Torrens River. Reform reached Australia after a gay academic drowned there in 1972. Two former vice-squad officers were charged over the drowning years later, both were acquitted.

No other state followed South Australia's lead though the House of Representatives, the Liberal Party in Queensland, a royal commission in Western Australia, the New South Wales Young Liberals, the Labor Party Women's Conference and the Anglican Church in Melbourne had all come out in support of reform. Lawyers, civil libertarians and the first brave men and women to identify themselves as homosexual were already campaigning across the country for reform. One timid attempt had even been made to deal with the issue in the New South Wales parliament where the Liberal backbencher John Dowd put a notice of motion on the agenda paper calling for reform of the Crimes Act. Dowd was a solicitor. Working in the courts had convinced him something needed to be done. 'You see life as it is.' His notice of motion was never debated.

Then came Kings Cross in 1978. The men and women who had gone out to celebrate and party that night, stayed around to fight. The bar culture met the political culture and the result was a unique Sydney fusion, that's survived to this day. But despite all the noise after 1978 the laws against homosexuality stayed stuck in a political logjam. It was a mystery. Here was Neville Wran, Labor's new face, glossy and articulate, the JFK of New South Wales, a civil libertarian who was on record saying these laws had to change — but nothing was happening. Wran assured Labor staffers that homosexual law reform was on the agenda. Once or twice he massaged gay delegations. That was all.

Hidden from public view was Wran's ambivalence. He came from a class and a profession, and was leader of a party that didn't, for the most part, *like* homosexuals. No one has to. Wran didn't. Those who knew him well knew he needed a push. His deputy, Jack Ferguson, was lobbying. So was his new wife, Jill Hickson. She was a woman from another generation and another class. 'I was on the case,' she says. 'We were both in sympathy. It was just a matter of getting the politicking done.' The question asked for the next six years of candlelight parades, police raids, court cases, parliamentary farce, twists and turns, church lobbying, brave gestures, pigheaded treachery, stunts and tears was, what was all this politicking really about?

Wran had had only a tiny majority in the State's Legislative Assembly but four months after the Mardi Gras the 'Wranslide' elections delivered him absolute control of parliament. Reformers had been sympathetic to Wran's problems before but now he had the numbers. Yet as the Attorney-General, Frank Walker, got to work preparing a general program of reform, Wran told him to back off on abortion and homosexuals. 'It will send the right wing mad.' Walker believed the premier was still promising homosexual law reform. But when? Sometime later.

Out at Sydney University, in the grey, brick barn of the Merewether Building, a bunch of irritants wouldn't leave the issue alone. They were lecturers in the Government Department. Their leader was Lex Watson, a prickly, brilliant academic living in a dark room full of newspaper clippings. His motto: 'If you teach politics, you should know how politics works.' His fellow lecturer, Craig Johnston, would be the steady presence throughout the campaign. Together, they organised a fractious alliance of homosexuals, lawyers and students into the Gay Rights Lobby to keep pressure on the government.

A bizarre situation was looming. New 'genderneutral' rape provisions would threaten men raping men with jail for seven years, while the old sodomy provisions of the Crimes Act might still punish men making love to men with jail for fourteen years. Rape would be a useful defence to the crime of love. Newspapers took the problem seriously. The Gay Rights Lobby enlisted the old socialist George Petersen, 'the conscience of the party', to take 'gender-neutral' reforms to their logical conclusion by proposing parliament remove all the old homosexual offences from the statute books. Men and women, in whatever coupling, would then be treated equally by the law.

Support poured down on Petersen from beyond Macquarie Street — from the Society of Labor Lawyers, the Young Labor Conference, the Council for Civil Liberties, the New South Wales Teachers' Federation and the Labor Women's Committee. Watson and Johnston had also won the support of the New South Wales Labor Council. But Wran wanted none of this. Petersen's amendment was ruled out of order. There was no debate. Petersen was warned by the whips that if he moved dissent, he would be expelled from the ALP. The gallery erupted in jeers and hissing. 'Sham,' they called. 'Gutless wonders.' Afterwards, in private, Wran promised Petersen his support for a full reform bill — after the *next* elections. The result was never in doubt. Labor couldn't lose. But Wran didn't want to go into the campaign with the church on his back.

Cardinal Sir James Freeman was an old bloke with a simple faith who wielded unique political power. He set the temper of his diocese. Catholic bishops can do that. The Anglicans of Sydney and Melbourne and Adelaide are what they are because of their synods and hardly change from bishop to bishop. But the political impact of the Catholic Church differs from diocese to diocese, bishop to bishop. That Melbourne's Archbishop, Sir Frank Little, and Sydney's Cardinal Freeman were very different men shows in the extraordinary contrast between Sydney and Melbourne in the narrative of gay law reform in Australia. Little gave the nod to reform. He wasn't approving the sin but recognised it didn't have to stay a crime. The Anglicans in Melbourne were already actively canvassing the change. The only organised opposition to the Victorian Government's plans came from the little Protestant congregations, but without the backing of Anglicans or Catholics they could only detach about a dozen Liberals from the party line. All the rest and the entire Labor caucus in both Houses supported a reform bill which was signed into law just before Christmas 1980.

Freeman, on the other hand, fought the change. He was a likeable, pious old figure who drank and smoked — His Eminence was notorious for cadging cigarettes — and enjoyed a good day at the races. This knockabout image wasn't contrived. He was the son of a tram driver, boxed for a while and followed Rugby League all his life. Freeman was a man of his time, but his time was the 1950s. He had risen through the ranks of the church, not by grappling with the subtleties of faith but as an astute bureaucrat. He was a man of the corridor as much as the altar, and the political instincts that took him to the College of Cardinals were at the service of his faith in New South Wales. He didn't need to be directed from Rome on the issue of homosexuality: in his cut and dried faith it was simply wrong, a sin so terrible it must also be a crime. Always.

He wasn't shy of challenging Sydney's politicians. In the 1978 elections, Freeman had demanded the leaders of all parties state their position on plans to redefine 'spouse' in New South Wales anti-discrimination legislation so that spouses might, for some purposes, include same-sex partners. For the church this is not a small point. Bishops around the world were arguing that making life easier for homosexual couples was imperilling the sanctity of marriage and family. The cardinal pronounced Wran's 'spouse' proposals, 'completely unacceptable to all who regard the family as the basic unit of society'. The definition was withdrawn and the church has been able to hold this line across Australia ever since.

Freeman was a uniquely powerful prince of the church in Australia because the local Labor Party was still full of Catholics. They hadn't fled in the 1950s Split as they had in nearly all the other states. Catholics were still there, manning the party's invincible right wing machine. Most of the Labor Left were once Catholics too. The

Left/Right divide in the party roughly marked the line between lapsed and active Catholics. This didn't mean Freeman could get on the phone and direct Wran's government. But in New South Wales there was a powerful sense of mutual obligation between church and party that had survived nowhere else in Australia. When the atheist Neville Wran became Premier in 1976, his Left-wing deputy, Jack Ferguson, warned this newcomer to Macquarie Street, 'Labor governs New South Wales with the permission of the Catholic Church'. He was exaggerating, but the division between church and state was often hazy.

Wran, as the first non-Catholic to lead Labor for 50 years, needed to reassure the church. For this he used his right-hand man Gerry Gleeson, the state's most powerful bureaucrat and a source of constant political advice to the Premier. Wran said, 'If Gerry had a view you had no chance of avoiding hearing it'. Gleeson's Catholic faith was orthodox and keen. For him, homosexual law reform was a topic freighted with religious significance. Years later, Wran admitted the biggest fight he ever had with Gleeson in their often stormy relationship was over homosexual law reform. 'He wasn't conservative on most matters but on some, like homosexuality and abortion, he was. We had arguments and disagreements, but we were able to have the acrimonious debate and then go and have a bite to eat.'

Church defence of the Crimes Act rested on the claim that homosexuals were only very rarely prosecuted. 'Most of those are for assaults where young children are involved or lack of consent is an issue,' said the cardinal. In this he spoke for all the Anglicans and all the other hostile congregations. These crimes were to stay on the books, they argued, as official expressions of disapproval. The laws against sodomy were there not for persecution but education. These churchmen were not listening to the lawyers in their ranks and their benign picture of the law overlooked the violent mayhem of that march through the Cross, an educational experience from which others had drawn rather different lessons. Cardinal Freeman piously cautioned police dealing with homosexuals to exercise particular clemency.

What followed was not a tale of intricate conspiracy. Freeman pulled strings and Gleeson threatened and the Protestants backed them up. But the Catholic Church, having put so many years into making the men of the Labor caucus, didn't have to do much to kill reform. The caucus that met after Wran's third election victory in September 1981 was still a typical New South Wales Labor caucus. It could jolt newcomers. 'Coming into parliament was like being thrust into the company of all my Irish uncles,' said Legislative Councillor Ann Symonds. 'Those Catholic boys! Half the poor blokes went to Christian Brothers and Marist Brothers schools. No wonder they're so confused about sexuality at any level.'

Old George Petersen quickly discovered Neville Wran's promises of support evaporating. Whatever arguments the premier might once have made about the precarious position of his leadership or his party were now exhausted. Wran was all but unassailable. In every factional corner of his caucus it was acknowledged that this non-faction, atheist, silvertail barrister from Woollahra was Labor's lifeline. But Neville Wran was not going to venture any of this authority by making good his promises to Petersen or the gay lobby or to the public.

So Petersen drafted a bill of his own with Lex Watson's help. Their aim was simple equality for homosexual men and women and heterosexuals. The mark and symbol of this equality would be a common age of consent for both gay and straight sex. Sixteen was the age the law already recognised for heterosexuals, so it should also be sixteen for homosexuals. Petersen was under immediate pressure to 'protect' young men by raising the age of consent for homosexuals to eighteen. This was the churches' fallback position. They couched their rhetoric in terms of sheltering immature men from dangerous experience, but the symbolic purpose of the shift was to demonstrate difference, danger and disapproval. Petersen refused to accept this. To make such a distinction between straight and gay would be, he said, 'more objectionable and more offensive than this parliament's previous neglect to change archaic laws'.

In the mad history of the New South Wales parliament there have been few exercises as ludicrous as the wrangling over homosexuality in the summer of 1981. The atmosphere was all the crazier for the election to the Legislative Council at the poll just past of the brawling preacher Fred Nile. This was the issue that gave Nile his head start in politics. Fighting homosexuals was his first crusade. In hard political terms his vote in the upper House never mattered but he set the standards of ferociously uninhibited debate and his fascination with sodomy gave the proceedings a peculiar pungency.

Wran was looking for another bill even before Petersen's reached parliament. Michael Egan, who later became Treasurer in Bob Carr's government, volunteered for the task. In a hurried day, with the help of Chris Sidoti, the secretary of the Catholic Bishops' Commission for Justice and Peace, young Egan cobbled together a bill designed to meet the principal objection of the church. It kept all the old offences. Only when homosexuals had been arrested, prosecuted and found themselves in court could they plead in their defence that they were adults and sex had happened in private. Egan says now: 'It was a horrible bill.' But back then he thought it would be accepted by the church and the Right of the caucus. His bill was waiting for Petersen's to fail.

The first day of debate in late 1981 was the first time the NSW parliament had ever in its history discussed such reforms. It was a wild day. Gathered outside in Macquarie Street were men and women who had been bashed and arrested at the first Mardi Gras. Inside the House, the lines of battle were confused because Labor members had been allowed a conscience vote which released Catholics in the ranks to speak against Petersen's bill. The free vote was an acknowledgement that on this issue, party discipline couldn't be imposed in New South Wales as it had been in Victoria. Petersen saw at once that he didn't have the numbers for the equal age of consent but he soldiered on for a few days before facing the tactical need to change. Almost alone amongst the gay activists, Lex Watson supported the shift to eighteen for homosexual men. This was the start of a deep split within the gay rights movement, a split that has never entirely healed.

The sight of the monolithic Wran Labor Party stumbling around in this way in public gave the Opposition deep pleasure. The Nationals were adamantly opposed to reform, so hopes for change rested on the liberal Liberals led by John Dowd. After Dowd's earlier brave stand, the support of his faction was assumed. But in an act of sheer political bastardry, the Opposition voted en bloc to kill the Petersen bill. Egan's effort was debated immediately. He was baffled at the time by the 'unholy alliance' opposing him but homosexuals believed no bill was better than legislation that entrenched shame as Egan's did. They lobbied the Left to reject the bill and Jack Ferguson — who called Egan's legislation an invitation to 'persecution and discrimination' — sat the Left down with the hard Right and the National Party to kill it 65 to 28. 'As it turned out,' says Egan, 'the Left made a wise decision.'

Wran had taken no lead in any of this. He spoke to neither bill and voted for both of them. Nor did he offer leadership in the embarrassing aftermath that summer as the factions searched for some sort of compromise. Barrie Unsworth, secretary of the Labor Council, had his own power base in the party and his own seat in the upper House. His boys were at St Leo's but his Catholicism was relaxed. In the vacuum after the defeat of the first two bills, he proposed a bill of his own. It was a softer version of Egan's but still preserved the offence of sodomy. 'I believe there must be a clear distinction,' he told the Legislative Council, 'between heterosexual practice which is natural in physiological function, and homosexual practice which is not.' This formula of shame was opposed

THE HIGH PRICE OF HEAVEN

absolutely by gay lobbyists, but this time the Left was looking for just about any legislation to support.

Unsworth made a few compromises. The cardinal did not attack the bill. It passed the Legislative Council after a brawl with Nile that Unsworth remembers as 'Bible studies for the upper House'. Down below, Jack Ferguson reluctantly sponsored the legislation as the only bill with 'any real chance of being passed'. But it wasn't. A few of the Left who remained loyal to the gay cause joined the farmers and Labor's hard Right to kill the bill. Clinching defeat were the liberal Liberals whom John Dowd led once again into opposition. For all his vaunted support for the cause, Dowd never voted for reform. Wran on the other hand was voting for every bill but showing leadership with none.

Labor was traumatised. Gay activists were exhausted. Splits and acrimony marked all involved in the failed campaigns. It was a truly terrible political mess. One thing was absolutely clear: reform wasn't going to happen in the face of opposition from the Catholic church and couldn't happen without Liberal support. In the midst of all this parliamentary drama, a few days before Christmas 1981, the London *Times* carried a little report that began: 'An unexplained epidemic of infections and cancer among young male homosexuals is causing growing concern in medical circles . . .'

Letting his eyes adjust to the gloom, the man from the Vice Squad wandered among the patrons of Club 80. 'A strong smell of sweat was evident,' he later told the Ombudsman. 'There were moans and groans, together with low-toned conversations.' Then he flashed his torch: 'Two men were continuing with what appeared to be sexual intercourse. I leant through the doorway to the cage and said, "We are from the Vice Squad. Stay where you are". The male on top rolled over and I could see both persons had an erection, which subsided very quickly.'

The claim that police left consenting adults alone was looking shaky. Crime statistics showed New South Wales had, in any case, the highest prosecution rate of homo-sexuals in Australia. A Sydney magistrate in August 1981 fined a man $50 for the 'serious affront' of tongue-kissing another on the dance floor of an Oxford Street club. The bashing of gay men continued, barely investigated. The park beside St Mary's Cathedral was a beat where men had gone to have sex with each other for decades. 'Sometimes at night I could hear cries coming from that direction,' said the critic and commentator Father Ed Campion, who lived in the presbytery then. 'In the morning there was certainly blood on the steps of the cathedral where they'd been beaten up.'

Why did the police bother with Club 80? It was only one of half a dozen clubs in Sydney where men went for sex. Perhaps, as police claimed, a citizen wandered in unawares one night, climbed those flights of stairs and was affronted. Perhaps there was a darker purpose. Giving evidence to the New South Wales parliament's Prostitu-tion Committee later that year, Terry Goulden of the Gays' Counselling Service reported widespread feeling in the community that someone had failed to pay protection money. He speculated that this also explained the fires in

Oxford Street the previous year. 'In a sense, the homo-sexual community has ridden on the back of crime for a long time.'

The Club 80 raids reunified and mobilised the gay community. By the time the place was closed down as a disorderly house a few months later, hundreds of men had been questioned, scores taken to police stations and dozens charged with an ancient common law offence of 'causing scandalous conduct'. Times had changed: none of these names was printed in the *Herald*. Protests over police conduct sparked a number of official inquiries. The Ombudsman upheld complaints of rude, improper, unrea-sonable and illegal behaviour by police. More than ever, the press was on side. When the Gay Rights Embassy — a four-berth caravan — was parked outside the Wrans' Woollahra house in August/September, its doings were reported without derision. The cake stalls and garden parties were a joke, but a joke on Wran. On the John Laws show during all this hoopla, the premier volunteered that laws against homosexuals were a 'grave anachronism'. But he still did nothing.

The hostility of the churches had become a little more frantic after Mardi Gras moved from winter to summer and began to attract big crowds. This was not about Stonewall any more. Gay and lesbian Sydney was celebrating itself. And the crowds were there to enjoy something that went beyond the sexual politics of the occasion: Mardi Gras's ruthless Australian sense of humour. Patrick White was not alone among the city's homosexuals fearing a respectable backlash if poofters 'wave their handbags in people's faces'. But the sexy glitz of Mardi Gras was achieving what respectable civil libertarians and brave politicians had still failed to win: the affection of the city. For concerned Christians, however, the annual parade was evidence, every year more damning, that Sydney was the Gomorrah of the South Pacific.

Wran was distracted. Early that year, the *National Times* published the first details from illegal police tapes which suggested, in the words of the new Chief Stipendiary Magistrate, Clarrie Briese, 'an exceptionally serious criminal conspiracy operating in New South Wales for some time'. One of the dramatis personae on the tapes was Wran's close friend and old Labor colleague, the High Court judge Lionel Murphy. Wran was resisting calls for the further investigation of this worrying evidence against Murphy by arguing that what mattered most here was the illegality of the taping. According to Wran, this wasn't a corruption but a civil liberties issue.

In retrospect, he was probably not the man to have as guest of honour at the 21st birthday dinner for the Council for Civil Liberties. But Wran had been a founding member of the council and these were men and women whose approval still mattered to him. The guest list was distinguished. The room was full of judges and Queen's Counsel. Sitting at the main table with the premier were the new Opposition leader, Nick Greiner, the Chief Justice of the state, the attorneys-general of both the state and the Commonwealth, plus the embattled Lionel Murphy. What happened that night came as a surprise to all onlookers. Instead of celebrating the work of the council, Wran tore into its members for offering no more than a 'squeaky voice' of protest over the police tapes. 'I'm just staggered that we're all here this evening and that we could have tolerated what was going on in this country for so long.' There were jeers and catcalls from the guests. Bread rolls were flying. Wran shouted: 'This whole meeting is appalling, this is a very abysmal night for the Council of Civil Liberties.' When guests began to question Wran's own record — including his dismal record on homosexual law reform — he launched into an attack on George Petersen. John Marsden, about to become president of the council, remembers the atmosphere that night as 'pretty vicious'. Murphy sat there with his head in his hands.

Two days later, Wran and his wife left for a fortnight in Europe. At Sydney Airport on their return, he announced that he would immediately introduce his own bill for gay law reform. He'd decided to act: partly from conviction, partly out of pride and partly to refurbish his civil liberties credentials for the looming battles in defence of his old mate Lionel Murphy. And then he showed what a superb political operator he was. He told Gerry Gleeson it was going to happen. He told his caucus that if the bill didn't go through he was going to strip them of their conscience vote at the next state conference. He told his cabinet he expected its backing with or without a conscience vote. He told some of the hardest hardliners to stay away. He threatened Fred Nile with contempt of parliament if he now set up a Mothers' Embassy outside his house.

Wran might still have failed but for two vital changes — at the top of the local church and the local Liberal Party. Cardinal Freeman had by this time retired to the

St John Vianney Hostel for Retired Priests in Randwick. His successor, Edward Clancy, conceded that 'all sins are not necessarily crimes'. He wasn't going to fight to the finish in defence of the Crimes Act. Of the big congregations, only the Anglicans remained resolutely opposed to reform. But not all Anglicans — only the evangelical Anglicans of Sydney. From Newcastle, the Anglican bishop wrote to all members of parliament with seats in his diocese reminding them that his synod supported reform. The only sop for the churches in Wran's bill was the age of consent: while heterosexuals could still have sex once they turned sixteen, it would be a very serious crime for homosexuals until they turned eighteen. Wran refused a last-ditch appeal for age equality from the gay political movement. As a result they decided neither to support nor oppose the bill but sit on the sidelines.

The other change at the top had brought Nick Greiner — a Jesuit-educated Catholic — to the leadership of the Liberals. He emphatically supported the reform. 'It had to happen.' Greiner saw there was still a strong Anglican presence in Liberal ranks, 'proud of their homophobic attitudes' but he was determined to get their ideas off the party agenda. 'I was trying to modernise the Liberal Party, trying to make it acceptable as a government. I thought it was important for the party itself to make this move towards the centre.' He and Wran were not on speaking terms, but the whips arranged that Wran would move the bill and Greiner would follow in full support. That's how it happened.

Debate raged with undiminished fury for two days in May 1984. The same verses of the Bible were endlessly debated. The only new element was AIDs. 'It may be as well,' said the Liberal Member for Wagga Wagga Joe Schipp, 'if they do not find a cure.' The final vote showed that neither the Labor hard Right nor the Nationals from the bush had budged on this issue from start to finish. But they were beaten by recruits from the moderate Labor Right joining the Left and the Liberals that Nick Greiner brought with him across the floor of the House. The Governor signed the bill into law in June 1984. It was the Queen's Birthday weekend. That was Wran's little joke.

Catholics and Anglicans never fought shoulder to shoulder again after their defeat in Sydney. Three states — Queensland, Western Australia and Tasmania — were still holding out against change, and religion played a big part in the outcome in these reluctant jurisdictions. But sometimes the big churches supported rather than fought reform. God spoke in bewildering ways on either side of state borders. The most reliable enemies of change — and often the best-organised — were the little Protestant churches, particularly those upright congregations which had declined to join the Uniting Church. The worst fears of these Baptists and Continuing Presbyterians were confirmed in 1987 when the Uniting Church took a first step towards acceptance of homosexuality by deciding, 'All baptised Christians belong in Christ's church and are to be welcomed at his table, regardless of their sexual orientation'.

Five attempts at reform in Western Australia failed, killed by the conservative Legislative Council. The

Anglicans in the West weren't opposed to change but would press for it. By the late eighties, the Catholic Archbishop of Perth, William Foley, was privately lobbying for a bill along New South Wales lines but with a very high age of consent. The sixth attempt was heading for failure too but scraped through the upper House in 1989 after a brief denunciation of homosexuality was attached to the top of the bill and the age of consent was raised to 21 — where it still stands, the highest in the world.

Joh Bjelke-Petersen was a man of rock-hard Calvinist faith. While he was in power, there was no prospect of reform in Queensland. He campaigned against homosexuality as one of a trinity of Southern vices from which he must protect his state: homosexuality, atheism and socialism. He did the churches' work for them. By the time Bjelke-Petersen and then his party lost power in the late eighties, only the little churches in the Bible belts around Queensland's scattered cities continued to fight homosexual law reform. But they fought vociferously. The Anglicans came out in support of reform and the Catholics signalled clearly enough that they weren't going to fight Labor's plans to make the change. Reform became law in December 1990 with an odd quirk that still survives: sixteen is the age of consent for both straight and gay sex in Queensland, but anal intercourse remains a crime for the under eighteens.

The long struggle in Tasmania ended only in 1997 after Canberra called on a United Nations convention to compel Hobart to fall in line with the rest of Australia. This long delay was not essentially the work of the churches, though Archbishop Joseph D'Arcy and the shock troops of the Catholic Women's League were absolute in their opposition to change, and could call on the loyalties of Ray Groom, the Premier and Attorney-General for much of the nineties. The little Protestant churches were terriers for the status quo and a couple of their preachers were among the most colourful opponents of reform. But as the eighties turned to the nineties, both the Uniting Church and the Anglicans came out in support of reform. Victory, when it came for the gay cause in Tasmania, was complete: not only a law with an equal age of consent, but strong anti-hate and anti-discrimination laws.

The Vatican's response to the wave of anti-discrimination legislation around the world in the eighties was to prepare 'a set of observations' to assist bishops in protecting the church from these laws and 'to promote family life and the public morality of the entire civil society on the basis of fundamental moral values'. As anti-homosexual laws were repealed state by state in Australia, the churches put their political energies into opposing laws that offered lesbians and homosexuals protection from discrimination — alone or as couples.

Rome noted that the chaste homosexual does not draw attention to his 'orientation' and so requires no protection. Virtue is its own reward. The state might restrict the rights of homosexuals just as it does the freedom of 'contagious or mentally ill persons'. The letter particularly encouraged measures taken against homosexuals in the 'placement of children for adoption or foster care, in the employment of teachers or athletic coaches, and in military recruitment'. The bedrock on which these instructions from Rome rest is the fear that legislative kindness to homosexuals could 'encourage' those who were hitherto chaste to start having sex and even, 'seek a partner in order to exploit the provisions of the law'. Anti-discrimination measures were to be opposed as occasions for sin.

Four years after this letter was officially published, the new Catholic archbishop of Perth, Barry Hickey, killed stone-dead a bill to extend anti-discrimination laws to homosexuals and lesbians in Western Australia. There had been little controversy over the issue until the day of the debate itself in parliament in 1996. Hickey issued a fax to all members of parliament vociferously condemning the dangers the legislation posed to the family and children. That was the end of the bill. It has never been revived.

Everywhere else on the mainland the churches have succeeded — effortlessly — in saving themselves from anti-vilification, incitement to hatred and anti-discrimination laws. What the churches see at stake here is the right to go on doing what God had called them to do in the Third Book of Moses, the writing of St Paul and the resolutions of the Lateran Council — to teach that homosexuality is a particularly disgraceful sin.

The Catholic bishops have retreated from the early hardline instructions from Rome but they ferociously and successfully — except in Tasmania — oppose any laws that redefine 'spouse' to include same-sex partners. The church will allow couples to be 'helped' by the law but not 'recognised'. Bob Carr's 1999 legislation on the property rights of same sex couples was not opposed by the churches once a Fred Nile amendment was grafted onto the legislation to declare the bill had nothing whatever to do with marriage. Even after so much has changed in Australia, laws about couples remain fundamentally shaped by religion.

So laws on the age of consent. Justice James Wood of New South Wales is no pin-up in the gay world. But at the end of a ruthless inquiry into paedophilia, he could find: 'no reason to perpetuate a distinction between consensual homosexual and heterosexual activity, or to suppose that legislative change to achieve uniformity in this area would bring about any behavioural shift, or that it would, in real terms expose any more children to the risk of paedophile activity than are presently exposed to that risk.' Most adolescents are sexually active by the age of sixteen, Wood said, and the law should recognise the fact. It was moving into 'shaky territory' to forbid such 'consensual conduct . . . upon purely moral or religious grounds'.

The laws of most States and territories allow everyone once they turn sixteen or seventeen to begin to have sex. But in some states, homosexuals must wait — in Western Australia for five years, in New South Wales for two. And the most extraldinary passions are brought to bear by the churches to defend this cruelty. Once again the churches promote the fiction that the laws are not enforced. They are. Young men of sixteen and seventeen are threatened, exposed to blackmail and prosecuted in Western Australia, Queensland and New South Wales for what is perfectly legal over the border. If men go to prison as a result, that doesn't worry the Catholic Church. Monsignor John Walsh of Rose Bay who is spokesman on this subject in New South Wales said, 'If it's against the law there has to be punishment of some kind'.

Only two of Wood's many recommendations were not accepted immediately by Bob Carr's government — those on safe injecting rooms and the age of consent. Since the Sisters of Charity have agreed to open a shooting gallery at the Cross, Carr is holding out on just this last one. In October 1997, the Premier allowed a pantomime test of parliament's attitude to closing the age consent gap. Jan Burnswoods was allowed to introduce a private member's bill in the Legislative Council. Once again demonstrators with candles filled Macquarie Street. Again Fred Nile shouted abuse across the House. Again the Liberals were bound by their party to oppose the bill absolutely and unanimously. Again there was no backing from the Labor leadership. Half a dozen members of the council spoke eloquently in support. None spoke against. Then the bill was abandoned. Burnswoods puts this down to the 'cowardice and superficiality' of New South Wales politicians when confronting fundamental moral issues. 'And I don't see any difference across the parties.'

NINE

DISPATCHES FROM THE REPUBLIC OF SALO

*'I'm actually over the moon that the artists have been pulled
back into line . . . You must remember I'm National Party —
artistic merit doesn't mean much to me.'*

Senator Julian McGauran

DECEMBER 1996

Bill Deane opened the floodgates. I told him so the
last time I met him and he smiled that amused smile
of his that might be disbelief but more likely pity for
someone bothering to remember one brief he'd argued
in a long career at the Bar. He's Governor-General now.
Back then he was Penguin Books' QC, telling a couple
of juries that poor sad Portnoy in Philip Roth's little
masterpiece of masturbation was a saintly comedian,
something like St Augustine with a dash of Jerry Lewis.

All around Australia, moralists, columnists, politicians,
cops, headmistresses, magistrates, priests and juries had
united in declaring *Portnoy's Complaint* an obscene publication. Sydney was the last stop. You can't ban a book
in Australia unless you can ban it in Sydney. I was the
dogsbody of the defence team, fetching books and herding
witnesses. This was the highlight of my very brief legal
career. Patrick White was our star witness. I met him for
the first time on a hot morning in the corridors of the
Central Criminal Courts in Taylor Square. We were
running late and my orders were to go out and 'keep
him calm'. But he kept himself amused telling me yarns
about his new life at Centennial Park where he'd spied
local kids biting the heads off day-old chicks. Then he
was called into court and cross-examined about the

wanking and shitting and foul language of *Portnoy*. He told the jury, 'Worse things happen in Sydney'.

That first meeting with White and the little part I played in censorship's downfall makes the subject personal for me. I'm defending one good thing I had a small part in doing a long time ago. Two Sydney juries refused to convict *Portnoy*. We have no idea if those anonymous men and women fairly represented the Australian community. We don't even know how they voted. But back in 1970 they ended book censorship in Australia. Soon after, Don Chipp, the Minister for Customs, gave us the 'R' certificate and that was the end of brutal censorship of film.

But time rolls by. Patrick is dead, Bill Deane is now at Yarralumla and Canberra is once again cutting and banning. State arts ministers are anxious to vet scripts of festival performers. Cartoons are solemnly being classified for parental guidance. Regional galleries are culling travelling exhibitions. And Senator Richard Alston has urged the ABC to consider seriously the complaints of 60 people who don't want the Mardi Gras telecast. This year, 650 000 people packed the streets to watch the parade and 1.2 million saw it on television, but Alston rated those 60 complaints 'a significant level of community concern'.

Among themselves, censors will concede they've virtually given up on 'bona fide' books. But *E is for Ecstasy*, on sale all over the world, has been banned in Australia not to guard us this time from the perils of sex but to save us from the pleasures of a party drug. Why? Because in the eighties and nineties censorship rules were redrawn to play their part in the War on Drugs. Perhaps we'll look back one day and see how bizarre this is. Not even at the height of Prohibition was Hollywood forbidden to show drunks misusing drink. But even those films which by law can show gross violence mustn't give 'detailed instruction in the use of proscribed drugs' or so suggest that drugs are part of everyday life as to 'offend against the standards of morality, decency and general propriety generally accepted by reasonable adults'.

The battles we thought were won nearly thirty years ago are breaking out all round us again. We've not retreated to what we were in the sixties, the Ireland of the South Pacific. God knows, even Ireland couldn't go back to the sixties again. But familiar combatants are back on the field and we can't afford to be weary at the prospect of taking them on once more. Now isn't simply a replay of then. Attitudes and laws have changed since *Portnoy's Complaint* was in the dock. Juries don't decide these issues any more and art has lost its clout. Back then art was a defence to obscenity. In the states that really mattered in censorship skirmishes — New South Wales and Victoria — an obscene book could still be published if it had high literary merit. Art was the key. But under the Commonwealth legislation that superseded thirteen old State and Federal censorship laws in 1995, art is no longer a defence. Art has been downgraded to a 'consideration', just one of the matters to be taken into account by the Office of Film and Literature Classification when tossing up whether to ban films, videos, books and magazines.

The OFLC had been around for about a decade but at this point it was given a single national censorship code to administer. Authority over the OFLC passed from the nine parliaments of the States, territories and Commonwealth to their nine 'censoring ministers' who are usually the attorneys–general. What they decide is law. When the legislation was going through the Senate, Brian Harradine protested. 'We need to have a bit of representative democracy about this.' But undercutting the power of grandstanding backbenchers like him was one purpose of the whole scheme. Now the rules are set by often-grandstanding ministers, kept a little in check by having to work by consensus. *Who's Who* tells us our censoring ministers in 1996 are mostly a bunch of lawyers who read a bit but rarely watch films. Football seems to be their real love. Denver Beanland, Attorney-General of Queensland, lists all four codes: rules, league, union and soccer.

The ministers set the rules and approve the appointment of the censors who work in two tiers: the 'classifiers' employed by the OFLC who day to day make the decisions that set the tone of censorship in Australia, and then the half dozen 'members' of the Board of Review who hear appeals from these OFLC decisions. Lately, appointments to all these positions have been more conservative, but not conservative enough for the Community Standards Committee which is pressuring the Howard Government to take censorship out of the hands of experts and city types and put it into the care of 'real' Australians. Who these genuine Australians are isn't clear. They're not those who love writing and film. The senators of the committee seem to put such people among the enemies of decency. Instead the senators want a representative sample of 'parents, teachers, churches, academics, women, youth, Aboriginal and ethnic

THE HIGH PRICE OF HEAVEN

representatives' to ride shotgun on the work of the OFLC. Real Australians, by definition, wouldn't let *Portnoy* off the hook. Or *Salo*.

Nothing has such repercussions in this little world as the 1993 decision of the Board of Review to release Pier Paolo Pasonlini's *Salo*. The board decided that *Salo* was brutal but a great work of art. Since the film's release, the notion that art can redeem what might otherwise be offensive or even dangerous is being demonised by the enemies of the liberty of the screen. Christian groups throughout Australia are raging against the film. They have been backed by Brian Harradine and the Committee for Community Standards. But the leading warrior in the fight against *Salo* these days is a maverick Catholic senator from Victoria, Julian McGauran.

He's a cheerful reactionary from an Irish family that's prospered for a century in pubs in Victoria. As well as hotels and motels, the McGaurans these days own a big patch of East Gippsland. The size of their empire isn't clear. As the recession of the early nineties was beginning to bite, their fortune was put at $30 million. But in 1993 the banks sent the family's prize pub, the Canberra International, into receivership. That was the year Julian McGauran returned to the Senate after a brief absence and *Salo* became his latest enthusiasm. He's made his name with these sorts of causes. McGauran has never held any portfolio. In the late eighties he was part of a push to restrict Medicare payments for abortions. This failed. He broke with his party to oppose the deregulation of the wheat market. Another failure. He opposed bans on tobacco advertising. Failed again. He was a lone voice in the Senate demanding all Chinese students in Australia be sent home after the Tiananmen Square massacre. Again he wasn't listened to. But McGauran seems to have found his audience with *Salo*.

He didn't quite last the distance himself at a Toorak cinema in the first week of the film's release. He left before the end. Later he declared: '*Salo* is a case of the vile meeting the evil . . . censorship laws in this country have taken a leap to the outer bounds, or we have no censorship laws at all.'

MARCH 1997

Hustler magazine fought all the way to the United States Supreme Court for the right to publish a spoof Campari ad that ridiculed the hellfire preacher Jerry Falwell. They made a film, *The People v. Larry Flynt,* to celebrate the victory. Now you won't believe me — but you should — when I say that the spoof Campari ad has been censored in Australia, not on behalf of the Rev. J. Falwell but for the sake of Australia's children.

Back in 1984, Campari was running an elegant series of ads with celebrities chatting about their 'first time' drinking the drink. In *Hustler*'s spoof, Jerry Falwell gets it all wrong and 'confesses' instead to the first time he had sex — supposedly with his mother, in a back dunny in Lynchburg, Virginia. A disclaimer in tiny print read: 'Ad parody — not to be taken seriously.' The preacher sued for $45 million but in 1988 the Supreme Court unanimously upheld the magazine's right to publish. This decision may not be, as Australian *Hustler* claimed, 'one of the most famous cases in legal history', but it had

THE HIGH PRICE OF HEAVEN

important consequences for the liberty of ridicule in the United States.

Not here. As *The People v. Larry Flynt* hove over the horizon in January, the editor of *Hustler*'s Australian edition, Simon Firth, began cranking up publicity for the film on orders from head office in America. Of course, he wanted to run the ad. That was the point. But that was the trouble. The planned issue of *Hustler* contained many photographs of breasts and vaginas, a clutch of crude yarns and a number of coarse cartoons. They were all okay by the Office of Film and Literature Classification. But not the spoof ad. Firth was told it could be published only if a certain word was blacked out.

And the word was 'mom'.

The office declared all references to 'mom' and 'mother' were 'unsuitable for minors'. So the ad appeared with a scattering of little black patches. The magazine praises its owner extravagantly for fighting the case to the US Supreme Court — 'lesser men might have bowed to the massive social, financial and legal pressure put on him, but Larry Flynt . . . etc'. But Simon Firth caved in to the Office of Film and Literature Classification. He explained, 'If I piss these people off they make our life hell.'

APRIL 1997

As a practical politician, Fred Nile is excused the usual Christian ideal of showing humility in triumph. 'Niles Claim Major Victory over New South Wales Education Department', trumpeted the press release he issued after hearing that Gillian Mears's *Fineflour* and Caryl Churchill's play *Top Girls* are to be dropped from the New South Wales Higher School Certificate.

Fred and Elaine Nile have put six years of their lives into the fight against *Fineflour*, *Top Girls* and Peter Goldsworthy's novel *Maestro*. Ignoring ridicule from parents and English teachers, they've denounced the works at hundreds of public meetings held year in and year out in country towns and outer suburbs. When the campaign was flagging last year, Elaine Nile delivered an attack in the Legislative Council that even her husband describes as 'ferocious'.

Victory in the end came through an alliance between the Niles, a couple of Sydney radio talkback hosts, a campaigning *Daily Telegraph* columnist, the Liberals' shadow minister for education — despite his party in government putting the texts onto the HSC in the first place — and a blundering Minister for Education, John Aquilina, who set up a committee under the chancellor of Sydney University, Dame Leonie Kramer, to deliver the coup de grace.

Having buckled, the minister is discovering what all politicians dealing with the resurgent moral minority are learning: giving in earns you no thanks. Aquilina's office seems baffled by the sudden public support for the books, the other talk-show hosts are furious because the minister has gone to ground, and the Niles are still after his blood, calling for 'an urgent review of the selection process of the high school texts . . . How did a play such as *Top Girls* get selected? Who selected it? Who should be sacked?'

When the HSC list was put together in 1991, the

Niles objected to 22 of the 26 proposed English texts. They were ignored. Fred Nile now admits they'd only had a 'gut reaction' at first and over the years sometimes wondered if their judgement was 'haywire'. But then along came this endorsement from Dame Leonie's committee. 'You can't do much better than that.' Though they aim to try. Kramer's committee acquitted Goldsworthy's novel *Maestro*: 'an excellent book . . . a good example of a text which would be rewarding to teach and rewarding to read.' But the Niles do not accept this 'extreme' verdict. So the most popular text on the HSC list remains in the Niles' sights: 'We will certainly continue to campaign against *Maestro*.'

Call to Australia campaigns hard that these texts are studied by 'children', but by the time most of these students sit for their exams they will be old enough to vote, fight, drink, smoke, drive and marry. Bill Symon, president of the English Teachers' Association of New South Wales, deeply upset by the course of events this week and a keen teacher of *Top Girls*, pointed out: 'This text is set for a very small group of kids, the really sophisticated ones who love English and are responsible and socially aware. These kids are not impressionable kids. They are young adults, the cream of the crop.'

Nile is unimpressed with such talk. He admits frankly he is campaigning for the right of pupils from 'protective Christian families' to study English without being shocked by what they read. He profoundly disagrees with an academic he remembers saying a few years ago that teachers should be unpacking 'the cotton wool' that cocoons such kids. Nile says, 'That's not the role of English.'

The principal target of the preacher's long campaign was always Churchill's *Top Girls* which has been performed all over the world since its London debut in 1982. At the play's centre is Marlene who is revealed to have betrayed her child, her family and her deeper self to become a successful businesswoman. When choosing between greed and compassion, family and career, Marlene makes all the wrong choices. Even those who don't much like the play tend to praise Churchill's moral argument here. This week Leonie Kramer struck a fresh note when she found 'contempt for religion' in the text.

But Angie brought *Top Girls* undone. Angie is the abandoned daughter. She is, 'a bit thick. A bit funny'. She swears. Far from endorsing her bad language, Churchill uses it to show that poor Angie is destined for nowhere. In a scene set in a backyard cubby, Angie licks menstrual blood from the finger of a young friend. This scene and the swearing — unexceptional and scattered — have been the ammunition the Niles have used to batter the work all these years. They have judged it not by its achievements but its sins: swearing and shocking.

Top Girls was never a compulsory HSC text — the only compulsory text this year is Shakespeare's study of incest, revenge and suicide, *Hamlet* — and there appear to have been very few complaints about it in the five years it has been taught. Last year the minister's office was aware of only two complaints about the Churchill play and Bill Symon said, 'I make it my business to know and I would have heard if there were murmurs. Even through the HSC marking operation — where you get a very good idea of how students are reacting to texts —

I haven't heard of teachers getting suggestions of kids being shocked.'

But the Niles were soldiering on. They made no real headway until last year when Martha Clark from the central coast of New South Wales brought the Niles copies of the complaints she'd been making about *Top Girls* and *Maestro* to her daughter's school, her local member, and the Minister for Education, John Aquilina. She objected to the play for using bad language and undermining parental authority and to Goldsworthy's novel for arousing sexuality. She'd won the support of her local Uniting Church and her local Liberal member in the swinging seat of Gosford, Chris Hartcher, who describes himself as 'an active Christian'. Hartcher had forwarded her complaints to Aquilina but was unable to discuss the play when I rang this week. 'I'm under a complete disadvantage,' he said. 'I haven't read it.'

The Niles made good use of the Clark correspondence, sending it out with their regular press releases. One of these chunky dispatches landed on the desk of Norm Lipson, producer for Sydney 2GB talkback host and former sports reporter Jon Harker: 'I looked at it and thought this is not a bad story.' They invited Aquilina onto the show on 25 February. Neither producer nor presenter read the play but Harker went on air and endorsed the complaints about *Top Girls* as 'absolutely valid'. Aquilina defended the moral thrust of the play and the swearing — 'it's reality' — but conceded he would not be happy having his daughter read it. His daughter is six years old.

Rumbustious *Daily Telegraph* sports writer and

columnist Ray Chesterton heard about the play from a friend and at least he tried to read it — 'I'm not suggesting I understood it. I found it incomprehensible' — before publishing a column on March 10 headed 'Putrid Play for School Study'. He wrote, 'This play reads like a collection of the back doors of toilet cubicles.' The paper was waiting on Alan Jones' desk before dawn that day. He had not read the play but at 7.12 a.m. on Radio 2UE he declared *Top Girls* was 'the bottom of the educational birdcage' and demanded to know when Aquilina would remove it from the HSC syllabus.

The rule of the Carr government is to solve the problems Jones causes by the start of that working day. When Aquilina went on air that morning there was no fight in him at all. 'I am not defending this book,' he said over and over again as Jones savaged him. The minister made a bizarre claim that he had heard about *Top Girls* only 'last week'. He was well prepared for capitulation. Before limping off air, he announced Leonie Kramer would examine the problem. Once again, issues of great sensitivity were being decided on the run in response to nothing much more than the rage and froth of talkback radio.

Dame Leonie once made a great reputation for herself by standing up for the independence of the ABC, but it was the other Kramer, the dour professor of English, who sat down with two North Shore headmistresses and the Director of the Catholic Education Office of NSW to examine *Top Girls* and other 'problem' texts. This was a committee designed to reach the verdict it did. They were damning about *Top Girls*: 'It expresses contempt for

THE HIGH PRICE OF HEAVEN

religion, portrays life as meaningless and introduces gratuitous violence in banal and crude language.' And they had little better to say for Gillian Mears's *Fineflour*. Not only did they recommend both be thrown off the HSC — the only texts to meet such a fate in NSW in the nineties — but they called for every book on the HSC list in future to be one that 'needs' to be there and 'furthers the literary and linguistic development of the students'.

Fred and Elaine Nile are not the only ones claiming victory. Jon Harker, Alan Jones and Ray Chesterton are also proud of the result. Ray Chesterton is relieved. 'Morals are getting too elastic for my liking.' Bill Symon, who's teaching *Top Girls* at an inner-city Sydney school, said: 'I can't cry because it's too silly for words.'

EARLY JUNE 1997

Salo is doomed. Pier Paolo Pasolini's film has been stalked by the forces of censorship ever since its release in Australia four years ago. Somehow it has survived, playing to smaller and smaller houses around the country, but a bit of tit-for-tat politics in Queensland is delivering it back, trussed and bound, to the Office of Film and Literature Classification for banning.

Perhaps 50 000 Australians have seen *Salo*. It was never a *Titanic* or a *Terminator II*. 'Most of the people who want to see it on a cinema screen have seen it by now,' said its distributor Michael Walsh of Premium Films. 'It's an old film.' The season at the Valley Twin in Brisbane was so poor the film was about to be pulled off after only a week when Labor's Judy Spence — shadow minister for Women, Aboriginal and Islander

Affairs and Consumer Affairs — went to an evening session and emerged after 20 minutes to release next day a statement headed: 'Borbidge Must Act on Sex Film that Glorifies Pedophilia.'

This was a payback. Spence went to the movie 'to expose the hypocrisy of this government. Borbidge made such a fuss of it when it came out in 1994, telling Goss that if he cared about Queenslanders he'd have it off the screen that afternoon. And really I wanted to expose the fact that there is a National government in power and the film was still on, and nothing had changed.'

Denver Beanland, Queensland's Attorney-General, has announced he's 'moved with all haste and power' to have *Salo* brought back before the Office of Film and Literature Classification. 'There is no doubt that *Salo* is a depraved and disgusting film that should never have received an R rating in the first place. I am a firm believer that most adults are mature enough to decide what they want to watch. However, outright brutality and pedophilia are not acceptable.'

He has not tried to see the film in the four years since the Classification Review Board decided unanimously to lift the seventeen-year ban on *Salo*.

'It was not a task we relished,' said the board's convenor Evan Williams, film critic and arts bureaucrat. '*Salo* contains scenes of concentrated foulness such as few of us might have imagined, and I doubt if anything would persuade us to watch it again. Yet we reached our decision with surprising ease and a reassuring unanimity.' He acknowledged *Salo* went 'to the heart of the dilemma facing all censorship bodies in a free society' but he and his colleagues on the board could find 'no valid reason' for preventing adult Australians from seeing it.

'It is the duty of the censor to protect the young and warn the innocent. It is the task of the artist, at least occasionally, to shock the old and the complacent. There are times when the serious artist will ask us to plumb the depths, to contemplate both heaven and hell. All of us have the right to flinch from doing so, but a mature society will not deny us the choice.'

Art was the central issue. They all considered *Salo* a serious work of art pursuing a serious political purpose by depicting the degradation of young men and women at the hands of authority: officials of Mussolini's rump fascist state of Salo. Father Michael Elligate, a Melbourne priest on the board, still rates the film as 'perhaps the most powerful modern critique of the whole issue of fascism and the totalitarian state'. So Australia joined Italy, Germany, Sweden, France, Japan, Britain, the United States of America, the Netherlands, Spain, Israel, Greece and six other countries in allowing Pasolini's film to be shown uncut to adults. Here the film has had an 'R' certificate — restricted to adults eighteen years and over — and a unique ban on its release on video, though pirate videos without subtitles are circulating illegally and have been ever since the film's original release in Italy.

The uproar over early Australian screenings of *Salo* came with a good dash of comedy. The national premiere in the 1993 Adelaide Film Festival caused church and civic protests and an angry debate in parliament. Mrs Patricia Draper, mother of three young boys, tried to buy all 1200 tickets at that first screening as an investment, she said, in her childrens' future. 'I was prepared to use our mortgage money to buy all the tickets so that no one would be there. Unfortunately the tickets were all sold out in the first few days.'

South Australia then put *Salo* in limbo, allowing it to be screened only at film festivals. No theatre has ever been willing to show the film in Tasmania. Western Australia banned *Salo* outright using old censorship machinery it never gave up when the states joined Canberra in the new national classification code. Under Wayne Goss, Queensland did abandon its own film censorship board, for which the Nationals hammered the Labor government when *Salo* had its first sell-out season — 'in the Year of the Family' — at the Boomerang Theatre in Annerley. Wayne Goss called it 'appalling trash' but the screenings went on. So did the attacks led by Beanland. It was the political embarrassment of these that Judy Spence was revenging.

Goss did promise to pressure Canberra to review 'the composition of the Commonwealth Film Board of Review'. That pressure from a number of quarters has since been unrelenting, mostly because of *Salo* but also because the board refused to bow to militant Christian demands for the banning of *The Last Temptation of Christ*. Indeed, Martin Scorsese's film was given an M classification — suitable for fifteen year olds — which the Board of Review also gave Jonathan Demme's *The Silence of the Lambs*. These decisions made the board a target of Christian, political and pro-censorship action but the focus of discontent has always been *Salo*.

The unbanning of Pasolini's film is turning out to be

the most effective weapon conservatives have had to force changes to Australian censorship — changes of mood, regulation and personnel. Senator Julian McGauran called it 'The defining moment'. The key upper House Committee on Community Standards has used *Salo* as a 'window' to examine the whole classification apparatus. Evan Williams was grilled at public hearings after its release about the effect of such a film on crime. 'The answer was as shallow as, there's no evidence of it,' recalled McGauran. 'Anyone will tell you some of your best mass-murderers have come out hooked on porno-movies, and he won't even concede that. Well who wants him as chairman?' Williams was not invited (as was the custom) to sit again when his first term expired shortly afterwards. The veteran film critic was replaced by Barbara Biggins, an expert on children's television. Senator McGauran sees the non-renewal of three members of the board at this time as having, 'A big effect and started the ball rolling on all the other charges'.

Salo's opponents refuse to acknowledge that its release is an exception justified by Pasolini's place in cinema. They don't think much of Pasolini and they don't see evidence of art in this film. Instead they argue its release in Australia set new low standards of extreme sexuality and violence that today's 'out of touch' censors might allow in any R-rated film. They misrepresent *Salo* as the classification norm. Few of them have actually seen the movie so summaries of the plot have been the raw material of debate. These precis range from the clinical to the absolutely lurid. Some contain details of an incident with a rat which is not in the film at all but seems to have wandered in from Brett Easton Ellis's novel *American Psycho*.

At the Office of Film and Literature Classification, the director John Dickie has been offering no resistance to those who want regulations tightened post-*Salo*. Dickie told the Senate committee in 1993 that the film was 'wallowing in depravity' and two years later, after a number of rule changes inspired by the film, he reassured senators that *Salo* would now be refused classification, i.e. banned. He didn't even want it shown at film festivals or studied at film schools. 'In my view *Salo* is a refused category film under any circumstances.' Further tightening of the rules in early 1997, though directed against porn videos, made *Salo's* position more perilous still by forbidding 'unacceptable fetishes' on the screen and prohibiting the use of young actors of either sex in sequences that are sexy, violent or concentrate on drugs.

It is the age — or apparent age — of the actors that particularly offends the Brisbane politician bent on revenge. Judy Spence came away from the 20 minutes she saw of *Salo* convinced the actors looked like teenagers and behaved like teenagers. 'To me teenagers are still children. Banning the film won't protect children but basically we don't want to encourage people to make films of this kind, and use teenagers to make them.' Spence knows little of the long history of *Salo* nor, she admits, has she thought much about the repercussions of what she's done on film censorship in Australia. This was really just a little stoush with the Nats.

The rush of publicity after Spence's protest rescued *Salo's* failing season at the Valley Twin. Despite a personal plea by the Premier Rob Borbidge, the run was extended for a few weeks before the print — the only print in Australia — went down to a rather drab season at Melbourne's Capitol Theatre and thence to a cupboard at Premium Films waiting for its next engagement, in the theatrette of the Office of Film and Literature Classification. What follows will be a pioneering effort. Provisions allowing the office to take a second look at a film have never been used before. Until now, a classification has stuck with a film for life. But once *Salo* is rebanned, classifications are likely to become more fluid and more frequently challenged.

It's still going to take a little time. Advertisements are appearing nation-wide calling for public submissions. The censors are due to make their decision later this month. Whatever they decide will be appealed to the Review Board. Only two members of the board survive from the six who released the film in 1993 'with surprising ease and a reassuring unanimity'.

Once Premium Films hands over its scratched and battered print in the next few days, Australians will have to catch *Salo* on their holidays in Europe or North America or Japan. Back home, those pirate videos remain widely available in Italian video stores. Laser discs are also about. The book of the movie, the Marquis de Sade's *120 Days of Sodom*, will be available as always among the Penguin Classics in all good bookshops.

LATE JUNE 1997

The obituaries for *Salo* came too soon. By a close majority, the Classification Board of the Office of Film and Literature Classification has refused a request from Queensland's Attorney-General, Denver Beanland, to ban Pier Paolo Pasolini's 1975 film in Australia.

The majority found *Salo* 'a serious artistic work which deals with oppression and abuse but which does not depict these things for the enjoyment or titillation of viewers . . . Accordingly, in the board's opinion while the film may offend some sections of the community it does not offend against standards generally accepted by reasonable adults to the extent that it should be refused classification (banned).'

An angry Senator McGauran said later: 'They've had their second chance. They've bombed. They've learnt nothing. They are as negligent as always. There is no reason possible under the sun for *Salo* not to be rebanned.' An appeal has already been lodged by Denver Beanland, who accused the board of making 'a mockery of the Federal Government's election promise to remove sadistic sex and violence from cinema screens . . . this film's portrayal of brutality and sexual degradation can serve no purpose in a modern society.' The Queensland Attorney-General has still not seen *Salo*.

The appeal will be heard by the Board of Review. One of those welcoming the film's reprieve was Evan Williams, now head of Bob Carr's Arts Ministry but convenor of the Board of Review back in 1993 that released *Salo*. 'This is an enlightened and sensible decision. It should be welcomed as a timely defence of artistic and individual freedom at a time when many other liberal traditions are under challenge.'

The enemies of *Salo* have carried the day. A majority decision of the Board of Review has once again banned Paolini's study of the degradation of innocent youth at the hands of the Fascist state. The incongruous result of all the politicking to get to this point is that no film director, local or foreign, can claim such a unique impact on politics and the arts in Australia as an Italian poet, communist and homosexual, dead now for over 20 years.

Barely mentioned in the 1993 deliberations of the Board of Review was the issue that would eventually bring *Salo* undone: the youthfulness of Pasolini's actors. It was not an issue back then. One member of the board, Father Michael Elligate, did remark over sandwiches that day in 1993 that Pasolini was not using children but young people. 'Whatever this was, it's not pedophilia.' Yet the uproar that followed was overwhelmingly on behalf — or so it was claimed — of vulnerable children. A former crown prosecutor in Victoria, Richard Read, took two police with him to a screening and reported in the Melbourne *Herald-Sun*, 'We must await the copy-cat torture crimes of innocent children'.

The *Salo* row — plus the long-running Christian war against porn videos — has produced new regulations banning any film likely to offend reasonable adults by using actors who 'appear to be' under sixteen in dealing with issues of 'sex, drug misuse or addiction, crime, cruelty, violence or revolting or abhorrent phenomena'. This goes beyond protecting young people from unscrupulous movie makers. The new ban applies to whatever actors are doing and whatever their ages so long as they *appear* to be under sixteen and what they do on the screen is *likely* to offend reasonable adults. So what counts now are a couple of difficult guesses — about the age of the actors and the spectators' threshold of offence.

This law threatens to cut deep. The film industry wonders if Louis Malle's *Pretty Baby* and Martin Scorsese's *Taxi Driver* could survive a strict application of the new law. Almost certainly contrary to the legislation is Visconti's 1971 *Death in Venice* and Volker Schlondorff's 1979 *The Tin Drum* in which a six-year-old kid has sex with an adult woman. The law is so wide it's possible even Baz Luhrmann's 1996 *Romeo and Juliet* could be threatened. The actors look young, deliberately young, perhaps to some eyes they even seem under sixteen. And wouldn't some reasonable adults be offended by the sex, drugs and violence in this hectic version of Shakespeare? Bob Carr, Premier of New South Wales, was offended enough to ask Luhrmann to cut the drug scenes before the film was shown in schools. Luhrmann refused.

And how are we to assess the age of these young adults? I consulted Dr Peter Bradhurst of the New South Wales Institute of Forensic Medicine. While confident we can tell a child from a teenager 'just by looking', he gives the professional opinion that there is no scientific way of telling the difference between a fifteen and sixteen year old by sight. Even if you conduct a post mortem, 'You would have to know about their skin care, how they look after themselves, what sort of disease processes that have afflicted them in their life'.

After the Classification Board of the Office of Film and Literature Classification refused to ban *Salo* last June, an appeal to the Review Board — a kind of High Court of censorship — was inevitable but then delayed for six months while fresh appointments were made to bring the board to full strength. From the day *Salo* was released, Senator Julian McGauran has been pressuring the government to get rid of 'intellectual arty types' on the board. Now he wrote to the prime minister, pointing out that the film was up for review and there were four more vacancies to fill. 'I was unashamedly coding it to say I would like four members of conservative values that had a community touchstone.'

When the Attorney-General Daryl Williams announced the new team just before Christmas, the only member connected to film was the solicitor Ross Tzannes, an ex-president of the Sydney Film Festival. Gone were the film critic Keith Connolly and film maker Sue Milliken. The chief professional interest of the new board is children: Brent Waters, the only survivor of the board that released *Salo*, is a child psychiatrist. Robin Harvey is a children's psychologist in Western Australia. Convenor of the board for many years has been Barbara Biggins, president of the Australian Council for Children's Films and Television.

The new board met on 13 February to watch the film. Striking a position of absolute independence from the critical mainstream of the world and from the old board's decision in 1993, the new board has decided by a majority that *Salo* fails as a work of art because Pasolini hadn't shown an 'effective connection' between the horrors of the film and late Italian fascism. So art could not now be brought into the argument, as it was in 1993, to give point to the distressing and offensive spectacle of young people being abused at the hands of generals and bishops and bankers in Mussolini's rump republic.

Once the film was declared an artistic failure, the question of the age of the actors became crucial. If a majority of the board thought they looked under sixteen then the film *had* to be banned as inevitably offensive. But the majority wasn't there. It seems Barbara Biggins had the support of only one other member of the board in thinking the actors looked too young. So the special knockout blow designed to get *Salo* failed — on the facts. Biggins now shifted the goal posts. She argued that even if the actors looked over sixteen, they were still so youthful that reasonable adults would find the fetishes inflicted on them particularly offensive. That's not in the regulations, but the argument persuaded a bare majority of the board to ban the film. It was a close-run thing. *Salo* was officially banned, according to the reasons which have only now been published, for containing cruelty, sexual violence and, 'a large number of offensive fetishes, the offence of which was increased by the involvement of young people who, if not clearly under sixteen years, nevertheless looked like persons under the age of eighteen'.

Veterans of the old board greeted the result with sadness and disbelief. Keith Connolly found the decision, 'absurd, utterly absurd'. Michael Elligate said, 'The new Review Board sensationalises this into children being abused. Now I'm not defending abuse. I've spent some time among abused people.' He is holding to his 1993 verdict, 'Whatever this was it's not pedophilia'. But after four determined

THE HIGH PRICE OF HEAVEN

years stalking this film, Julian McGauran was delighted with the result. He told the *Sydney Morning Herald* journalist Lauren Martin that he didn't care 'two hoots' about artistic freedom. 'I'm actually over the moon that the artists have been pulled back into line . . . You must remember I'm National Party — artistic merit doesn't mean much to me. The Sydney-style view . . . doesn't amount to a row of beans.'

JUNE 1998

Labor is back in power in Queensland and the national search for acceptable fetishes, held in check for twelve unhappy months, can get underway at last, to everyone's relief.

The Howard government rode to office on a core promise of getting rid of porn (X-rated) videos but once in power discovered porn was a principal industry of the Australian Capital Territory, that it was constitutionally almost impossible for the Canberra government to root it out and — so far as such things count in these arguments — lots of Australians like porn. Lots. So the federal Attorney-General, Daryl Williams, came up with a plan to satisfy both Christians and consumers. X-rated videos would be purged of 'unacceptable fetishes' and then rechristened and reissued as Non-Violent Erotica. Queensland would have nothing to do with this under Rob Borbidge and Denver Beanland. They saw it as the transparent political gambit it was and sided with those Christians who called for porn videos to be banned and burnt and their owners put in jail. Labor in Queensland has other ideas. Labor will cooperate in the national classification of fetishes, acceptable and unacceptable.

But which to keep and which to ditch? Australia has reached a stage of such exquisite refinement in assessing the moral gradations of fetish that one wonders whether the skills developed here might not be exported for the good of the world. We have now evolved four cardinal rules of fetish: the mouth rule, the dog rule, the blood rule and the rule against pink flesh.

The mouth rule. Coprophilia used to be okay so long as turds didn't drop into the mouth. This was a health measure, a question of harm. Now coprophilia is totally banned from sex videos, a result that was a particular enthusiasm of John Dickie, the previous director of the Office of Film and Literature Classification. Golden showers were also thought to be okay so long as the mouth rule was observed, but then along came *Salo* which was banned a few months ago in part because of breaches of the mouth rule described as 'sexual activity accompanied by offensive fetishes'. There are many breaches of the mouth rule in *Salo*, including the forced eating of faeces — which I'm told were Suchard Chocolate mixed with crostini — but also cited against the film was the scene 29 minutes in of a girl pissing onto a man's face. The face was held to be unacceptable. Under pressure from the moralists, the mouth rule seems to be turning into the face rule.

The dog rule. Magazine censorship in Australia was transformed a couple of years ago by the dog issue of *Picture* magazine. Christians and some feminist factions combined to condemn this offensive image of a woman on all fours in a dog's collar being led along on a lead. It wasn't actually a dog's collar but that hardly matters in the history and folklore of censorship in this country. Now *Salo* has further expanded the dog rule to include posture as well as accoutrements. Among the many scenes the Review Board found demeaning of the young persons involved were 'being forced to line up naked and on all fours so that the best arse could be chosen' and further 'being forced to act like dogs'.

The blood rule. You can smash a woman to pulp and have blood ooze down the streets of Chicago, so long as no one seems to get any pleasure from it. Pleasure in connection with blood is banned. For instance in *Hustler White* we were allowed in Australia to see the sad client of the said hustler burnt with cigarette butts — 'exquisite dear boy' — but not allowed to see the same hustler cut the same client lightly with a razor blade. Of course that was fake blood running down his poor old torso, but it was banned.

The pink flesh rule. Once you could paddle till you raised welts so long as it was absolutely clear that the 'victim' was happy being abused. Consent was the only issue that worried the censors. Now another exquisite shift of moral concern has seen any sign of harm — which means any sign of tissue damage — being banned. Indeed the Office of Film and Literature Classification considers any reddening of the buttocks a sign of possible damage, so these days you can't even paddle pink. Further restrictions on spanking have appeared lately. The Office of Film and Literature Classification tried to ban an edition of *Searchlight* magazine for running a short item about a woman being spanked in a lift. It was one of those fake letters to the editor: 'Dear Sir, I was in a lift the other day and you'll never guess what happened. A man put me over his knee . . . etc.' This number was banned as demeaning to women but on appeal the Review Board allowed it to be sold wrapped in plastic, on restricted premises, only to over eighteens.

The Christians aren't fools. Measured against their moral absolutes, tinkering with X-rated videos to turn them into Non-Violent Erotica is a con. They were told they would be banned and they want them banned. They will continue to campaign for them to be banned — and mount a parallel campaign to have them stripped of fetishes. But the prospect of the censoring ministers solemnly sitting down at their thrice-yearly meetings to run through a schedule of fetishes to decide what's unacceptable to the nation is too wonderful. Rarely do governments give such opportunities for comedy. And once they start this remarkable moral exercise they must, to safeguard themselves, explore every chink of humanity's perversity to work out whether they approve or disapprove of every variety of strange behaviour. This sort of thing is usually left to filmmakers and writers. Australia faces the prospect here of it being done, instead, by a sub-committee of the nation's attorneys-general.

The raw political logic of the exercise will be that everything not banned will come with a stamp of government approval. Imagine the scene in the House of Representatives as the Member for Blaxland rises to ask a question without notice of the Attorney-General: 'We note your government bans pissing on the face, but are

THE HIGH PRICE OF HEAVEN

you telling the people of Australia that you approve of pissing on the neck?' And so it will go on, part by part to the toes.

A Sydney madam recently gossiped about a strange fetish she'd lately dealt with. A man from the lower North Shore who collected sandshoes would bring a sack of them over to the brothel and cover the bottom of a bath with a layer of Nikes and Adidas, then run a couple of inches of water in the bath then — dressed in tracksuit pants and a pair of sandshoes — squelch up and down while she beat him with another sandshoe. At some point he would ask her to leave the room and she presumed he masturbated. The first thing to ask is, would we vote for a government that approves such a fetish? The second question is, would we vote for a government that gives a damn?

MAY 1999

The Howard government has ordered the Office of Film and Literature Classification to find more 'ordinary' Australians to appoint as censors. In an unprecedented move, apparently to placate the morals campaigner Senator Brian Harradine, cabinet has rejected an entire list of candidates for censorship positions with the Office of Film and Literature Classification and demanded fresh names more representative of the community.

By 'representative', cabinet is understood to mean 'ordinary' citizens, outside the professions and outside Sydney, who understand the concerns of people in rural and remote areas. Senator Harradine has long argued that these people must be brought into the censorship process to end 'permissive' decisions. He has most recently protested angrily over the Office of Film and Literature Classification releasing the controversial new *Lolita* after it consulted psychologists and child-welfare experts. 'Where were the ordinary people?' demanded the senator. 'Where were the ordinary people?'

Candidates for Office of Film and Literature Classification positions are not usually considered by cabinet. For an entire list to be rejected is unprecedented. The list was prepared over six months by the office with the assistance of headhunters Chandler and McLeod Consultants. Dymphna Austin-Perry of that firm told the *Herald*: 'I felt the standard of candidates was good.' Cabinet thought otherwise. The rejection was of the *list* rather than individuals.

The candidates not 'ordinary' enough were: Andrew Harvey, 31, of Sydney, a social worker in the intensive-care unit at Royal Prince Alfred Hospital; Cathy Johnstone, 39, of the Australian Capital Territoy, an officer in the Department of Foreign Affairs and Trade; Graham Shirley, 49, of Sydney, documentary maker and oral historian, father of three and currently employed by the Office of Film and Literature Classification on a temporary contract; Bronwyn Healy, 41, of Sydney's western suburbs, mother of two, health and welfare consultant; Peter Epifano, 33, from regional Victoria, a parent and teacher; Rachel Williams, 30, of Ipswich, Queensland, a volunteer worker in the education and accommodation of young and homeless people; and from the Australian Capital Territory a fluent Cantonese speaker who is also an expert on violence and crime. (Ten

THE HIGH PRICE OF HEAVEN

per cent of the films classified by the office are in Cantonese.)

The seven were chosen from about 700 who answered advertisements last June. They were interviewed and auditioned over several days, assessing films and publications in the presence of senior staff of the Office of Film and Literature Classification and representatives of the states. Ten months' work went into the selection. Early this year the names were circulated among the states. It is understood the states had no objection. But cabinet did. No new advertisements have since been placed. Chandler and McLeod instead picked a few other names from further down the short list with special emphasis on candidates from remote Australia.

Senator Harradine may yet be disappointed. Previous plans promoted by the senator to have committees of 'ordinary' Australians vetting censorship decisions led, earlier this year, to a trial that demonstrated contact groups of ordinary Australians were not less, but slightly more liberal than the censors of the Office of Film and Literature Classification. But they were city folk. The bush may yet be the answer to Harradine's prayers.

JUNE 1999

The future of political ridicule in Australia remains in limbo following the High Court's refusal to consider the ABC's argument that the ban on the Pauline Hanson spoof 'I'm A Backdoor Man' is wrong in law and infringes fundamental rights of free political discussion. This is the third court that has failed to see the joke.

The song by satirist and Senate candidate Pauline

Pantsdown (a.k.a. Sydney communications lecturer Simon Hunt) was a cult sensation on ABC Triple J for a few weeks in 1997 before Ms Hanson had it banned by the Queensland Supreme Court. Evidence was given to the court that her schoolboy son was being teased about 'I'm A Backdoor Man' at Ipswich Grammar.

The ban was confirmed by the Queensland Court of Appeal a few days before the last Federal election. Ms Hanson wept as the song was played in court. Pantsdown/Hunt made a dash from Sydney in full drag to remind the press that the song was 'trivial' compared with the 'unimaginable pain' Ms Hanson had caused Aboriginal people. But the court declared the song 'patently defamatory', 'grossly offensive' and 'a mindless effort of cheap denigration'.

'I'm A Backdoor Man' is collage for the airwaves: odd fragments of Hanson-speak cut and pasted together so it seems she's claiming to be a man, a member of the Ku Klux Klan, a transvestite, a homosexual, and 'a very caring potato'. The ABC argues this is clearly satire but the Queensland Court of Appeal thought a jury might take it to be literally true and so inevitably defamatory.

Where this leaves cartoonists, satirists and impersonators is unclear. Ridiculous, broad, painful, exaggerated lampooning is their trade. They batter reputations. They mean to wound. They ridicule public figures as tarts, butchers, gladiators, drag queens and executioners. No one takes this sort of political abuse to be literally true — no one except, it seems, these Queensland judges.

Of course in America 'I'm A Backdoor Man' would be protected by the same constitutional rights of free speech that let *Hustler* ridicule Jerry Falwell going at it with his mother in a back dunny. But that's in America . . .

The High Court refused to release 'I'm A Backdoor Man' which means the ban stays at least until a jury hears Ms Hanson's defamation case against the ABC. Appeals could still take it all the way to the top. At least the High Court has already conceded that Pantsdown's lyrics might not be taken to be literally true by Triple J fans. Hunt and Pantsdown have jointly declared: 'Any reasonable listener would not accept that Pauline Hanson believes she is a potato.'

TEN

THE SPIRES OF
ST MARY'S

'Democracy does not mean that there is no ultimate truth.'

Pope John Paul II

Cathedrals are built to remind politicians they're not the only power in town. It works. A strange, late-nineties political phenomenon in Australia is throwing public millions at a cathedral.

St Mary's, on the edge of Sydney's Hyde Park, is putting on its spires with the help of $5 million from Bob Carr on top of an earlier $5 million pledged by Paul Keating to repair the old stonework. No private building in Australia has had so much public money thrown its way. Bigots will dissent and citizens of that city might wish $10 million more could be found for the sick and the poor, the arts or learning but when those stumpy little spires are complete, Sydney will be delighted with the sight. The city will celebrate with fireworks and Masses. Tickled pink, also, will be the Japanese tourists who flock to photograph St Mary's, the biggest gothic pile anywhere near Tokyo.

Those public dollars are a measure of the raw power of the Catholic Church in Australia, power essentially undiminished by the end of the Harradine era. For most of this decade the church has had unique leverage because this Catholic Independent, unfettered by party discipline, has held a crucial vote in the senate. Not that Brian Harradine was operating under orders. Harradine is an odd kind of loner even within the church. His loyalties are to great figures of the past, long dead now, like Archbishop Guildford Young. When the new senators arrived in Canberra in 1999, a smiling Harradine posed for press photographers with a feather duster. This was typical Harradine, self-effacing and self-promoting all at once, the rooster of the senate pretending his day is over. It isn't. Nor is the influence of the church on Australian politics fundamentally affected by the shift of power in the Upper House. In secular Australia, the church remains a formidable lobbyist. The euthanasia debate demonstrated its awesome capacity to achieve a result that's deeply reassuring for Catholics and other Christians but opposed by something like 70 per cent of the population.

It's pointless to complain about church entanglement in politics. It's been going on since the year dot. How else could the Church of Rome have survived to become the oldest political machine on earth? Both sides of Australian politics take for granted that they can't win government if the Catholic vote is solidly against them. Once tribally loyal to Labor, then since the 1950s drifting towards the Liberals, the Catholic vote is now split. Conservative Catholics have joined the Liberals and have made the Coalition side of politics more conservative as a result. The more radical Catholics have stuck with Labor. But between the two sides is a volatile wedge of the Catholic vote that is crucially important in deciding who governs Australia.

That was so in 1993. John Hewson's plans for a 15 per cent goods and services tax (GST) were condemned by the Catholic Social Welfare Commission. The commission's verdict was backed in turn by the bishops. Their quarrel with the Liberals was another round in a long brawl between the church and politics over free-market policies which have brought no unprecedented prosperity but opened a gap between rich and poor that Australia has never known before. The church declared the GST unfair, regressive, tough on the poor and easy on the rich. Paul Keating ran with a line he took from the Social Welfare Commission: 'God help you if you're a Catholic renter with an appetite because you are really marked down for extinction.'

On election day, Catholics returned to Labor in droves. Bob Hawke had won in 1990 with 47 per cent of the Catholic vote. But exit-poll figures showed Catholics gave 55 per cent of their primary votes to Labor in 1993. Paul Keating scraped back home. The reprieved Prime Minister spoke more wisely than he realised when he claimed victory in the name of 'the true believers'. These exit-poll figures prepared for the Australian Electoral Study by Dr Clive Bean, now a senior academic at the Queensland University of Technology, underline the continuing relevance of faith to politics. 'Sociologists are saying religions don't matter much these days,' he told me. 'But we're finding even nominal affiliation has an impact on how people see politics.'

Australian governments now work in the shadow of that 1993 result. Even Catholics among old Liberals rage at the memory of that election, particularly at the part played by the Social Welfare Commission. 'I thought they were a bunch of shysters at the time,' said Hewson frontbencher Fred Chaney at a seminar organised in 1999 by the Jesuit priest Frank Brennan. 'There is, to my mind, a total intellectual incoherence in what the church has said publicly on these tax issues over a long period, and I think that in that sense they have muddied debate, they have slowed the pace of sensible tax reform. I think their contribution has been nil on the moral front, and on the political and economic front, negative.'

Catholics are now secure inside the strongholds of power, not just of the Labor Party but the Coalition too. The Jesuits educated four or five of John Howard's Cabinet. This strength of representation around a Coalition Cabinet table would have been unimaginable even twenty years ago. But so would the policy outcomes of this Catholic presence. As Frank Brennan says, 'We've arrived and the policies bear no resemblance to what Catholics say they're about'.

The traditional social agenda of the church — concern for fairness, for the poor, the marginalised and the immigrant — has made little impact in Howard's Cabinet. The GST and Wik compromises were victories for the church, but imposed on Howard's government by the Opposition parties and the fluke of Brian Harradine's vote. But it's a little window into the strange political position of Catholicism these days that not all the bishops were happy with the GST result. Some even dissented very privately on Wik. But Harradine was there speaking and voting as Catholics had long imagined Catholic politicians should speak and act, trying to reach some sort of truce between today's economics and the old Catholic social agenda.

The hostility of modern politics to that agenda leaves the church weaker in pressing its case for a fairer society, but all the stronger in lobbying for more obviously

Catholic issues. Unable to please the church where it most counts, the parties are left to please it where they can. What became caricatured in the press after 1993 as bribes for Harradine — censorship, family planning, tax concessions — are also evidence of this wider Catholic leverage.

The political objectives of the church divide above and below the belt — social above, genital below.

Above the belt, Howard has been at loggerheads with the church over the economy, race and immigration. The Catholic Church is an immigrant church immensely strengthened by postwar arrivals. It wants more immigrants, not fewer, a more generous refugee policy, and fairer treatment for those caught up in immigration disputes. Under Howard that's not happening. But above the belt, Howard has helped kill off euthanasia, and backed Catholic commitment to the health system, not only to Catholic hospitals but to public health. 'There would be a major showdown over Medicare,' says Brennan. 'In the end, any deliberate policy of the church will be for universal health cover for all Australians, regardless of their means. And Howard knows that.'

Then there are the schools. If anyone doubts the clout of the Catholic Church in today's politics, they only have to look at the privileged position of its schools. The Federal government is changing the way it funds private schools, moving to a system that pays according to census-based calculations of wealth. The poorer the kids, the more state cash. The new system is generally considered very fair, but the Catholic Church did its sums and opposed the idea. Peter Tannock, chairman of the National Catholic Education

Commission, declared the new scheme would have, 'undermined the integrity of the Catholic system'. Anglican, Presbyterian, Lutheran schools will all have to comply. But in the 1999 budget, Catholic schools were not only exempted but promised an increase under the old system — in itself usually very difficult to obtain — of $85 million a year for five years. This is power.

Come below the belt and you enter the world of peculiar Catholic obsession. At the end of the century of Freud, Lawrence, de Beauvoir, Kinsey, Proust, Cavafy, Nabokov, Masters and Johnson, Joyce, Genet, Stein, Foucault, Jung, Baldwin, Schnitzler, and Thomas Mann — the Catholic Church still *officially* insists that only men and women may have sex together, and only within marriage, and only if a child may result. And the church still *officially* expects governments to protect — with legislation if necessary — their notion of sex viewed through this narrow slot.

So censorship is always on the political agenda. So is making life tough for lesbians and homosexuals, if only to put them on the path to heaven. So is an underlying prejudice against mothers working. So are taboos against contraceptives. In the case of condoms, this taboo is so fierce it extends to putting lives at risk from AIDs rather than allowing men to use rubber prophylactics when they're having sex with each other. The fear of death is part of the armoury brought to bear against homosexuality, just as it is deployed against drug-users. In all the talk of right and wrong messages, the message of the ban on condoms is shape up or die.

Nothing, however, matters so much as the perpetual

quest for effective laws against abortion. The trouble is the two last Catholic-inspired attempts have left the church little better off. Terminations are even easier to get in Western Australia as a result of new laws introduced after botched attempts to prosecute Perth doctors. In the ACT, women can still have a pregnancy terminated, even if they are first forced by new laws to look at sketches and photographs of developing foetuses. This has happened despite the unanimous advice of a committee established to advise the local health minister. 'Let's face it,' said Dr Stan Doumani who represents about 300 local doctors, 'This is just trying to lay a guilt trip on these ladies.'

Above and below the belt, the Catholic Church remains a difficult beast to please.

Father Brian Lucas is a fleshy man who doesn't see much sun. He's like a figure glimpsed in a Vatican corridor — dark, intent, impersonal, sharp and pale. There's a quiff of hair in front of a balding head, and a comfortable roll of fat under his chin. Lucas is very good at his work. One day he will be a bishop. Meanwhile, he's the lawyer priest, Sydney-trained, who is the official spokesman for the church in that archdiocese. There is no one quite like him in Australia. Admirers and detractors alike call Lucas 'the cardinal's man', which he doesn't quite deny. 'You may get the situation where the cardinal says, "Will you please give the following message to someone . . ." '

You can't put a new question to Lucas and you can't get a new answer. You know that before you enter the room. He's an old hand at a very old game. His reproaches are almost as old as time: beware mistaking voices within the church for the voice of the church itself. 'This is where your profession needs to be more cautious: a very nuanced, subtle, sophisticated statement by an expert in social welfare gets translated into a headline, "Yesterday the Catholic Church said . . ." That is unfair both to the person making the statement and to the rest of the Catholics of Australia, who may legitimately not agree with it. It's also then misleading to the government, because the government is put in a position of seeming to be either for or against the church.'

Put that another way: the bishops in Australia for whom Lucas speaks have often been at loggerheads with the commissions of the church over the years. The bishops are conservative, the commissions — on welfare, education, social justice etc. — are more radical. Not very, just more. Where they judge it necessary, the bishops will use, or even cultivate, division in Catholic ranks to undercut the commissions. Headstrong bishops, like George Pell, of Melbourne, will even undercut the corporate authority of the bishops.

The campaign against the Northern Territory's euthanasia law showed just how powerful the church is when it speaks with a single, clear voice. Lucas calls the campaign, 'an example of good education'. That's a magnificent euphemism. The Vatican spoke through its official newspaper, *L'Osservatore Romano*. The cardinal spoke in Sydney. The bishops spoke. An alliance of Catholic politicians led by the redoubtable Sydney Labor conservative Johnno Johnson, and businessmen led by the former banker Jim Dominguez — a man close to both Howard and the church — plus leading Anglicans came together in an ultra-low-profile group called Euthanasia No. It didn't lobby directly itself but recruited experts and friends to approach MPs in both Sydney and Canberra. It didn't use the press. Lucas says, 'It wasn't a media event because most of the media commentators are pro-euthanasia'.

Profound doctrinal belief lay at the core of the campaign, but the language used by Euthanasia No was resolutely secular. It argued euthanasia was a 'human rights' issue. What it wanted to avoid was the line, 'If the church debates on religious terms and you are not religious, you can reject what the church is saying'. This worked. The debate did not turn on the fundamental issue of the right of the churches to impose their views on the secular public. Out there, euthanasia was overwhelmingly supported, but in the senate the cause was lost by a handful of astutely cultivated votes. 'Right is right even if nobody's right,' says Lucas, musing on that victory over popular opinion. 'But wrong is wrong, even if everybody's wrong.'

When John Howard became Leader of the Opposition he set about restoring good relations between the Coalition and the church. His links through Dominguez and other Catholic businessmen were important, but the hard work was done by the federal director of the Liberal Party, a Catholic, Andrew Robb, who had set out to 'remove the barriers we erected for ourselves in 1993'. Robb established links with both the commissions and the bishops through the Coalition's Catholic MPs. 'We were determined to ensure that once we got into a campaign there would be no surprises, no problems,' says

Robb. 'We discussed a range of issues, particularly education, but also health and industrial relations. The family focus of our policies resonated very strongly with the churches, particularly with John Howard articulating them.'

In 1996 the Coalition won office after promising the GST was off the agenda forever. Exit-poll figures showed the Catholics deserting Labor: only 37 per cent of them gave the ALP their primary vote. Once in office, Howard's challenge was to maintain Catholic support while pursuing a number of policies certain to cause trouble with that constituency. That Harradine had a crucial vote in the senate only dramatised the underlying difficulties Howard faced. But the prime minister also had the unhoped-for advantages of a wave of new Catholic Liberal MPs in parliamentary ranks, who, in turn, represented a Catholic constituency more prosperous, more conservative and more in line with his thinking. The federal Coalition had probably never had such a feel for what the church would object to, what it would live with and what it wanted — above and below the belt.

The immediate result was the Howard government's keynote emphasis on 'family values'. Here Howard's values and Catholic values knitted seamlessly. For the first year in office, Howard also offered dramatic support for Catholic doctrinal positions on fertility control. Cuts to Medicare rebates for IVF and the slashing of overseas aid for birth control programs were important victories for Harradine and the church. The climax of this phase was the effective banning of the 'morning after' pill, RU486, and then the blackballing of the man who had recommended its release, scientist and committed Catholic, Dr John Funder. He had been offered the chair of the National Health and Medical Research Council but at the last minute this appointment was blocked in Cabinet at Harradine's insistence. The Funder crisis brought down a wave of ridicule on the government and marked the end of this avenue of cultivation.

Two years later, the GST was back on the agenda. The church seemed united in its disapproval. The bishops backed the Catholic Social Welfare Commission in declaring this a regressive tax. No such tax could have the support of the church. If the government persisted in its plans, then the GST must not apply to 'the essentials of life'. As decisions go in the Catholic Church in Australia, this was about as all-embracing and official as they get. But a couple of days after this declaration, Archbishop Pell of Melbourne issued through his public relations firm a statement: 'There is no one Catholic position on an issue as complex as taxation.' With that he sabotaged church unity. Howard went straight onto 'AM' to say the church was divided. Pell's intervention was a political godsend.

The true Catholic voice on tax, when it came, was Brian Harradine's in the senate, ten months later. Scholars of Catholic rhetoric can identify in Harradine's now-famous 'I cannot' speech the words of Catholic teachers going back to Pope Leo XIII. More to the point, it was firmly based on the bishops' verdict before the elections. In the aftermath, Harradine found himself feted at football matches, his hand pumped, his shoulders patted. The tactical effect of his vote was to flick-pass the tax issue to the Democrats who saw to it that the GST didn't apply to what they defined as those 'essentials of life'.

The GST campaign left George Pell more powerful but even more resented in the church. A bishop willing to strike out on his own, has peculiar authority because the political clout of the church depends so much on consensus at the top. Pell is a wild card and quite fearless in his political dealings. He nails his republican colours to the mast despite Howard. He denounces gambling despite Kennett. He denounces safe injecting rooms, needle exchange and heroin trials despite the Sisters of Charity. Pell is the walking proof that on difficult social issues there is not only division in the Catholic hierarchy but a gulf between the hierarchy and the workers out in the field. Sometimes it's as if two churches are operating under the same Catholic banner. The important political question is: which has the ear of governments? The believers in the field or the conservative bishops and their bureaucrats? Canberra listens to the bishops when they speak with a single voice. Where they're divided, Canberra listens to those who offer political comfort. What Pell has to say about drugs is another godsend to John Howard.

But Pell and his fellow bishops offered the Prime Minister no comfort on Wik. Howard faced an unprecedented public attack from nearly all the churches for his Ten-Point Plan to strip Aborigines and Torres Strait Islanders of rights acknowledged by the High Court and granted by the Native Title Act. Howard responded with an audacious counterattack on the churches, even publicly sympathising with National Party calls for boycotts of the pews. He appears to have been shrewdly advised on division in church ranks. Catholics gave a public impression of solid opposition to Howard's native title plans, but the outspoken bishops were causing what Lucas calls 'some pain and suffering' in the ranks: 'Catholic pastoralists obviously had a point of view.'

Race was not an issue like euthanasia, where the church could ring the bell and the faithful would assemble for duty. The churches — particularly the Catholic Church — showed determined courage in revealing Australia's inherent racism. National consciousness was raised, but Catholic forces weren't united in opposition to Howard's Ten-Point Plan. While the bishops were flaying the government publicly, one or two bishops from the bush were making representations to Harradine on behalf of the Catholic graziers. Brian Harradine forced a compromise on the government that sat, as Lucas remarked, 'very comfortably within the principle of Catholic social teaching'. And the senator achieved his stated aim of saving the country from the ravages of a double dissolution election based on race. But it was not just the fabric of secular society that was at risk. There was also the fabric of the Catholic Church. As one senior layman involved in these matters remarked, 'Think what a One Nation campaign could have done to Catholic Australia'.

That Howard scraped home in 1998 is testament to his shrewdness and to the hard work the government had put into cultivating the church. He won by not entirely alienating the Catholic vote, despite the Ten-Point Plan and despite the GST. Exit polls suggest a strong return to Labor by Catholics, but the Liberals lost only about half those Catholic voters who had deserted Keating in 1996. Enough stayed behind to stop Kim Beazley getting over the line.

John McCarthy, QC, flanked on all sides by lawyers, opened the Gospel of St Matthew at chapter 25 and read to the New South Wales Industrial Relations Commission the promise Christ gave to his followers on the Mount of Olives. If they feed the hungry, tend the sick, comfort prisoners and clothe the naked they shall sit among the righteous by the throne of God. Those who fail in these duties, 'will go away into eternal punishment, but the righteous into eternal life'.

McCarthy is one of the leading Catholic lawyers in the nation. His fields are the Labor Party, the church and native title. A fifty acre claim he won on the north coast of New South Wales for the Dunghutti people was the first native title victory on the mainland. He advised Harradine during the Wik debates. He is briefed to man the legal frontiers where secular values threaten the privileges of the church. That brought him in July 1998 to the Industrial Relations Commission with his Bible open at St Matthew as supreme Authority for the proposition that the work of the church can't be divided between spiritual objectives on one hand and educational or social work on the other. It is all one.

New South Wales was broadening the definition of 'family' in provisions for compassionate leave to include de factos and same sex partners. McCarthy and his team of lawyers were there to save the church from having to acknowledge that it employed men and women whose sex lives lay outside its own strict rules. The church lawyers were unembarrassed by fighting the battle over, of all things, compassionate leave. There was a principle at stake. McCarthy told the commission that to express the obligations of the award in that language would put the Catholic Church 'in a position of formal cooperation with what they regard as a moral wrong . . . of enormous seriousness'.

The leave 'problem' was solved with a little deft hypocrisy. Catholic Church bodies in New South Wales offered to give the same people the same leave under a different formula — 'pressing domestic necessity'. But that left the much bigger question unanswered: is everyone employed by a church body engaged in propagating religion? If they are, religious rules apply to their employment. If they're not, then they may have secular protection of the law against church bigotry.

Catholic employment practices are not some little side issue, a minor enthusiasm of the civil liberties lobby. The Catholic Church is now the biggest employer in Australia outside government, and is everywhere defending its right to *appear* not to employ those in de facto relationships, any homosexuals and lesbians, any un- married mothers, any remarried divorcees whose first marriages have not been annulled by the church, any adulterers or fornicators and any atheists. That they *do* employ these people is not denied. Indeed, the church could not run hospitals, charities, schools — and perhaps even seminaries — without them. But for moral reasons that are extremely hard for outsiders to grasp, the *reality* has to be kept under wraps. The known atheist and the known adulterer will not be hired and should their circumstances become known when they're in the job, the church asserts the right to sack them. It's not for nothing that employees of the Catholic Church — and churches generally — are among the keenest unionists in the nation.

Patrick Lee of the New South Wales Independent Education Union has been dealing for fifteen years with the churches. 'The Catholic Church gets more notice because they run more schools,' says Lee. He talks of the 'entrenched operating hypocrisy' of a system where the real lives of teachers are known 'to a reasonable degree' by fellow staff members, principals and even parents. 'De facto partners and gay partners are welcome at staff functions. That's not entirely novel.' But promotion beyond a certain point is denied to those who live outside the Christian rules of marriage, or there's 'a bit of a purge', or a woman has a baby out of wedlock, or a teacher is glimpsed marching in the Mardi Gras — and they're out. Most states have anti-discrimination laws to protect employees from just this sort of treatment, but the same states have always given bodies 'established to propagate religion' exemptions to allow them to go on doing the same things — but on religious grounds. The law fights bigotry in individuals and privileges it in the churches.

Back in the eighties, the Independent Education Union fought noisy test cases around Australia. Those fights made martyrs. The official position of the churches didn't change. So these days, while the union will still stage a public brawl if necessary, it's usually left to negotiate practical solutions and quiet departures. 'It gets hard when the teachers are really committed members of their church, committed to the social justice objectives and the values of Catholicism — and then their church turns on them. One of the hardest things is nursing a teacher through this. While you're trying to advise them on the options they have, we're also having to deal with their devastating reassessment of the church when the values they thought were rooted in their religion turn out to be dispensable when they come up against this other reality.'

In 1993, Jacqui Griffin challenged that reality by complaining to the Human Rights and Equal Opportunities Tribunal in Canberra that the Catholic Education Office back in Sydney wouldn't take her on as a teacher. She turned to Canberra because federal anti-discrimination laws at least compel churches to stand up and publicly justify why they won't employ a woman like Griffin, a former co-convenor of the Gay and Lesbian Teachers Association, GaLTaS. The case was deeply embarrassing for the Catholic Church. It had to concede that the GaLTaS aim of protecting homosexual and lesbian kids from harassment squared with the church's own teaching as laid down by the Congregation of the Doctrine of the Faith, 'It is deplorable that homosexual persons have been and are the object of violent malice in speech or in action . . .' The tribunal was given no evidence of Griffin promoting the joys of lesbian sex nor any evidence she was sexually active. Commissioner Chris Sidoti declared the church's assertions to the contrary, 'gratuitous and scurrilous'. But still the church maintained the sheer presence of a lesbian teacher in a Catholic school would imply, 'Acceptance of his or her lifestyle [that] may well influence a student to follow that model and engage in a similar lifestyle'. In dismissing the church's case in March 1998, the commissioner declared the idea of role models recruiting kids in this way, 'contrary to all research of which I am aware'.

Sidoti didn't have the power to compel the church to employ Griffin. He could only find she had been discriminated against. But the church had not enjoyed the experience. Frank Brennan remarked that the sight of an officer of the state deciding what was and what was not injurious to the religious susceptibilities of Catholics was 'a touch Orwellian'. In the aftermath of the case, representations were made to the federal attorney-general that all bodies established to 'propagate religion' should be given the same automatic exemption from Canberra's anti-discrimination laws as they enjoy in the states. Meanwhile, back in New South Wales, the local Anti-Discrimination Board was using the compassionate leave case to try to narrow those exemptions dramatically by arguing that not every Catholic organisation was established to 'propagate religion'. Nurses nurse the sick. Physics teachers teach physics. Drivers for St Vincent de Paul drive trucks. They should be protected from discrimination.

This is what brought John McCarthy QC and his team of hard-hitting lawyers down to the IRC to read St Matthew to the commissioners. According to McCarthy's interpretation of Matthew 25, verses 31 to 46, every single person employed by a church body is employed in the propagation of the faith. One of the commissioners expressed his doubts: 'What you have quoted is I mean obviously very profound but it's also very general . . .' McCarthy was unfazed. The Anti-Discrimination Board backed off. Perhaps the lawyers did a head count of the bench and feared a majority of Catholics. Chris Puplick, the president of the board, denies this. 'A judgment was made in all of the circumstances, taking into account all of the material factors, not to press the point.' So it remains the case in Australia today that no one working for the largest private employer in the nation is protected from discrimination, except on the ground of race or disability.

The problem of privileging the bigotry of the churches is wider than this. Governments across Australia are using church charities to do work once done by the Public Service. It's a deliberate policy of the Howard government. Ask Brian Lucas for an assurance that the Catholic Church would distribute government aid in a strictly non-discriminatory way, and that assurance doesn't come. Already Puplick has seen problems in New South Wales. A Uniting Church group in Newcastle, taking over part of the work of the Commonwealth Employment Service, was advertising for staff with 'Christian values'. A church charity in Sydney distributing public money for homeless youth was doing so in a way that clearly discriminated against gay young people.

For some years now legislation sponsored by the Democrats has been hanging fire in the senate. It's not radical. On the one hand it proposes to give some teeth to the sort of declaration of discrimination won by Jacqui Griffin. Under the proposed law, she would get her job. The churches could discriminate still in employment, but only if they are willing to stand up in public and prove that refusing a job, say, to a single mother is a necessary expression of religious belief. A second arm of the legislation lays down the principle that religious bodies distributing public assistance must do so on absolutely secular lines.

A senate enquiry into the bill drew hundreds of submissions from across Australia that make a survey of sorts into the state of homophobia in this country. The difficulties of single mothers, atheists and the remarried divorced were all but forgotten. What the Christians asked for most urgently in their submissions was an automatic exemption to let them fire and refuse to hire homosexuals. Yet there were wonderfully encouraging submissions. The Quakers said: 'We don't see the necessity for religious bodies to be exempt from any provisions of the bill.' The Anglicans of Western Australia supported them: 'Churches and related institutions should not be exempt.' The Uniting Church wants no exemptions in church schools, hospitals and charities. But the general mood of the submissions was anger and surprise that the national parliament would think of legislation that issued such a challenge to church prerogatives. The Catholics and most of the Protestant congregations are demanding to be as free from the working of this new law as they are of the present state laws. Genesis and Leviticus figure heavily in the submissions, along with those familiar dreams of purity and nightmares of disgust that have haunted the church for so long.

Labor says it will support the bill, but the going is likely to get very tough once the churches flex their political muscles. As this book went to press, a spokesman for the federal Attorney-General, Daryl Williams, told me the government was still considering its own position. If by some secular miracle the bill makes it through parliament, my guess would be that John McCarthy QC would be standing before the High Court within months briefed by the Catholic Church to challenge that law on the ground that discriminating against single mothers, lesbians, fornicators and homosexuals is an expression of the 'true exercise' of religion guaranteed by the Constitution. The only difficulty counsel for the church may face is finding clear directions along these lines from Christ.

Meanwhile, stone by stone, those spires are going up on St Mary's Cathedral for the decoration of Sydney and the glory of God. There they stand to remind the city and its leaders of the power of the church, and its historic claim to represent a force for fairness and goodness in Australia's rough-and-tumble society. There are Muslims among the stonemasons who pause at appropriate moments through the day, point themselves to Mecca, and pray. The church was happy to employ them and for Australia to know they were working on the spires. Indeed, the church earned a little pleasant ecumenical publicity when this story was aired on the radio.

But let there be no *known* adulterers among the masons, no *known* lesbians, no *known* fornicators . . .

ELEVEN

YOUNG MINDS

'But when Jesus saw it, he was much displeased, and said unto them, suffer the little children to come unto me . . . '

St Mark

The Christians of the North Shore are muttering about Judith Wheeldon and the noise is being heard all over town. 'She's a Jew', or 'She's not what I call a Christian', or 'She's told the school chaplain to preach atheism'. Wheeldon — who is not Jewish and never issued such instructions — runs an Anglican girls' school called Abbotsleigh that sits above the frost line on Sydney's North Shore where magnolias and Bible studies flourish. The details of Wheeldon's faith aren't a private matter any more: she's a vigorous new appointment to an important school in a system under siege from radicals within — and she doesn't pretend to be devout.

All that's controversial about her — the way she was appointed, her public profile, the changes she has already made at the school, the expulsion of some girls of 'good family' caught drunk in public, the twin peculiarities (so far as the North Shore is concerned) of being born in Oklahoma City and having a former Labor senator for a husband — is being boiled down to the single question of her faith. Is Judith Wheeldon a Christian?

The same loaded question is being asked from coast to coast wherever church schools find themselves caught these days in a tug o' war between faith and learning. The contest is old but there's fresh urgency now as public money pours through these schools and the radicals among the faithful ponder how they might make better use of these assets to turn out more Christians. The conundrum of church schooling has always been that it doesn't produce Believers. The men and women who emerge from St Peter's Adelaide, or Xavier in Melbourne or Churchy in Brisbane or Abbotsleigh in Sydney know the *Book of Common Prayer* or the Missal and one day they'll be married in church and have their children baptised — but if they're true to type, they won't be keen Christians. For those who've been through these schools, the explanation is fairly simple: after being harried about sin and damnation all through your teens, you've usually had enough.

But the radicals with their deep faith in Faith search for deeper explanations for the failure to deliver converts. They believe church schools aren't exposing young minds powerfully enough to Christ. The leader of the Evangelical radicals in the Sydney Anglican synod — the church parliament — is Phillip Jensen. He rates the traditional Anglican schools of the diocese like Abbotsleigh as no better than 'semi-Christian'. Jensen is mustering the strength in synod to try to impose tough new doctrinal rules to guarantee schools have 'a Christian council that will appoint a Christian principal who will engage Christian teachers and so establish a Christian ethos in the schools'.

All-Christian schools are the ideal of the radicals in whichever church they're at work. But the Protestants have particularly frantic worries about the *type* of Christian to employ — when only the right type will do. It's an issue where purity of doctrine merges seamlessly with pursuit of power. So in the last decade we have seen a heresy trial in Sydney after the ordained master of

St Andrews Presbyterian College at Sydney University voiced doubts about the infallible myth of the Bible and questioned St Paul's sexuality. He returned to Scotland. Finding men and women of precisely acceptable beliefs is a challenge for a church that lost the better part of its strength to the Uniting Church but kept a number of fine schools and colleges of its own to run across Australia. The key to jobs and preferment here is doctrine.

The Anglicans of Sydney are caught up in the same squabbles. No other Anglican diocese on earth is quite like Sydney. It's the biggest and richest of them all and probably the most fractious. The watered-down Catholicism of the church in England never took root in Sydney. From the time of the First Fleet, Sydney was the territory of evangelical missionaries who brought with them a simple faith for a rough society. The city and the church have grown, but the diocese still operates on the half-articulated suspicion that in Sydney it's dealing with humanity at its worst. Salvation lies through God's rules, but the true path laid down by the Bible is almost as hotly contested in Sydney today as it was when Queen Mary was burning Anglican bishops at the stake. Where you worship matters enormously. Adjoining parishes in Sydney can regard each other as un-Anglican, un-evangelical, even un-Christian. In such an atmosphere, the precise doctrinal commitments of the men and women who run the Anglican schools is counted as crucially important.

Being the wrong type of Christian would make life difficult enough for Judith Wheeldon at Abbotsleigh, but she didn't claim to be much of a Christian at all. 'There are others who would be better able to lead the worship and the doctrinal life of the school than I would,' she said and cited as her main concern, 'the moral and spiritual as opposed to specifically doctrinal' leadership of the girls and staff. It was as good as heresy.

Phillip Jensen sits on a sunny afternoon drinking mugs of tea under a scalding electric light. The room is full of books and the venetians are shut tight. For all his energy he gives the impression of a man who has yet to hit his stride. He clowns a little, as if flexing his muscles for other purposes on more serious occasions. His easy laugh mixes confidence, professional friendliness and straightforward pleasure at his own points well made. 'Gotcha' says his grin as he QEDs another conclusion into place. Jensen candidly admits that his interest in schools is as a Christian: 'I am not an educator.'

Headquarters is this big house in a sandy suburb close to both the University of New South Wales and to St Matthias parish in Centennial Park. Jensen has turned both into powerhouses of the most active Christianity. St Matthias leads a loose network of 'gospel' parishes across the Sydney diocese and beyond. They're booming, all the more so because they invest all their cash and zeal in further spreading the Word. When the Anglicans were looking for a new archbishop in 1993, the clergy put this man on the shortlist but he didn't have the lay votes to stay there. Both clergy and lay must agree on a candidate. So Harry Goodhew got the job — from which he must soon retire. Phillip Jensen is once again considered a leading candidate to head the mighty Sydney diocese.

Jensen deals in absolutes. He believes the Bible is true and that God speaks through its pages and that the pronouncements of Moses, Isaiah, Christ and St Paul are all true for all time and form a code of absolute rules and vetoes. He admires Islam's way of holding to absolutes too. He derides liberals and 'relativists'. Obedience is the mark of a Christian: wives are subject to their husbands, children to their parents. Only men can be ordained ministers and lead a parish. Purity must be guarded, by censorship if necessary. No sex outside marriage. No sex ever for homosexuals. Sundays are for worship, but so is every day of the week. Jensen is a leading combatant in the doctrinal guerilla campaigns around these propositions in the Sydney diocese. He is rarely defeated.

Jensen has wounds. He went to the Presbyterian Scots College in Sydney's Bellevue Hill where 'bagpipes and rugby' were king and life turned ugly for the boy when he was converted at a Billy Graham crusade. 'When I stood up and declared myself a Christian I was a leper. When I bowled Shore out I was a hero, but as a Christian . . . ' He rated only one Scots teacher a true Christian, and this man fled from the school after breaking down in tears in front of the boy, broken by the treatment dished out because of his faith. Jensen concludes, 'There are some church schools that don't have much to do with Christianity'.

Others might draw more complex lessons from this experience about boys, discretion, other ways of expressing faith, other notions of being Christian. But to Jensen the lesson seems blindingly obvious: these schools have to be Christianised top to bottom with Christian principals and members of council and teachers. Syllabuses need to be tweaked to acknowledge a 'coherent Christian world view'. Science is not such a worry, though Darwin is not part of the world view of his sort of Christian. There are some 'insensitive' English texts set for the Higher School Certificate that need to go and a particular problem with Ancient History: the need for proper respect to be shown to St Paul in the Year 12 option, The Rise of Christianity. The truths of St Paul are not to be read as secular teachers read them in the context of their time: they are all true and for all time.

While there's something deeply attractive about the idea of shaking these Anglican schools out of their prosperous torpor, Jensen's purposes are narrow. The schools must change he says, they must live up to their mottoes, must practise what they preach for in this atheist and materialist world, there's work for them to perform for Christ. The work is urgent. 'It's crazy to go on being semi-Christian.' So Jensen wants to put a bomb under them for Christ? He rolls this extravagant question round in his mind for half a second, spreads his arms wide and with a great smile says, 'Yes'.

Every Ascension Day — the day of Christ's exit for heaven via the Mount of Olives — the principals of all the Anglican schools in Sydney gather for dinner at Bishopscourt, the little Gothic palace on Darling Point that is Harry Goodhew's official residence. Twenty or so men and women sit down together. They are a mixed bunch. Some are from schools only 'associated' with the church and are untouched by the threat of Jensenite

Christianisation; some welcome the prospect; some deeply resent the control already exercised by the church. One of these last startled the diners a couple of years ago by raising his voice to the archbishop. He demanded, 'When are you going to forget what happened to SCEGGS in the seventies?'

The SCEGGS debacle is the key in a locked door. Dreams of perpetual endowment lured the council of the Sydney Church of England Girls' Grammar Schools into extravagant property developments in the late sixties just as the latest Sydney land boom was about to go bust. When the worst happened, the council — and the five girls' schools it ran — was $7.5m in the red and the council treasurer, Richard Geoffrey Glanville, had fled to Rio. It was discovered that he'd siphoned off more than $100 000 for his own shaky property deals. Glanville was and remains a Christian. These days he's an Assembly of God pastor in South Australia but at the time of the great crash of 1974 he was a leading member of the Australian Lawyers Christian Association. 'His knowledge of the Bible is phenomenal. Incredible,' said his girlfriend while waiting for his extradition from Brazil. 'We used to have long discussions about "Jesus Christ Superstar". We saw it about eight times.'

The church closed one school, sold two, sold real estate, settled the trade debts and left the parents — enthusiastic volunteers — to raise the cash to keep the Darlinghurst and Redlands schools running. The church kept only a small stake in both, just enough to secure a couple of seats on their councils. This seemed a niggardly investment at the time and there was much rancour over the church's meanness. But as the independent SCEGGS schools prospered they came to value their distance from the synod very highly. They can watch the ideological brawls knowing these disputes have nothing much to do with them. They make their own policy. Religious criteria hardly count in hiring teachers or finding citizens to serve on their councils. By the measure of academic success — very attractive to those paying the fees — it's clear that the further a school is from synod control, the better its academic prospects. The 'associated' Anglican schools are always nearer the top of the heap than the synod-owned, synod-controlled schools. The only regular exception to this sobering rule is academically excellent Abbotsleigh. Of course, the best academic bet among the private schools of Sydney remains the absolutely secular Ascham and Sydney Grammar.

After the SCEGGS mess the radicals in synod wanted to unload all the schools. They argued it was indecent for a church to hold these extraordinary assets for the benefit of the rich children of Sydney. Shouldn't the church be where most children were: in the public schools? But the traditionalists counter-attacked and carried the day. Instead of letting the schools go, they brought them under tighter church control by setting up backroom machinery to supply them with the professionals they needed on their councils — synod-approved lawyers, accountants, architects, etc. — while also loading the councils with clergy. 'This caused a lot of frustration because they didn't throw their weight into the work of the schools,' admits one of the bishops from those days. 'But they were there to keep an eye on things.'

Jensen and the radicals turned their attention instead to establishing new Anglican schools — low-fee and emphatically Christian — in the outer suburbs. This was part of a movement in which most of the Australian churches were taking part, to move Christian education into the new suburbs of Australia's cities. These were prosperous times and as Canberra's commitment to secular education faltered in the nineties, money was flowing into the new church schools from the State. There was a slightly uneasy relationship between the new and old Anglican schools in Sydney. Snobbery played a part in this. So did the fear that should synod fall into the wrong hands, half a dozen new schools might be built on the proceeds, say, of Shore's spare real estate and an oval or two from King's.

So successful were the new schools by the mid-nineties that the radicals began to turn their attention back to the rich old schools they'd once given up as a lost cause. 'The mood changed and the schools were seen as perfect ground for sowing the seed,' said Justice Peter Young of the Supreme Court of New South Wales, a council member of a couple of Anglican schools for the last fifteen or twenty years. 'The feeling was, "This is ours and this is our mission field". And that mood is still the current mood of synod.' The bishops now lost control of the machinery supplying professionals to school councils. A school that needed an architect was getting a man who was very good at prayer. To deal with the problem, Peter Young and half a dozen men with long experience on school councils formed a synod 'review committee' in 1995.

They were working essentially on a set of housekeeping

proposals for smaller councils, fewer clergy and a permanent synod committee to liaise with schools when Abbotsleigh announced that Judith Wheeldon would be the school's next headmistress. She arrived in late 1996 to take up her post bringing with her two great danes, two cats and her husband, the former Labor senator from Western Australia, John Wheeldon. What happened in synod thereafter was all about Abbotsleigh.

In the 'Freedom Summer' of 1964, Judith Shaw left the University of Wisconsin, where she was studying, to spend three months doing voter registration work among black families in Mississippi. A knife was pulled on her one night in Carthage and she escaped after a wild car chase down rutted roads. That summer she wore a Quaker's little lace cap. Voter registration is the sort of work Quakers do, but the more extreme evangelicals in both the United States and Australia would look on this as a wasted opportunity for doing the only thing that really matters — spreading the Word.

'I grew up in a family which was not religious,' she wrote in the *curriculum vitae* she presented many years later to Abbotsleigh council. 'But in my teens my own interest in religion made me try many churches. I spent a long time with the Quakers before finding I felt most at home in the Episcopal Church which since age seventeen I have attended most regularly.' That's all she had to say about her religion in the CV: a sense of being 'at home' with the Anglicans of America, but no deep profession of faith. In Sydney terms, this is hardly a profession of faith at all.

A few years after Mississippi she was in Perth, married

Wheeldon and didn't move east until the mid-eighties, when she taught briefly at Abbotsleigh before landing the job of setting up the Yeshiva Girls' High School in Bondi. The policy of the Lubavitch community that owns the school is that teachers have either to be the right kind of Jew — ultra-Orthodox — or not a Jew at all. After a couple of years at Yeshiva, she left to rescue a school for girls in Mosman that was in deep decline. Queenwood is one of that handful of Sydney private schools that have no religious affiliations at all. The staff was unhappy at her appointment and many left in her early years — this has happened again at Abbotsleigh — but by the criteria that matter most to the parent customers, Wheeldon was a success.

She became a public figure, speaking and writing for the press to boost herself and Queenwood. Wheeldon could be depended upon for forthright conservative views on the dangers of drugs, greedy and neglectful parents, violence in schools and porn in the community. She was one of Leonie Kramer's committee that pulled Caryl Churchill's *Top Girls* and Gillian Mears' *Fineflour* off the Higher School Certificate after Fred Nile's long campaign against these texts. But she was also a public enemy of corporal punishment and welcomed legislation banning the cane in New South Wales — legislation that was eloquently opposed by the same sort of Christians who want 'filthy' texts banned from English courses. She was not afraid of controversy, easy with the press and running a flourishing school.

Abbotsleigh — crest: fleur-de-lys (purity), lion (strength), fish (Christianity) — received 65 applications when it advertised for a new headmistress here and abroad in 1996. Judith Wheeldon's was not one of them. The academic headhunters Philip Roff and Associates, of Melbourne, were employed to advise. Eight or ten candidates were interviewed by a subcommittee of the school council led by the merchant banker James Graham of Gresham Partners. After four months' searching, Graham asked Judith Wheeldon to apply and three weeks' later she had the job. Announcing the appointment, Graham said: 'She is an inspired leader.' The church was astonished.

All sides agree the most important work a school council ever does is finding a new principal. Synods can (and do) white-ant them over time but that's a messy business. Better to ensure from the start that the right sort of Christian gets the job. For Anglican moderates it's the cast-iron guarantee that things will stay the same. For the radicals in synod the principal is the key to any strategy to Christianise these privileged institutions.

It was said Wheeldon's appointment was sprung on the church and that it came even as a surprise to Archbishop Goodhew. That's not so. But clearly the clout of the church on the Abbotsleigh council — nine representatives out of a total of fourteen — had been whittled away by the committee procedure used to select the new head. So now the synod committee came up with fifteen recommendations to deal with the 'problem' of school councils, including the astonishing idea of having every councillor and all future principals sign the Thirty-Nine Articles, the Elizabethan definition of Anglicanism which contains, apart from some tricky theology, Article XXXVII endorsing both the monarchy and capital punishment. 'The laws of the Realm may punish Christian men with death, for heinous and grievous offences.'

This wasn't enough for Phillip Jensen's party. For fourteen months he led a counterattack and by September 1998, Jensen's forces had rolled the original recommendations and set out their own proposals to set the schools on a Christian course. The Thirty-Nine Articles were ditched, not for being ludicrous but for placing doctrinal obstacles in the path of other Protestants of acceptable faiths — Uniting Church, Salvation Army, Baptists etc. — who might want to work in Anglican schools. Now all candidates would be required to produce a 'testimonial from their own church minister outlining the person's participation in the life of the church'.

This was the flashpoint with the schools. Already worried they couldn't rely on synod to provide the professionals they needed, the schools saw the prospect of losing all parents', old boys' and old girls' representatives — usually the most active members of the school councils — who weren't active Christians in the right sort of parish. Mark Webeck, speaking for The King's School Old Boys' Union, says his members would be 'most concerned' that requiring testimonials of this kind may disqualify 'some otherwise appropriate old boys from serving their old school'. Jensen sees this sort of response as beside the point. 'If you are not a churchman, why be on the council of a church school?' But what useful information can be learnt from these testimonials? 'Church practice is something of an indication of what sort of person they are. The church they chose to go to will tell us something about them, too.'

Jensen doesn't mind if there aren't enough Christian lawyers, accountants, architects, educators and managers to go around. His long-term objective is to strip school councils altogether of experts who are not his kind of Christian. 'Old boys and experts,' he reckons, are subverting the synod's voice on councils. 'The trouble with experts is that they tend to expand their expertise beyond their expertise. The powerful non-churchgoers have been able to have a disproportionate say.' Schools can *employ* the professionals they need. 'Councils are for policy. That comes from the heart. What is crucial is the council's Christian world view.'

While Jensen agrees that remarkable qualities are required of school principals, he insists they must be chosen from a pool of Christian candidates. The mistake schools have made in the past, he explained, 'is to start their search in the education community instead of starting in the Christian community'. He insists the talent is there among Christians. 'That's not faith, it's statistically true.'

By definition, Christian principals will want to employ Christians. 'Only Christian teachers can teach with a consistent Christian world view.' For Jensen, formal academic qualifications are not irrelevant but not decisive in deciding who should be employed to teach. 'Say there is one applicant who is a Christian with a B.A. and a non-Christian with an M.A. A Christian principal would go for the man with the B.A. but tell him to *get* his M.A.' Teaching is a natural career for Christians, says Jensen, and teaching doesn't depend on degrees. 'You're born a teacher.'

Ultimately this fight is all about who gets to stand at the blackboard. The freedom most prized by the associated schools is not having to worry about the religious qualifications of their teachers. 'We can make up our own minds,' said one of the associated heads. 'Religion is a trivial basis on which to choose between teachers. Schools need diversity. Of course, all the teachers are expected to support the ethos of the school, including its Christian ethos. But you have to appoint excellent teachers.' Excellence is also the criterion that counts most in Justice Young's experience on the councils of synod-owned schools. The 'customers' demand excellence. 'You reach a dangerous point, to my mind, if more than 40 per cent of the staff are card-carrying Christians. You have to have a good mix of ideas for young minds.'

Jensen disagrees with this line. 'The materialist philosophy of life is governing the curriculum. Our society is besotted with the idea of getting a TER of 99 to get into university. Christians have other values.' But what would he say to a parent about to invest $10 000 a year for the next six years to give his son a better chance of reaching that university? 'I would try to get him to see the Christian world view. If that doesn't work, I'd recommend Grammar.'

The archbishop's palace rather embarrasses the Anglican Church but at last the Heritage Commission has allowed them to bury the garden under flats. So ugly. So profitable. But until the heavy earth moving equipment comes, the Goodhews have the place to themselves. The archbishop sits in his study with a mug of Lavazza in his hands. His eyes are slightly liquid behind rimless glasses. The shirt-front is cardinal pink but the episcopal ring on his right hand is Protestant plain. An Italian desk lamp shines down on his papers but light enough is drifting in through high windows. At no point this afternoon does Goodhew name Phillip Jensen. But then the archbishop is dealing with something far larger than the impatient enthusiasm of a single cleric. Jensen would be nothing if he did not command the very wide admiration he does in the diocese, particularly among the clergy. Goodhew says, 'I don't think it's altogether easy to determine what will happen'.

There's nothing much about the latest proposals he seems to find necessary. 'As the archbishop of the diocese I would like to see, by what ever means are possible, the schools pursuing academic excellence under the guidance of warm-hearted, clear-headed, Christian educators.' He is a very Anglican bishop. He talks about 'a culture of expectation' rather than laying down quali-fications, 'in black letter law'. He doesn't like the sound of those parish testimonials. He knows there are those in the diocese who would fear a factional backlash if they had to flag their parish in writing. But he concedes that synod must do more to give the schools the professional councillors they require. And they should be professionals: 'I find it hard to think that anyone would take exception to the fact that school councils ought to have people with experience.' He wants women and men who have expe-rience in 'accounting, law, someone who knows a bit about schools, people who are generally able to run large organisations. And I think it's good to have some clergy there, you know, to take particular note of that order of the school's life.'

Goodhew says he's never seen any figures that suggest 'in any way at all' that schools employing only Christian teachers produce more Christians. He suspects it's not good for a school to be staffed entirely by 'Christians of that very active kind . . . I have heard some people express the view that a few staff members who don't necessarily dot i's and cross t's keep the rest of the staff honest.' But school principals *must* be Christians. Goodhew talks of men and women of Christian conviction whose faith lies: 'within the structures of Anglican — and hopefully Anglican evangelical — expression, and that it's a living thing and not just a historical faith, and that it's blended with a high level of educational competence — someone who can run a school and someone who, respecting the individuality of the youngsters who come through the school, seeks to expose them to the fact and expression of the Christian faith and help them when they wish to respond to do so. Now people like that come in different shapes and sizes . . .'

Has Abbotsleigh appointed one of them? 'I support the efforts of the principal of Abbotsleigh in every way I possibly can.' But is that an answer? 'I presume that the question is asking whether I agree with some people who feel that the current headmistress is not necessarily a good choice?' The archbishop pauses. 'The council has made its choice and I think the current principal is well motivated to be as helpful in the area of Christian things of the school as she possibly can be.'

Goodhew can't force his views on the diocese. He can veto a synod decision, but such a veto has been exercised only rarely and over 'very substantial matters'. The archbishop does not rate the schools issue one of those great issues where he might block the wishes of his synod. 'There is a lot of water to go under the bridge. A lot of water.'

We spoke on an afternoon in the summer of 1998 and the story I wrote about the Jensen forces appeared a few weeks later. It was the middle of speech-day season, that time of year when parents turn out to watch their kids collect prizes. Prayers are said and hymns are sung and principals deliver flattering endorsements of their own fine efforts to produce young men and women fit to face the world — this world. When you're talking to parents who sign the cheques you emphasise this world over the next. But there's talk of Salvation, too, which parents let drift by as they always have, the small Christian price to be paid for having kids at these schools.

At that point the hopes of the radical reformers had never stood higher. But there was urgent talk at those speech days. Parents spoke to councils. Councils spoke to synod. Instead of the lawyers sitting down to draft the new regulations for the consideration of the schools, the issue was sent back for reconsideration. Over the next six months the Jensen agenda was cut back hard. Ditched were those parish testimonials and the fears they raised of doctrinal witchhunts. Instead it was decided all lay men and women on the councils — the mothers, fathers, accountants, judges, architects, stock brokers, etc. — must put their signatures to a binding declaration of faith. But what should they sign? The Apostles Creed was the obvious contender but the radicals were unhappy with the creed alone. It says a great deal about the forces inside the Anglican church that the creed which has defined the Christian faith for a couple of millennia wasn't considered — enough. Two more propositions are to be added for signature. 'In particular I believe (a) there is only one way to God which is through his Son, Jesus Christ, who died for us the death that everyone deserves; and (b) that God's word, the Bible, is the one final authority in all matters of faith and conduct.'

It goes without saying that the fundamentalists will keep on pushing for more. When eternity is at stake the delay of a few years is nothing. And it hardly needs to be said that the pledge now going round for signature has absolutely nothing to do with education.

TWELVE

SHAME AND
FORGIVENESS

'I am a 26-year-old male and have been in Courage for one year and eight months . . . My prayer life has improved. I worry less. My chronic masturbating habit has decreased some.'

Barry

I was fourteen, standing on the deck of the ferry wearing a snazzy pair of white pants, as it chugged across Port Hacking towards Camp Howard. What I couldn't admit to myself then is what I most vividly remember now: the erotic charge in the air. It was frightening and compelling. That week of messing about in the bush, swimming in deserted bays, sleeping out and listening to the Word, was suffused with the promise of sex. Nothing happened but a lot happened. Some of it was ludicrous. One night in the dining hall we were given a sex education lecture. The slides weren't of men and women, but chooks. I remember still a cross-section of tubes and eggs and dislocated talk of reproduction as that hen glowed on the screen.

Afterwards over cocoa — here's the point — a serious, handsome young man spoke intimately to a dozen or so of us about committing ourselves to Christ. I was deeply drawn to the idea of a man who could love me knowing all my faults, indeed who could love me *for* my faults, even for the worst of them. One day I would need to be saved but Judgement Day seemed a long way off in 1961. On that night and at that moment I needed to fall in love and here was this counsellor — a radio sports commentator in later life — telling me there was a man available: Christ. By a miracle which seemed obvious then, Christ would satisfy me and cure me and protect me from the worst fears I held for myself. I didn't have the courage to come forward over cocoa. Two did. I piked. But as I walked back to the tent I shared with half a dozen other boys on the edge of the bush, it struck me that I had committed myself at that moment to Christ. The future would be different now, pure, thrilling and safe.

The school chaplain had already been pursuing my soul for years, hammering on about sin and salvation. Three times a week we assembled in the chapel to be taught the only lesson Anglican schools in Sydney teach thoroughly: the need for all of us awful human beings to be forgiven. I wasn't convinced. There didn't seem anything worth forgiving, until sex came along. Uneasiness at thirteen was turning to shame at fourteen. This was the raw material I took across the water to Camp Howard. I couldn't have been the only one. We were there to be recruited and the counsellors knew what they were doing, setting us free in that stretch of bush and talking sin at the same time. They challenged us to take Christ into our hearts but that first required deep acknowledgement of shame. First shame and then forgiveness. That's their business.

You don't have to be a young queer for this to work. There's a trace of self-disgust in most of us that can be worked up into shame, especially in those most difficult, precious years when we are on the threshold of sexuality. But a young homosexual is particularly easy pickings, fearful of himself, his family and the disapproval of his world. Christ offers a gay kid consummation of a kind, strength to resist sin, the minor heroics of teenage self-sacrifice, and a chance — important for children living day to day with an undertow of shame — to do good. That was the Christ I took into my life at the age of fourteen. It was a kind of falling in love, tepid by comparison with the real thing when that came along, but it was love nevertheless. What followed were a dozen wasted and painful years. I wasn't very brave. My circumstances weren't desperate and I got out the other side with most of myself intact. But it's left me unable to forgive those Christians who are still at work, inflicting misery on kids.

At puberty the churches reach out to us with their ministry of shame. The timing is everything. These years of doubt and confusion are the best chance they'll ever have of winning us over. Religious zealots are keen to get control of church schools essentially to be on hand in these crucial years. The message they bring could hardly be more familiar or less welcome. It's the message Christians have been working on since the first evangelists for chastity headed out into the Roman Empire — sex is intrinsically shameful. This isn't easy to cope with whether you're growing up straight or gay. It's bleak if you're a girl. Deep down in this Christian ministry is still the suspicion that women are to blame — for shame, for sin, for our expulsion from Paradise. They can make up for it by being mothers. Gay men and lesbians have no way to make good except, officially, to forsake intercourse altogether. This calculus of shame comes mixed with a great deal of admirable ethical baggage. But it is perverse, needless and cruel. Such refined cruelty.

Where does shame come from? I look back to my

childhood and can't remember anything being said. My parents had no idea what was happening. Children like me were bred in other suburbs to other families. Homosexuality was a vice too dark for the Anglican Church to detail. All I heard from the pulpit were grim hints. I knew it was a serious crime and the afternoon papers had stories of disgraced men caught in lavatories. The only instruction my school ever gave me came when I was seventeen and the senior year was in the assembly hall for a talk by the school doctor. It wasn't much of an advance on cross-sections of chooks. 'You can tell a homosexual,' he said and by my calculation about a dozen boys must, like me, have frozen with curiosity and terror. 'You can tell them by the decor of their flats.'

Though this advice has not been entirely useless . . .

Silence was the most potent source of shame in my childhood. Preachers like Fred Nile claim Christians have the right to keep their children 'wrapped in cotton wool' and campaign for the state to collaborate in that. For years I used to scoff at the pointlessness of trying to keep the young innocent in this way. My answer to the Fred Niles was that, try as they might, our subversive bodies will always tell us the truth. But I was missing the point. What censorship is really designed to achieve is the sort of silence that turns what our bodies tell us into shame. This calls for more than censorship of books and films. It also needs the censorship of learning. Those many Christians who still oppose sex education, use the rhetoric of intimacy, innocence and faith. What they're fundamentally about is cultivating shame.

Silence is breaking down. For eight centuries no one

stood up in public to say that Christian demonising of homosexuals was nonsense. But then came Kinsey, Wolfenden, the 'sixties, Stonewall, Gay Liberation, the drowning of George Duncan in the Torrens and the vicious police response to Sydney's first Mardi Gras. Christians had to watch as ordinary human beings stood up and said: I am gay, I am lesbian, I am one of these. The invisible had become visible. Suddenly, in the third quarter of the twentieth century, Christendom was caught up in a public debate that the forces of silence and shame had postponed for the eight centuries since the rules against homosexuality were set in concrete by the Third Lateran Council. Most faiths were entirely unprepared for this turn of events. Some were open to new definitions of what mattered in Christian sexual morality. The rest dug in their heels.

In 1975 the Catholic Church issued a conciliatory statement about homosexuality. Three years later Karol Wojtyla became John Paul II. Soon the Congregation of the Doctrine of Faith was working on a corrective letter to the bishops which appeared in 1986, complaining of a 'grave' crisis brought on by 'an overly benign interpretation' being given to church teaching. The letter reminded Catholics that homosexuality remains an especially grave sin. Like all Christians, Catholics are careful to say they distinguish between the sin and the sinner, but in the case of homosexuality the Catholic Church declared even celibate unsinning homosexuals are 'disordered' creatures with a perpetual tendency towards 'intrinsic moral evil'. The sin is lodged in the sinner for life. Absolute sexual abstinence is the church's fundamental rule for homosexuals. They must be as celibate as priests. If they fail, they threaten the 'lives and wellbeing' of themselves and others on earth and deny themselves a chance of Everlasting Life.

Everywhere in the churches, there are men and women who reject this bigotry. But it remains the official teaching of Catholicism and the dogma — in rather different language — of most branches of Anglicanism and most of the little Calvinist churches which regard homosexuality as striking evidence of mankind's sinfulness. In Australia churches have privileged exemptions from anti-discrimination and anti-vilification laws to go on promoting these views. Distaste for homosexuality is a widely held view in the community, but the churches are the *only* bodies left in Australia cultivating and endorsing that attitude. They say they only hate the sin, but that's a theological distinction we're not good at grasping in the real world. You don't often hear it said that we love murderers, love embezzlers, love rapists while hating only their sins. Human beings have a way of personalising these things, and the churches have been around long enough to know that. If we're taught to hate the sin, we'll come to hate the sinner.

It began to be argued a couple of decades ago that time and good sense would see disapproval of homo- sexuality wither away in the churches, that they would drop it just as they managed to ditch support, say, for slavery after centuries of finding excuses for the trade in the Bible and Christian tradition. But that hasn't happened for homosexuality, because the core business of churches is sin and you don't lightly give up a burn-in-hell-forever sin. Between now and eternity there's a lot of shame to be provoked and forgiveness to be measured out to the sinners of the church. When Archbishop George Pell talks about reviving traditional and fundamental values, the cardinal value he's talking about is shame. Pell is always instructive in these matters. When he chastises the church for being afraid to give 'the hard teachings of Christ', he observes that softness pleases onlookers, 'but it doesn't win converts'.

Those who attack Pell as a dinosaur and a bully, flinch from the fact that the Pope's man in Australia is in touch with a truth as old as the church: that shame is a great recruiter. The challenge for men like Pell in this secular age is to make shame work. We know too much for silence to operate as smoothly as it once did. What once seeped silently into kids' souls is now a matter of vicious playground abuse. This is the age of AIDS. Homophobic harassment is turning the school days of kids like me who were once all but invisible into playground purgatory. Even in tolerant Australia, kids are dying. For the church to be preaching against homosexuality — the sin, of course, but not the sinner — is risky. For big figures in the church like Pell to be revving up the rhetoric of denunciation is daring. At stake is more than packing the pews with the faithful coming back and back for forgiveness. There's also the question of vocations.

If the clergy I met while I was a keen young Christian had been a more inspiring lot, I might have joined them. I was a shame-driven kid hungry for a spiritual life but all I heard were Sydney Anglicans, hammering out their formula for salvation. Even so, I thought a lot about joining the church in the year or so after Camp Howard. My reasons were muddled, but strong in the confusion was a sense that the church might be somewhere to shelter while I set myself right. It would be a respected response to my troubles. A cover and cure. But I knew so little of what service to a church might mean, that all I saw was a prospect of Anglican boredom for the rest of my life. My vocation was stillborn.

Talking to priests and ex-priests, trying to puzzle out why men commit their lives to religion, I heard over and again the familiar note of gay shame. Often it was hidden or deeply disguised at the time it was doing its work. Nor did their shame entirely explain how these gay men came to feel they had this vocation. But it was so often there. Anthony's experience fits the pattern perfectly. He was a kid in a country town in the seventies who didn't know he was gay. 'There was no name for it, there was no name, but you knew it was wrong.' From the age of twelve or thirteen he was strongly attracted to the idea of being a priest. At boarding school he was 'a pious prick' and now he knows those hours spent praying and reading hagiographies was him 'wanting to get away' from his sexuality. He decided to join the Jesuits. The decision was powerfully reinforced by, 'This very strong desire to cloak myself with this aura of goodness, this vow of goodness, as a way of hiding who I really am from myself and from everyone else around me as well'.

At first glance it seems an incongruous way of dealing with vilification, to join the church of the vilifiers. But that's the beauty of shame. It drives you inwards towards the pain because somewhere in there is also the promise of relief. The churches offer pain and shame, but provide the mechanism of forgiveness and relief. Catholicism differs from other churches only in offering guilty young men the supreme reassurance of celibacy. For those who fear their sexuality, that vow of abstinence for life looms like a bulwark against temptation. Mark Jordan wrote in *The Invention of Sodomy in Christian Theology*, 'The closet, far from being a construction of the present century, is a very old ecclesiastical dwelling place'.

Richard Sipe, a former monk, has written a couple of studies of celibacy that the Catholic Church takes seriously. After counselling priests in America for twenty or so years he estimates that 30 per cent of them have 'a homosexual orientation' and that without these men 'the church as we know it would cease to exist'. He argues that being homosexual can bind them to their vocation. 'As one priest put it, "The church demands celibacy of homosexuals anyway. If I'm homosexual and I have to be celibate, I might as well be a priest and be useful." Therefore, to maintain equilibrium, these men reason that prayer, humility, and reasonable vigilance of their lifestyle will keep them safe and save their souls.' These homosexual priests, Sipe concludes, are neither more nor less likely than heterosexual priests to hold to their vows. 'Roughly 50 per cent of homosexually oriented priests are celibate just as are the heterosexually oriented.'

That instinct to be useful is a key to many lesbian and gay lives. It helps explain the large number of teachers, nurses, social workers, nuns and priests who are homosexual. Something predisposes gay men and women to service. For some it's personal experience of suffering.

For some it's the shadow of shame working subtly in their lives, urging them to prove they are better people than their detractors claim. But there is also in gay lives a particular hunger for what the church calls transcendence: an urge to reach beyond the ordinary, to find the spiritual behind the physical. This isn't, of course, the prerogative of homosexuals but Janiene Wilson, a psychotherapist who works in a Sydney seminary, cautioned me to look beyond shame to transcendence as a way of understanding why so many gay men join the priesthood. 'There is a wound that comes with being homosexual that can be a source for longing for transcendence. If you find yourself as a person unacceptable, it can be a point of conversion.' She confirms that Sipe's findings on homosexuality are relevant to the Australian context.

Anthony was one of a dozen ex-Jesuits who spoke to Peter May — himself a former Jesuit — about their reasons for joining and leaving the order. For many of them — gay and straight — sexual denial, ignorance or inexperience was involved in their decision to join. Anthony only worked this out later. Jonathan discovered he'd joined the order in a kind of lingering pre-adolescent state. Daniel knew he was gay and joining was both 'a way of hiding from it' and finding security in a life where 'no sexual demands are placed on you'. Geoff eventually found he was straight but suspected the fear of being gay was one reason he'd committed himself to the priesthood. 'Was it shame and was it running away?' Some left the order reluctantly, but the rest were unwilling to live with the compromises that Richard Sipe's research reveals are the everyday reality of careers in a celibate church. 'You may think you put on this cloak of goodness, but you don't cover anything from yourself,' said Anthony. 'You may for a short time but it's going to come up again and you're putting the lid on the volcano. It will be all right for a while, then the pressure will build and it will burst. Put the lid on again, same process.'

The heroic prestige of celibacy has been shattered in the last decade with revelations of sexual abuse by priests, particularly their abuse of children. The damage done to those kids is incalculable. But there is collateral damage to society, too, from this priestly fetish for abstinence. These men, doing daily battle with human nature itself, are privileged commentators on the morals of the whole community. What celibates fear most, they condemn most harshly. The asceticism of the seminary becomes an official ideal for the community. So film and television and videos and books and magazines are condemned as if we were all locked in their do-or-die battle to stay chaste. With their own broken bodies they worship the broken body on the Cross. To insist that sex can only take place in marriage puts a second perimeter of barbed wire between priests and temptation. Over the centuries, no one has suffered more from these hothouse fears than women. But homosexual men have had a rough deal, too, for exactly the same reason: Christian men looking their way and struggling unhappily with desire. The particular mark of the Catholic Church is to try to inflict on society the double whammy of priestly fears: sex as a hazard both for our souls and their vocations.

George Pell stood at the west door of St Patrick's in full rig after another dramatic Pentecost. The archbishop loves the pomp of great cathedral occasions. For Pentecost 1999 this ecclesiastical showman had enlisted two or three dozen choristers and a squad of priests to join him in full regalia for the Mass. He'd also hired security guards. The archbishop had been informed — by letter and through the pages of the Melbourne *Age* — that rainbow-sashed homosexuals and their supporters would again be presenting themselves for communion. At Pentecost 1998 he'd denounced this 'ideological demonstration during Mass' and been loudly applauded by the faithful. This year he'd held his peace but once again in the sight of the press and the face of the St Patrick's congregation, Pell denied communion to fifty Catholics claiming their place at the Eucharist: gay men, their supporters, their friends and their mothers.

The denial was inevitable. They all knew that. What was happening here was a deliberate set-piece with advantages for both sides. The archbishop could show himself once more to be a fearless upholder of the church's traditional teaching, while the protesters could make the public hear what carnage those teachings can cause. As the rainbow-sash spokesman Michael Kelly wrote that Saturday in the *Age*, 'I think of Catholic kids trying to sort out their sexuality, of gay people who've suffered breakdowns or committed suicide, of all who've had their hearts broken by the church.'

At the first little demo in St Patrick's in 1997, one of the rainbow-sash demonstrators accused the church of contributing to the nation's 'appalling' suicide rate. 'I comment as someone who only narrowly escaped suicide during years of self-torture.' This was a few weeks after the death of James Anderson, a 19-year-old student who had been brutally vilified at his Catholic school in Melbourne. Among the 60 or 70 refused communion at Pentecost the following year was Anderson's mother. The details of the boy's ordeal as Michael Kelly set them out in the *Age*, are terrible but not exceptional. 'He was verbally abused and physically accosted on his way to school; he had rubbish thrown at him; threats of bashing were commonplace; human faeces were left on his door-step; abusive phone calls were made to his home. One day an entire class stood up and moved to the other side of the room when he entered — a full battery of teenage intimidation techniques was brought to bear. One of James's friends says a group of boys forced him to do sexual things for them, claiming that as he was gay he would enjoy it. In the face of this abuse most of James's close friends deserted him.' Teachers later said they saw and heard nothing of this. 'How could they not have known?' asked the boy's mother. 'I sent my children to Catholic schools so they'd be loved and nurtured and cared for. How could they let this happen?'

At Pentecost 1999, a few minutes before Pell appeared in scarlet at the west door of his cathedral, a wreath and a photograph were laid by the church railing in memory of young Australians who, said Kelly, have suicided or attempted suicide because of 'homophobia in church schools'. The cameras and reporters recording this little ceremony then saw Pell appear still in his robes and rather to their surprise found him willing to answer questions.

'I am enormously troubled by the number of youth

suicides in Australia,' he said. 'I haven't got good statistics on the reasons for those suicides. If they are connected with homosexuality it is another reason to be discouraging people going in that direction. Homosexual activity is a much greater health hazard than smoking. We all agree that we don't encourage smoking and very obviously the church does not encourage this style of life. We respect all people, but don't encourage and never will condone that sort of activity.' Pell added, 'We will do nothing to allow the spread of the gay agenda in Catholic schools. We will do everything we can to oppose it.'

Correctives rained down on the archbishop. Anne Jones, executive director of Action on Smoking told the papers, 'Smoking has killed more people than breast cancer, car accidents, AIDS, suicides, murders, falls and burns combined'. Joseph O'Reilly, president of the AIDS Council of Victoria, reminded Pell it was not homosexuality but unsafe sexual practices that transmitted disease. 'The most significant hazard for gay men and lesbians is the sort of prejudice, misinformation and ill feeling peddled by so-called community leaders.' Professor Bruce Tonge was heard on the 3LO news saying Pell's remarks were not helpful and may contribute to young men thinking their lives not worth living.

Pell pedalled hard over the next few days. More dangerous than smoking? 'One sexual encounter can cause AIDS, while one has to smoke for a long time for cancer to develop.' The gay agenda? Recruiting new members to the subculture, same-sex marriage, adoption rights, rejection of Biblical teaching, lowering the age of consent, government-subsidised IVF and avoiding 'the real reason' for youth suicide by laying the blame, 'anywhere except in the homosexual community'.

Pell's staff made an effort rather after the event to get some facts on youth suicide. Pell's secretary Michael Casey rang Tonge because of his comments on 3LO. Tonge is professor of Psychological Medicine at Monash University and a member of the Victorian Task Force on Suicide Prevention. Tonge explained the work of the Task Force and the state of scientific knowledge about gay youth suicide.

Suicide in general is one of the commonest causes of death in young Australians. We don't have the figures to tell whether young homosexuals are particularly vulnerable — coroners usually don't know and don't record the sexuality of victims — but everywhere the Task Force went, gay men spoke of problems with suicide. Harrowing accounts were heard of persecution, margin-alisation and abuse, particularly in the bush. Tonge explained to Casey that while the causes of suicide aren't known, there are three clear risk factors: having tried once already, being male and being depressed. For gay adolescents, a crucial cause of depression is the loss of self-esteem brought on by feeling rejected by family and community. American studies argue that young gay men are particularly vulnerable to such feelings as they develop their sexual identity. What we know about suicide suggests, therefore, that young gay men are especially at risk. Tonge concluded that key figures like Pell who have the capacity to form public opinion should be very careful not to excite further community hostility to young homosexuals.

Tonge heard nothing further from the archbishop.

How widely Pell consulted after the Pentecost 1999 remarks isn't known. But Pell might have benefited from discussions with psychologists, counsellors and teachers who know something of the reality of homophobia in Australian schools, especially as the Archbishop of Melbourne is responsible through Catholic schools for the education of about a third of that city's kids.

Pell could find it useful to read *Writing Themselves In* and talk to one of its authors, Lynne Hillier. He would find somewhere between 8 and 11 per cent of all young people in Australia are attracted — not always exclusively — to their own sex. The 750 'not unequivocally heterosexual' kids who took part in this discreet survey reported high levels of verbal and physical abuse, which was worst at school and very often didn't end when teachers discovered what was going on. Thirty of the kids volunteered they'd considered suicide. 'Verbal and physical abuse had a profound effect on these young people. It affected their feelings of safety at home and at school and was related to the use of drugs and reduction in their sense of wellbeing.' Things are tough enough for kids attracted to their own sex at state schools where there's an official syllabus of silence and an unofficial syllabus of abuse. Things are far tougher for boys in single-sex religious schools, particularly Catholic schools where the unofficial syllabus is still abuse but the official syllabus, instead of being silent, is negative. But they are not the worst off. Those having the roughest time of all living with their sexuality tend to come from Pentecostal and Evangelical families. Tough Christian homes, it seems, can be more terrifying than tough Christian schools.

But in ways unimaginable a decade or so ago, parents are now threatening to sue schools if they fail to protect their gay or lesbian kids from abuse. These children are 'out' to the parents and the parents are supporting them in the face of harassment at school. This is putting Catholic boys' schools, especially, in a very difficult bind. While condemning harrassment, the schools operate under a general direction not to 'promote' homosexuality and they continue to teach that it is an 'intrinsic disorder'. This encourages teachers to hang back from schoolyard violence, justifies the refusal to alert kids to homophobia — while teaching the dangers of racism and sexism as part of the syllabus — allows counsellors to avoid difficult issues of adolescent sexuality, and restricts school libraries from stocking basic information on the subject. *Writing Themselves In* showed most straight kids learn most of what they trust about relationships and sex from their schools backed by their parents, while gay students learn almost nothing from schools, less from their parents and have to glean what unreliable information they can from television and magazines.

As always in the Catholic Church there's a schism between dogma and what's really happening on the ground. Girls being taught by feisty nuns who operate outside the authority of the bishops have very little to worry about. And the more affluent and articulate the parents of both boys and girls, the less likely the school is to be sticking absolutely to the church line. But out in the suburbs and out in the bush, school days can seem brutish and long for kids whom God has dealt the same-sex card.

I asked the sociologist Maria Pallotta-Chiarolli who has been working for years in Catholic schools in Adelaide and Melbourne and written several books on adolescent sexuality, what impact religion has on the capacity of young people to cope when they realise they're turning into those abused figures, dykes and poofters? 'The reaction is either damn the church or depression and heartache.' Yet even those boys who stick with religion don't see themselves staying celibate for life as the church demands. 'They may feel deep down there is something wrong about themselves but that they have to live their life and hope to find a corner of the church where that's possible.' Many tell her of contemplating suicide.

Archbishop Pell's efforts are concentrated at the moment on a new religious studies syllabus which has copped flak inside and outside the church for wanting to take children back to a world of dogma and tradition that Catholicism elsewhere is leaving behind. Shame is an important element in the syllabus. There is to be a strong emphasis on the fall of Adam and Eve. A study topic for six year olds will be: 'Our first parents learnt to sin.'

At some point after Camp Howard I made a solemn pact that by the time I left school for university I would stop feeling this way. I devised a number of spiritual exercises to make certain. These included prayer, daily Bible reading, eating, staying clear of the beach and not letting thoughts of men come into my mind when I wanked. Keeping a blank mind while masturbating seemed a significant moral achievement. There was one image I had trouble keeping out: Johnny M. diving into a creek at cadet camp. His body hung in the air for a moment, naked and beautiful, before it hit the water. That split second has lasted forever, of course, but back then I thought I could lock it away with all my other troubles and contradictions, each in their separate cell. I suppose the idea was to turn myself into a prison, a sort of Pentridge for inappropriate emotions, then throw away the key and walk into university a free man.

I invested a decade of my life in the pursuit of a profound, sincere, determined and hopeless ambition not to be homosexual. It's an ordinary story with an ordinary ending. Christ failed me. So did alcohol. So did marriage. Whatever damage I did to myself along the way, I did worse to others I loved. Eventually the price of heaven proved too high and in my late twenties, with all these wasted years on my conscience, I set about doing what I might have done in my teens but for that problematic encounter with Christ over hot cocoa — I began to try to live as myself.

So I read Archbishop Pell's advice for saving gay kids from suicide with particular interest. He told the press at the west door of his church that if suicides are linked to homosexuality, 'it is another reason to be discouraging people going in that direction'. For a growing band of Christians like Pell it is an article of faith that sexuality is a matter of choice, something that can be manoeuvred with a little encouragement and discouragement. When Pell was explaining himself in the *Age* a few days after this encounter, he birched the homosexual community for not accepting some responsibility for young deaths. Doesn't the 'homosexual agenda' include recruitment of 'new members to the subculture'? Aren't they also to blame for the suffering that follows? 'Even young men have an intellect and will and are free to choose, to make themselves.'

In the real world of real lives, wrong choice doesn't explain homosexuality. But men like Pell have an urgent doctrinal need to argue against the best clinical evidence of the century that says once sexuality is formed it's fixed. Gay men and women in the church are asking why God would make them fully sexual beings and expect them to live without sex. The hardline Christian answer is to assert — not for the first time in the history of Christendom — that as a matter of faith the scientists must be wrong. 'Despite Freud,' says Pell, 'all Christians believe that each human person has a rational intellect and a free will, rather than being "a jungle chaos of hidden emotions and inner conflicts with an irrational character". We are free, in different measures, to build slowly an integrated personality, without gross contradictions.' We can choose chastity and we may work our way towards heterosexuality, but we can never choose to have sex with our own sex. What's at stake here is the whole authority of Rome on questions of sex and marriage. If dykes and poofters are allowed to fuck, the edifice of Christian teaching on sexuality crashes to the ground. Sex without the chance of procreation has been forbidden since Clement of Alexandria in the third century set the church and Western society down the strange path of demonising all sex unless its purpose is breeding. That's still Rome's fundamental attitude today. Gay men and women — particularly young gay kids — are the innocent casualties of a theological mistake.

The doctrine of choice has a bleak political side. All the laws designed to protect school kids from 'recruitment', and all the laws that forbid 'promotion' of homosexuality have their Christian origins in this idea that human sexual orientation can shift and change by choice. The cruelties involved are far-reaching and subtle. Kids need role models, but some of the most vulnerable kids in our society are denied the reassurance of knowing that the ordinary men and women who teach them metalwork and French are gay and living useful lives. They must hide their sexuality for fear of being accused of recruiting and promoting. That fear makes most of them ineffective in schools where homophobic harassment is rife. High ages of consent for homosexuals are justified on the clinically unsustainable view that young men might choose differently if they had a little more time. Lives are chewed up here, and lives are lost when Christians effectively oppose safe-sex campaigns because candid warnings 'promote' homo-sexuality. If there is an afterlife, I trust these Christians will find reserved for them a particularly uncomfortable circle of hell.

Out of America have appeared a handful of organisations dedicated to the theology of choice. These are now a force in American politics where millions are spent each year by Christian ministries attacking laws and city ordinances that make life safer or fairer for homosexuals. The message is that gay men and women have a choice: they don't need 'privileges' to go on living lives of sin, they can walk away and leave homosexuality behind them. Exodus International survived embarrassing sexual lapses by its leaders to become a powerful lobby in half a dozen countries and the most active of these rescue organisations in Australia. Exodus is hardline. Celibacy isn't enough. All Exodus members define themselves as 'ex-gay': their love has turned right around making them ready for marriage and children.

Catholics have Courage which began in New York in the early eighties as a chastity support group for devout gay men. It's very much the Pope's idea of the right sort of ministry to homosexuals. North America has lately become a battleground in which John Paul II is entangled in campaigns to discipline priests, nuns and bishops who minister far more sympathetically to gay and lesbian believers. The internal church politics of these campaigns are more than ordinarily vicious and have become unusually public. The great miracle of Catholicism — public obedience to John Paul II — is beginning to fail in the affluent white dioceses of North America. Most recently the Pope has silenced Father Robert Nugent and Sister Jeannine Gramick, a well-known team working for the past two decades with gay and lesbian communities. But Courage has His Holiness's backing. After a decade of assisting chastity through programs of prayer, reflection and frequent attendance at Mass, the movement has become more ambitious and now offers a program of 'reparative growth' for men and women wanting 'to leave behind not only the homosexual lifestyle but also the very feelings of same-sex attraction'.

Pell is a great supporter of Courage and celebrated mass at a three-day conference in Melbourne in late 1998 at which the movement's founder, Father John Harvey, was the star attraction. Courage boasts they have Pell's 'complete support' and the program of prayer, sacraments and ascetic discipline is very much in Pell's style. As the best evidence of its own success, Courage publishes testimonials and distributes tapes so tragic, so meagre they make it seem impossible Christ would want human beings to go through so much pain for so little.

Tom fought sex by visiting the Blessed Sacrament every day. He once went 39 days straight then fell and gave his life 'to Satan' for eleven years. Now through Courage he can share his 'pain and shame'. He has stabilised his life. Father Ralph has managed through God's grace to stay celibate but became an alcoholic. Courage gives him the support he needs to be chaste. 'It is still a struggle, but one I look forward to.' Paul was hoping to be a priest but was going to bars, reading porn and masturbating. Since finding Courage his 'destructive behaviour' has lessened. 'And when I do fall, I get up quickly — I don't despair.' Richard couldn't understand 'how God could harness me with the affliction of homo-sexual feelings' but now he no longer prays for removal of adversity, only 'the patience, strength and wisdom to deal with it'. Courage helped Andy turn his back on 'pseudo-scientists and supposedly compassionate priests' who told him to stop fighting his feelings. Barry's prayer life has improved and he's not masturbating as much any more. Greg has discovered that losing his family allowed him to love God more while 'suffering from attention deficit disorder became an opportunity to surrender my mind to the Lord'.

Courage is still in its early days in Australia, but a Courage breakfast at the Greek Club in inner Brisbane in

September 1998, heard the story of a 28-year-old, Catholic-raised, junkie transsexual who found God while doing time in a Queensland maximum-security prison. 'He had an overnight conversion and cut off his shoulder-length hair. One of his pleasures during the year was the fact that he was able to grow his first beard ever! He spoke with conviction and obvious authenticity and presented us all with the knowledge that God is able to do far more than we can imagine or even hope for.'

I'd hope God had more important things to do. He could stop his churches inflicting shame on children. He could remind the faithful that love is still love when it comes in all its human variations. He might try to convince priests and pastors to honour the whole of His Creation, including the great gift of pleasure. While He is at it He could immeasurably help mankind by working some miracle that would rob Christianity of its magic to cloak the worst motives of our politicians. And He could write across the sky in letters that never fade the message we keep forgetting: that the virtue Christ loved most was love, and the vice he despised was hypocrisy.

But that isn't going to happen. All those years ago when my faith in an all-good and all-powerful God suddenly collapsed at university, I had yet to discover the best evidence of all for His non-existence: that bully churches survive and bigots flourish. I hadn't then come across the Magees and Watters and Niles and Jensens and Lucases and Pells of this world. There they stand like station masters on a platform crowded with faithful waiting to catch the 9.35 to the Afterlife. No sign of the train but there's a queue round the block for tickets. The price is high — a slice of the only life we know for rumours of a life to come — but looking down the road to where the queue turns out of sight, it seems there are still as many customers as ever.

NOTES

The High Price of Heaven began as a number of articles and speeches written by me since I returned to newspapers in late 1996. All of them have been chopped about, expanded and reworked for the book. In the course of doing this, I saw that I needed to give some sort of personal explanation for why this subject means so much to me. So I wrote the opening 'Confession' and the closing chapter 'Shame and forgiveness'.

Lots of wonderful Christians have been button-holed by me over the years. I need to thank them for what they taught me and for encouraging me to translate my rage into enquiry. I've come to wonder if there are any other institutions on earth which contain such a mix of wonderful and appalling human beings.

My thanks to those who allowed me to interview them on and off the record, to my colleagues at the *Sydney Morning Herald* who endlessly and patiently briefed me on religion, race, education and politics, to John Sharpe who as editor of the paper's Spectrum section was midwife to much of this material and to my editor at the *Herald*, Paul McGeough, who has been reasonably good humoured as the weeks I took off to put this collection together turned into months. At the head of each of the chapter notes I've tried to give more detailed thanks, but in the end these debts can never be properly acknowledged. Let this, therefore, be what John Howard would call a 'generic' expression of gratitude.

To my partner and to old friends who were my sounding boards, special thanks: to Sebastian Tesoriero, Nick Enright, Mary Vallentine and Richard Barrett, now in San Francisco. No book of mine is fit to print until Rae de Teliga reads the proofs and contests every lower case that should be upper case and vice versa. She's done it again — and taught me the crucial difference between the Sisters of Charity and those of Mercy. And again my thanks.

ABBREVIATIONS

HRH   House of Representatives *Hansard*
SH   Senate *Hansard*
SMH   *Sydney Morning Herald*

CONFESSION

Packer: 'the other side', *The Rise and Rise of Kerry Packer*, Paul Barry, Bantam, Sydney, 1993, p.ix.

ONE
LEAVING THEM TO DROWN

First published in an earlier version, 15 May 1999 in the *Good Weekend* magazine of the *Age* and the *SMH*, p.14. I relied very heavily here on help from my colleague at the *SMH,* Paula Totaro.

Interviews
Wayne Magee, Howard Moody, Brian Watters, Bill Crews, Bishop Patrick Power.

Other sources
Moody: 'consciously or unconsciously', sermon preached, New York, March 1990. The exchanges between Watters and Brunt over syringe bins on Ansett: ABC Radio National's *Religion Report*, 18 November 1998. Brunt's reproach about 'saving lives': Melbourne *Herald-Sun* 4 March 1999, p.12. Nile on 'illegal activity going on in the Wayside Chapel': *Australian* 6 May 1999, p.3. Pell on 'stiff model': *Age*, 1 June 1998, p.3. Pell gave the inaugural Acton Lecture on Religion and Freedom to the Centre for Independent Studies, 4 August 1999.

TWO
NO MORE THAN THEY DESERVE

First published in an earlier version, *SMH* 4 July 1998, p.1 and Spectrum p.1 Here I relied heavily on advice from and the contacts of my colleague at the *SMH*, Debra Jobson. I also had important help from Steven Webb of the Uniting Church and from the staff of the Uniting Church Archive.

Interviews

John Howard, Sir Alan Walker, Ian Viner, Gerard Henderson, Rick Farley, Lowitja O'Donoghue and many others.

Other sources

Sheperdson: *The Missionary Review* November 1955, p.11. Craig McGregor: *National Times* 14 March 1982, p.12. Howard: 'It is a question' *SMH* 6 October 1984. Howard's condemnation of the treaty: 'cruel trick' etc., *SMH* 7 September 1987, p.8. Keeping Australia one nation: 'legal fragmentation', 'equal dispensation of justice' and 'valuable bond', to me 2 July 1998. Attack on ATSIC: 'If there is one thing' *HRH* 11 April 1989, p.1332. Denial of racism: 'Whenever one disagrees with the minister' *HRH* 11 April 1989, p.1330. 'Land rights is fundamentally wrong': *Bulletin* 6 September 1988, p.159. Wooldridge: 'We found numerous' *SMH* 27 Oct 1993, p.8. Asian immigration: 'It would be' to Paul Murphy on ABC Radio's *PM*, 1 August 1988. Peacock: 'fairer . . . more compassionate' *SMH* 10 May 1989, p.4. Howard: 'I stuffed up on that' *SMH* 31 January 1995, p.4. Blainey: 'black armband' Latham lecture 1993, *Quadrant* July–August 1993. Howard: 'by contrast the apologists' *SMH* 7 January 1993, p.8. 'Aboriginal industry': to Alan Jones, Radio 2UE, 2 May 1997. Katter: 'enviro-nazis' *SMH* 15 February 1996, p.9. Barnett: 'Whatever the merits' *John Howard Prime Minister*, Viking, Sydney, 1997, p.718. Howard: 'I don't agree' to Alan Jones and *SMH* 16 November 1996, p.45. Bi-partisan motion on racial tolerance: *HRH*, 30 October 1996, p.6156. Uniting Church: 'in a loving way', Standing Committee of the Assembly of the Uniting Church, September 1996. Howard: 'national lunacy' *Australian*, 12 December 1987, p.3. Howard: 'the bloke who ultimately wins' *SMH* 3 February 1996, p.30. Regret resolution: 26 August 1999, *HRH* p. 7046.

THREE
ORDINARY MEN

Delivered 25 May 1999 in an earlier version as the third annual Freilich Lecture on Intolerance and Bigotry at the Humanities Research Centre, Australian National University. Other chunks of that lecture are now in Chapters Ten and Twelve. For help with the law, I'm grateful to David Buchanan SC and Tom Molomby. For information on Don

Gillies and Mudgee I'm indebted to Yvonne Bucknell, Doug Paisley and many others in Sydney and Mudgee. For setting me on the right track with the theology of the body I'm indebted to Morag Fraser who recommended Peter Brown's *The Body and Society* and Mark Jordan's *The Invention of Sodomy in Christian Theology*.

Sources

Kirby: 'Immediately after his arrival' Green v. The Queen, 148 ALR 659 at p.700. Sirola evidence: Green v. The Queen p.666. 'I'm not like this': Green v. The Queen p.665. Green: 'I hit him again and again' at Green v. The Queen p.667. Green: 'Just that when I tried to push' Green v. The Queen p.667. Priestley: 'It is easy to see that many' Green v. The Queen p.664. R. v. McKinnon: unreported NSW Supreme Court, Studdert J, 15–19 November 1993. R v. Turner: unreported NSW Supreme Court, Grove J, 6–11 April, 1994. R. v. Dunn: unreported NSW Supreme Court, Ireland J 21 September 1995. R. v. Richards: NSW Supreme Court, Sully J, 30 August 1996. Boswell: 'neither the Roman' etc. *Christianity, Social Tolerance and Homosexuality*, Chicago University Press, Chicago, 1980, p.73. St Paul: I Corinthians 7–9, and 1. Brown: 'strict codes' *The Body and Society*, Columbia University Press, New York, 1988, p.60. 'Suffer Excommunication': Boswell, p.277. Brennan: 'When you say amorous', transcript, p.36. McHugh: 'it is a sexual', transcript p.36. Kirby: 'not technically' transcript p.46. McHugh: 'been convicted' transcript p.46. Kirby: 'he or she might' 148 ALJ at 714. Gummow: 'would undermine' pp.694 and 696. Brennan: 'terrifying' etc. p.665. 'disappointing' etc.: Graeme Coss, 22 *Criminal Law Journal*, February 1998, p.8.

FOUR

SOLDIERS OF THE CROSS

Delivered 20 June 1999 in an earlier version as the MacPherson Lecture, Sydney Film Festival. I'm very grateful for the help of Dr George Hazell, Coordinator Heritage Preservation for the Salvation Army, and Pam Williams, the author of *The Victory*, Allen & Unwin, 1997.

Interviews

Hugh Mackay, George Hazell and others.

Sources

Booth: 'the magic power' *The Victory*, September 1901, p.443. Alston: 'extensive community, industry', press release, 26 April 1999. Alston: 'easier for pedophiles', *SMH*, 8 May 1999, p.4. Roy Morgan Research Poll: Eros Foundation Media Release, 18 April 1999. John Elliott: 'It's not looking' and 'Sieg Heil', *Age*, 15 March 1993, p.13. Mary Whitehouse: 'the men and women of Great Britain' *Film Censorship*, Guy Phelps, Victor Gollancz, London, 1975, p.196. Booth: 'I saw at a glance', 'the greatest thing' and 'as the film opens', *The War Cry*, 18 August 1900, p.9. *Aggressive Salvation*, by James Hay, published by Gordon Hay, 1951, p.63. Harradine: 'women in general as being highly promiscuous and available', some recent references in *SH* 29 April 1988, p. 2182; 10 May 1990, p.305; 2 March 1995, p.1234; 28 April 1999, p.107.

FIVE
HARRADINE

I published a first profile of Harradine in the *SMH*, 1 February 1997, Spectrum, p.1. Subsequently I reported the Wik debate in the Senate and the new profile draws especially on my reports for the *SMH* 3 December p.11 and 6 December p.2. Other bits and pieces I've written about the senator over the last couple of years are also incorporated in this new profile. Particularly vital help was given to me in Tasmania by Andrew Darby, the local correspondent for the *SMH* and *Age*, and my colleagues Alan Ramsey and Margo Kingston in Canberra and Debra Jopson in Sydney.

Interviews
Brian Harradine, Fr Adrian Doyle and many others.

Other sources
Harradine: 'The greatest foul-ups', address to the St Thomas More Society and Lawyers' Christian Fellowship Law Week Dinner, 11 May 1998. 'Happy to stay here till Christmas': *SH* 28 November 1997, p.9790. 'A lawyer's picnic': *SH* 5 December 1997, p.10539. 'I have been giving this further thought': *SH* 5 December 1997, p.10549. 'I don't know what': *SH* 5 December 1997, p.10551. 'A lot of biscuits': *SMH* 10 November 1993, p.13. 'My father': *SMH* 27 November 1997. 'I was able to convince': *SMH* 22 March 1969. 'She shielded Harradine': *Australian* 17 February 1993, p.7. On embryos: see also *SH* 8 October 1986, p.975. 'Ranks of greats': *Sunday Examiner*, 8 December 1996. 'The theme is the same': *SH* 1 April 1992, p.1501. 'Ignorant . . . hoodwink': *SH*, 1 April 1992, p.1506. *R Classified Programs on Pay TV*, ABA, November 1994. 'Free to take poison': *SH*, 9 November 1988, p.2320. 'Pornographers right to freedom': *SH* 22 Octoberr 1997, p.7793; also 6 April 1989, p.1131; 9 May 1996, p.593 etc. 'Censorship is the application': *SH*, 9 November 1988, p.2320. 'Absolutely beyond the pale': *SH*: 2 March 1995, p.1250.

'Lame, sham excuses': *SH*, 9 November 1988, p.2320. 'Commercial exploiters', 'to make a fast buck' and 'he is either': *SH*, 11 May 1999, p.4744. 'There are people so dogmatic': *SH*, 17 May 1983, p.472.

SIX

ALEXANDRA'S SCREAM

This is a marriage of an address given at the Harold Park Raceway, 22 May 1997 to the Joint Council for NSW Professional Teachers Association, and an account in *SMH*, 10 April 1999, p.35 of the campaign against Channel 10's 'Sex/Life'. Again, Andrew Darby in Hobart gave me crucial help.

Interviews
Prof. Kevin Durkin, John Avery, Dr William Wilkie, Tony Branigan and many others.

Other sources
'Children who are': *SMH*, 28 September 1992, The Guide, p.13. 'There is far too much violence': *Age*, 31 October 1992, p.12. 'Unless we adopt': *SH*, 17 June 1991, p.4740. 'One can imagine': *SH* 1 April 1992, p.1504. Durkin: *ABA Update*, No. 29, March 1995, pp. 18–21. *Herald-Sun* reports: 30 April 1996, p.1 and 3 May, p.4. 'Case studies demonstrate': Australian Family Association, submission p.7. Avery: 'Mr Bryant described', R. v. Bryant transcript, 20 November 1996, p.349. Bryant to Mullen: 'my power' *Age*, 21 November 1996, p.1. Alston's threats of intervention: Sydney *Sunday Telegraph*, 5 May, p.2. Inconclusive link between violence on the screen and in life: Senate Community Standards Committee 1997 report, *The Portrayal of Violence in the Electronic Media*, p.18, recommendations 4, 5, 7, 12, 13 and 14. Justice Morland and Bernadette McNeilly *SMH*, 27 November 1993, p. 1. Wilkie: *Courier Mail*, 24 April 1999, p.25. 'Not that offending': 26 November 1992, p.5. For community attitudes on sex on TV: see 'Summary of ABA Research Findings: community concerns about sex and nudity on TV, 1994–97', prepared 15 June 1998. Alston: 'Sodom & Gomorrah' *SH* 28 May 1998, p.3370. McAlpine: 'I think Senator Harradine' *SMH* 24 June 1998, p.3.

SEVEN

HEAVENLY WISDOM

This first appeared in an earlier version in *Good Weekend* magazine carried in the *Age* and *SMH* 20 December 1997, p.16 following a visit to Istanbul in October that year which involved discussions with museum and UNESCO officials, builders and scholars.

Sources
Sullivan: 'form ever', *Lippincott's Magazine*, March 1896. Procopius: 'overwhelming to those' and 'the mind is lifted up' quoted by Rowland J. Mainstone, *Hafia Sophia*, Thames and Hudson, London, 1988, p.10

EIGHT

A NIGHT OUT AT THE CROSS

First published in an earlier version, *SMH* 28 Feb 1998, Spectrum p.1. This drew on my 8 July 1978 reconstruction of the first Mardi Gras in the *National Times*, 8 July 1978. Material on the age of consent first appeared *SMH* 6 February 1999, p.9, but has since been developed in an effort to keep up to date as the politics of this continues to move. My guides to the early years were Craig Johnston, Lex Watson, Senator Brian Greig, Greg Weir, Rodney Croome, Stevie Clayton, and many others.

Interviews
Justice John Dowd, Frank Walker, Fr Edmund Campion, Ann Symonds, Nick Greiner, Barrie Unsworth, Chris Sidoti, Michael Egan, John Marsden, the Dean of Sydney Boak Jobbins, Monsignor John Walsh, Jan Burnswoods.

Other sources
'The noise of chanting': *National Times* 8 July 1978, p.8. Wran: 'These sort of things', Channel 10 evening news, 25 June 1978. Kinsey: 'more or less exclusively', Kinsey, Pomeroy and Martin, *Sexual Behaviour in the Human Male*, W.B.Saunders & Co, 1948, p.651. Freeman: 'completely unacceptable', *SMH* 30 September 1978, p.1. Ferguson: 'Labor governs NSW', information to me. Wran: 'If Gerry had a view' and 'he wasn't conservative on most matters', Michael Grealy, *Sun-Herald*, 29 May 1988, p.27. Unsworth: 'I believe there must' *Hansard*, NSW Legislative Council 18 February 1982, p.2081. *Times* 11 December 1981, p.2. 'A strong smell of sweat': 'Report under section 28 of the Police Regulation (Allegations of Misconduct) Act 1978/85, 22 September 1986' par. 5.4, p.23. Goulden: 'homosexual community': transcript of evidence to the 1983 Select Committee of the Legislative Assembly upon Prostitution, p.60. Patrick White: 'wave their handbags' quoted in Peter Blazey *Screw Loose*, Picador, Sydney, 1997, pp.224–5. Briese: 'an exceptionally serious', statement to the first

Senate Enquiry into the conduct of Lionel Murphy, *SMH* 6 October 1984, p.1. Wran: 'a squeaky voice', 'I'm just staggered' and 'this whole meeting' *SMH*, 7 April 1984, p.1. Clancy: 'all sins are not' *SMH* 11 May 1984, p.2. Uniting Church: 'all baptised Christians', 1987 Standing Committee minute 87.46. Wood: 'no reason to perpetuate', *Final Report of Royal Commission into the NSW Police Force*, vol. 5, *The Paedophile Inquiry*, Chapter 14, pars 14.32 and 33.

DISPATCHES FROM THE REPUBLIC OF SALO

This diary of censorship is compiled from a number of pieces published between late 1996 and late 1999. They've been revised for publication here. I relied very heavily on Rebecca Huntley's research and insight into the fate of *Salo* and on the work of Lauren Martin, Mike Seccombe and Jon Casimir, my colleagues at the *SMH*.

Interviews
Bill Symon, Fred Nile, Chris Hartcher, Norm Lipson, Jon Harker, Ray Chesterton, Michael Walsh, Judy Spence, Evan Williams, Fr Michael Elligate, David Haines, Julian McGauran, Dr Peter Bradhurst, Keith Connolly, Dymphna Austin-Perry and many others.

Other references
McGauran: 'I'm actually over the moon', *SMH* 19 Feb 1998, p.14. **December 1996** First version *SMH* 4 December, p.12. White: 'Worse things happen', transcript of evidence, R. v. Angus and Robertson, 10 February 1971, pp.162–6. Alston: 'a significant level', *Age*, 5 November 1996, p.1. 'Detailed instruction' etc.: *Guidelines for the Classification of Films and Videotapes* (Amendment No.2). Refused Classification: 'little bit of representative democracy', *SH* 2 March 1995, p.1246. 'Parents, teachers, churches, academics': recommendation 4, *Review of the Guidelines for Classification of Film and Video*, October 1996. McGauran: 'vile meeting the evil', *Age* 10 July 1993, p.16. **March 1997** First version *SMH* 8 March, p.3. 'One of the most famous cases': *Australian Hustler* February 1997, p. 10. 'lesser men might': p.10 **April 1997** First version *SMH* 5 April, p.33. Kramer: 'an excellent book' etc., 'Report of the Review Panel on HSC Texts'. **Early June 1997** First version *SMH* 13 May, p.13. Beanland: 'haste and power', press release 15 March 1997. Williams: 'it was not a task we relished' etc., *Australian* 21 May 1993, p.8. Goss: 'appalling trash' and 'composition of the Board of Review', to Qld Legislative Assembly, 14 April 1994, pp7537–8. McGauran: 'The defining moment' etc.,

interview with Rebecca Huntley, 28 April 1995. Dickie: 'wallowing in depravity' and 'refused classification', evidence to Senate Select Committee on Community Standards and Electronic Technologies, 27 November 1995. **Late June 1997** First version, *SMH* 27 June, p.15. Classification Board decision announced 25 June. Beanland: 'a mockery', press release 26 June 1997. **May 1998** First version, *SMH* 25 May, p.15. Read: 'We must await', *SH* 19 May 1994, p.868. 'Appear to be': wording introduced into Classification Guidelines, December 1996. McGauran: 'intellectual arty types', interviewed by Rebecca Huntley, 28 April 1995. 'I was unashamedly coding it': *Age* 7 March 98, p.10. McGauran: 'two hoots', *SMH* 19 February 1998, p.14. Barbara Biggins dissented very vigorously from my interpretation of the final decision in a letter to *SMH*, 29 May 1998, p.14. **June 1998** First version was my contribution to a seminar on 'Censorship Follies' at the Sydney Film Festival on 15 June 1998. **May 1999** First version, *SMH* 8 May 1999, p.3. **June 1999** First version, *SMH* 25 June 1999, p.3. Australian Broadcasting Corp. v. Hanson, in Qld Supreme Court, see *Herald-Sun* 29 September 1998, p.13.

TEN
THE SPIRES OF ST MARY'S

First appeared, *SMH* 31 July 1999, Spectrum, p.1, but this revision includes further material on the anti-discrimination laws prepared for the third annual Freilich Lecture on Intolerance and Bigotry. My colleague Chris McGillion, religious correspondent at the *SMH*, was of crucial help to me in writing this piece, as was the earlier work on Catholicism and politics in the *SMH* written by Milton Cockburn. Thanks also to Adele Horin who after publication alerted me to funding changes for Catholic schools, and this new version draws on her *SMH* piece, 'How Catholics Beat the School System', 15 May 1999, p.45. I also had help and advice from many others including Clive Lucas, Robert Marr, John Davey, Simon Banks and John McCarthy QC, whom I know disagrees profoundly with the conclusions I reach.

Interviews
Fr Brian Lucas, Dr Clive Bean, Fr Frank Brennan, Chris Puplick, Patrick Lee.

Other sources
Keating: 'God help you', *SMH*, 10 October 1992, p.22. Bean's figures: *SMH* 27 April 1996, p.6 explained and expanded in discussions with me. Chaney: 'I thought they were a bunch of shysters', *Discerning the*

Australian Social Conscience, Jesuit Publications, 1999, p. 228–9. Tannock: 'undermined the integrity', *SMH* 15 May 1999, p.45. Doumani: 'guilt trip', *SMH* 4 September 1999, p.3. Robb: 'remove the barriers', *SMH* 27 April 1996, p.6. Catholic Social Welfare Commission decision on GST: *Commonwealth for Common Power*, September 1992. Pell: 'no one Catholic position' *SMH* 25 August 1998, p.15. Harradine: 'I cannot', *SH* 14 May 1999, p.5117. McCarthy: 'in a position of formal co-operation', State Personal Carer's Leave Case, IRC 2 of 1996, transcript, 21 July 1998, p.132. 'It is deplorable': *Pastoral Care of Homosexual Persons*, par 10. Sidoti: 'gratuitous and scurrilous', Jacqui Griffin v. The Catholic Education Office, Human Rights and Equal Opportunities Commission Report 6, 1998, p.19. 'contrary to all': Jaqui Griffin v. The Catholic Education Office p.20. Brennan: 'a touch Orwellian', *Discerning the Australian Social Conscience*, p.252. 'Conforms to the doctrines': *Sexuality Discrimination Bill* 1995, s. 28.Constitution, s.116.

ELEVEN

YOUNG MINDS

The first version published *SMH* 5 December 1998, Spectrum, p.1, since revised. My uncle, the late Jika Travers, had made problems with synod a matter of family discourse for me from the time I was old enough to eavesdrop. We spoke about it again in the weeks before his death. I was able to get cautious assistance from those women in my family who have between them a few centuries of experience at Abbotsleigh. Three colleagues at the *SMH*, Stephanie Raethel, John Sandeman and Julia Baird were also particularly helpful.

Interviews
Phillip Jensen, Justice Peter Young, Mark Webeck, Archbishop Harry Goodhew and many others who were peculiarly anxious not to be identified. Judith Wheeldon declined to be interviewed.

Other sources
'But when Jesus': Mark 10: 14. Wheeldon: 'There are others', CV given to Abbotsleigh Council at the time of her application for the job. 'His knowledge of the Bible': Sydney *Daily Mirror* 7 March 1975, p.41. The review committee submitted its proposals to the Standing Committee in July 1997; the Standing Committee's response was circulated to the full synod in September 1998; the revised version was settled by Standing Committee in July 1999.

THE HIGH PRICE OF HEAVEN

SHAME AND FORGIVENESS

This appears here for the first time. The chapter was written with the help of a great number of people over many years. They are gay and straight, priests, ex-priests, believers and non- believers, psychologists, Catholics and Protestants. But above all I'm indebted to the three friends who, from various states of belief and disbelief, taught me so much Catholicism over the years: Richard Barrett, Nick Enright and Rae de Teliga. For help in the research, I'm grateful to Michael Kelly of Rainbow Sash and Fergus Shiel of the *Age*, also to Robert White and Michael Crowhurst. To the very end I hoped Archbishop Pell would speak to me on the subject of sexuality and youth suicide. He declined.

Interviews
Professor Bruce Tong, Janiene Wilson, Peter May, Maria Pallotta-Chiarolli and many others.

Other sources
'Intrinsic moral evil': *On the Pastoral Care of Homosexual Persons*, Congregation for the Doctrine of the Faith, paragraph 3. 'Lives and well-being': *On Pastoral Care*, paragraph 9. Pell: 'the hard teachings' etc., remarks made after delivering the Acton Lecture on Religion and Freedom delivered in Sydney 4 August 1999. 'There was no name for it': Peter May 'Sexual Discoveries in the Society of Jesus', MA thesis, Melbourne University, 1997, p.132. Jordan: *The Invention of Sodomy in Christian Theology*, Chicago University Press, Chicago, 1997, p.165. 'A homosexual orientation': A. W. Richard Sipe, *Sex, Priests and Power: Anatomy of a Crisis*, Cassell, 1995, p.73. 'The church as we know it': Sipe, p.95. 'As one priest put it': Sipe, p.148. 'Roughly 50 per cent': Sipe, p.73. 'A way of hiding' and 'no sexual demands': May, p.43. 'Was it shame': May, p.47. 'You may think': May p.149. Pell: 'ideological demonstration', *SMH* 2 June 1998, p.12. Kelly: 'I think of Catholic', *Age* 22 May 1999, p.5. 'Appalling' and 'I comment': David Barker, *Age* 1 November 1997, p.4. Kelly: 'He was verbally', *Age* 23 November 1998, p.17. 'Homophobia in church schools': Kelly, *Australian* 24 May 1999, p.3. Pell: 'I am enormously', full text of the exchange from Fergus Shiel to me, excerpts in Shiel's report, *SMH* 24 May 1999, p.3 and Katherine Towers in the *Australian* 24 May p.3. Jones: 'Smoking kills', *SMH* 24 May 1999, p.3. O'Reilly: 'The most significant', *Age* 24 May 1999, p.5. Pell: 'One sexual encounter', *Age* 28 May 1999, p.15. 'Verbal and physical': *Writing Themselves In*,

published by the National Centre in HIV Social Research and the Australian Research Centre in Sex, Health and Society at La Trobe University, 1998, p.3. Pallota-Chiarolli of Deakin University published *Girls Talk: Young Women Speak Their Hearts and Minds*, Finch Publishing in 1998 and is preparing for Open University Press with co-author Wayne Martino, *The Stuff that Boys Are Made Of*. 'Our first parents': *Age* 23 May 1999, p.9. Pell: 'new members' and 'Even young men', *Age* 28 May 1999, p. 15. Pell: 'All Christians believe', Acton Lecture. 'Reparative growth' and 'to leave behind': Courage and Encourage pamphlet. 'Complete support': *Life Lines*, December 1998/January 1999, p.13. Testimonials from the Courage website 'http://world.std.com/~courage/tstmy.htm' on 12 May 1999. 'He had an overnight': *Life Lines*, December 1998/January 1999, p.12.

INDEX

Abbotsleigh, 241, 242, 248, 250, 251–2, 257

ABC, 41, 137–8, 211–13

Aboriginal and Torres Strait Islander Commission (ATSIC), 36–7, 46

Aboriginal Development Corporation, 34, 39

Aborigines: Coalition opposition to land rights, 42–3; Hanson on, 45; Howard's attitude towards, 27, 30–1, 35–44, 46–50; land rights, 33–4, 38, 41–3; Mabo decision, 41–3, 48; Methodist missions, 28–31, 38–9; policy of assimilation, 29, 46; stolen children, 38–9, 46–7; Wik decision, 47, 48, 228–9

abortion, 24, 223

Adelaide Film Festival, 195

Adelaide, homophobia in, 156–7

Age, 274, 275, 281

age of consent, 178

Aggressive Salvation (Hay), 86

AIDS, 8, 173, 222, 269

alcohol, 8–9, 10–11

Alston, Senator Richard, 75, 89, 90–1, 126–7, 135, 182

American Psycho (Ellis), 198

Amnesty International, 107

Anderson, James, 275

Anglicans: Anglican schools, 247–59; attitude towards homosexuality, 172, 173–4, 175, 268; choose archbishop (1993), 244; distance themselves from safe injecting room, 19; in Sydney, 242, 243; on proposed antidiscrimination laws, 236; organisational structure, 160; school principals' Ascension Day dinner, 246–7; synod requires school principals to sign articles of faith, 252–3, 259

Ansett Airlines, 11

anti-discrimination legislation, Church exemption from, 233–5, 268

Aquilina, John, 188, 191, 192

Arrau, Claudio, 155

Ascension Day, 246

Ascham, 248

Ashfield Uniting Church, 16

Atatürk, Kemal, 143, 149

Ausaid, 101

Austin-Perry, Dymphna, 210

Australian Broadcasting Authority, 113–14, 124, 133, 134, 135, 136

Australian Capital Territory: abortion laws, 223; pornography industry, 205

drugs, 6, 20–4; attitude towards homosexuality, 62, 174–5, 176, 267–9, 276, 279, 282–3; attitude towards safe injecting rooms, 19; attitude towards sex, 282–3; attitude towards Wik issue, 228–9; Catholic schools, 221–2; Catholics working with gay communities, 284; the Church as an employer, 231; desert Labor in 1996 election, 226; gays in the priesthood, 270–1; in Sydney, 160–3; in the Australian Labor Party, 161–3, 218, 220; in the Liberal Party, 218, 220, 225; on proposed discrimination laws, 236; political power of, 217–23; Vatican response to anti-discrimination laws, 175–6

celibacy, 64, 66, 273, 284

censorship, xii–xiii; appointment of censors, 184–5; attitude of political parties towards, 75–7; Christian rhetoric in favour of, 87–91; Dickie on, 119; elimination of art as a defence, 183; Harradine's passion for, 110–12; of literature, 181–2, 183, 187–91; rise of censorship on the political agenda, 79–82; *see also* film and video; television

Centennial Park, Sydney, 86

Centre for Independent Studies, 21, 22

Chan, Jackie, 128

Chandler and McLeod Consultants, 210, 211

Chaney, Hon. Fred, 219

Channel 10, 132–3, 135–6

charities, 235

chastity, 64, 66, 273, 284

Chesterton, Ray, 192, 193

Chikarovski, Kerry, 18

child protection, 89

Child's Play 2 (film), 126, 129

Child's Play 3 (film), 129–30

China, population policy, 102–3

Chipp, Don, 182

Christianity: appeal of to young homosexuals, 264–5, 270; author's experiences with, xi–xii, 269–70, 286; Christian attempts at censorship, 77, 82, 87–91; history of attitudes towards homosexuality, 62–7; in Sydney, 242–3; *see also* Catholics; Protestants

Church of England *see* Anglicans

Gay Rights Lobby, 159

Gillies, Don, 54, 56–9, 68–71

Glanville, Richard Geoffrey, 247

Gleeson, Gerry, 162, 171

Goldsmith, Tottie, 133

Goldsworthy, Peter, 188, 189

Gomorrah, 62

Goodhew, Archbishop Harry, 244, 246, 252, 255–7

goods and services tax, 218–19, 220, 226, 227–8, 229

Goss, Wayne, 194, 196

Goulden, Terry, 167

Graham, James, 252

Gramick, Jeannine, 284

Gray, Gary, 78

Green, Malcolm, 53–61, 68, 70–1

Greiner, Nick, 170, 172–3

Gresham Partners, 252

Griffin, Jacqui, 233, 235

Groom, Ray, 175

GST, 218–19, 220, 226, 227–8, 229

Gummow, Justice Bill, 69–70

Hagia Sophia, Istanbul, 143–50

Hamlet (Shakespeare), 190

Hanson, Pauline, 33, 45, 79–82, 211–13

Happiness (film), 90

Harker, Jon, 191, 193

Harradine, Brian, 95–116; anti-communism, 106; as a militant Christian, 81–2; as an Independent, 48, 99–100, 220, 226; blocks appointment of Funder to NHMRC, 227; Catholic tradition, 98–9, 101; childhood and background, 103–5; church loyalties, 217–18; concessions made to, 75–6, 221; doctrinal perils of bushwalking, 116; electoral success, 106–7; loses crucial vote in Senate, 137; mastery of rules, 105; opposes 0055 phone calls, 109–10, 123; opposes aid for population programs, 101–2; opposes contraception, 101, 107–8, 226; opposes GST, 98, 227–8; opposes members of Office of Film and Literature Classification, 209–11; opposes pornography, 88, 108, 110–15; opposes release of *Salo*, 185; passion for censorship, 110–14; pushes for greater television censorship, 134,

164, 178; opposes
homosexual law reform,
167; threatened with
contempt by Wran, 171;
wins amendment to
property rights bill, 177
Northern Territory,
euthanasia laws, 224
Nugent, Robert, 284

O'Donoghue, Lowitja, 49
Office of Film and
Literature Classification,
124, 183–5, 187, 194,
198–204, 207, 209–11
120 Days of Sodom (de
Sade), 199
One Nation, 33, 229
O'Reilly, Joseph, 276
L'Osservatore Romano, 224

Packer, Kerry, xi
Pallotta-Chiarolli, Maria,
280
Pantsdown, Pauline, 211–13
Parker, Janette *see* Howard,
Janette (nee Parker)
Pasolini, Pier Pasolo, 185,
193, 195, 197, 200, 201,
203
Passionist Fathers, 104
Paul, Saint, 64, 176, 246
Peacock, Andrew, 34, 40, 42
pedophilia, 177, 201
Pell, Archbishop George:
attitude towards drugs, 6,

19, 20–4; divides
Catholic opposition to
GST, 227–8; on Donald
Duck, 22–3; on
homosexuality and
suicide, 276–8, 281–2; on
shame, 269; prepares
religious studies syllabus,
280; refuses communion
to gay protesters, 273–4;
supports Catholics Have
Courage, 284–5;
undercuts corporate
authority of bishops, 224
The People v. Larry Flynt
(film), 186–7
Perkins, Charles, 39
Perry, Joe, 82–3, 84
Perry, Mrs (Joe's wife), 82–3
Petersen, George, 159,
163–6, 171
Philip Roff and Associates,
252
phone sex, 109, 110, 115
Picture, 206–7
*Playboy's Really Naked Truth
No 1* (television
program), 135
pleasure, attitude of Church
towards, 5–6, 8, 20,
65–6, 145
political correctness, 33, 44
population, 101
Population Council, 101
pornography, 76–7, 79, 88,
110–15, 205

Christianisation of,
245–6, 249, 253–4;
homophobia in, 275,
278–9, 283; private,
221–2, 241–2, 247–59;
see also specific schools
Scorsese, Martin, 196, 202
Seagal, Steven, 127
Searchlight, 207–8
sectarianism, 19–20
Senate Select Committee
on Community
Standards Utilising
Telecommunications
Technologies, 109, 113–14,
126–9, 133–5, 184–5
sex, on television, 132–7
Sex/Life (television program),
132–6
sexuality, Christian attitudes
towards, 64–6, 88,
265–6, 273, 282–3
Shakespeare, 190
Shaw, Judith *see* Wheeldon,
Judith (nee Shaw)
Shepherdson, H.V., 29
Shirley, Graham, 210
Sidoti, Chris, 165, 233–4
silence, cultivation of,
266–7
The Silence of the Lambs
(film), 196
Sipe, Richard, 271, 272
Sirola, Dean, 57
Sisters of Charity, 6, 19, 23,
178, 228

Smith, Wayne, 131
smoking, 276
Society of Labor Lawyers,
159
Sodom, 62
Soldiers of the Cross (film),
82, 84–6
Soros, George, 7
South Africa, 34
South Australia:
homophobia in, 156–7;
partial ban of *Salo*, 196
Spence, Judy, 193–4, 196, 198
St Mary's Cathedral,
Sydney, 217, 237
St Matthias parish, Sydney,
244
St Patrick's Cathedral,
Melbourne, 273–4
St Thomas More Society, 99
St Vincent's Hospital,
Sydney, 19
stolen children *see* Aborigines
Stonewall Bar, New York,
153, 156, 267
suicide, 274–8, 280–1
Sullivan, Louis, 143
Sunday Examiner, 108
swinging voters, 78–80
Sydney Church of England
Girls' Grammar Schools
(SCEGGS), 247–8
Sydney Grammar, 248
Sydney Morning Herald, 205
Symon, Bill, 189, 190, 193
Symonds, Ann, 160–3

THE HIGH PRICE OF HEAVEN